Australian Army C[ampaigns]

THE OTTOMAN DEFENCE AGAINST THE
ANZAC LANDING

25 APRIL 1915

Mesut Uyar

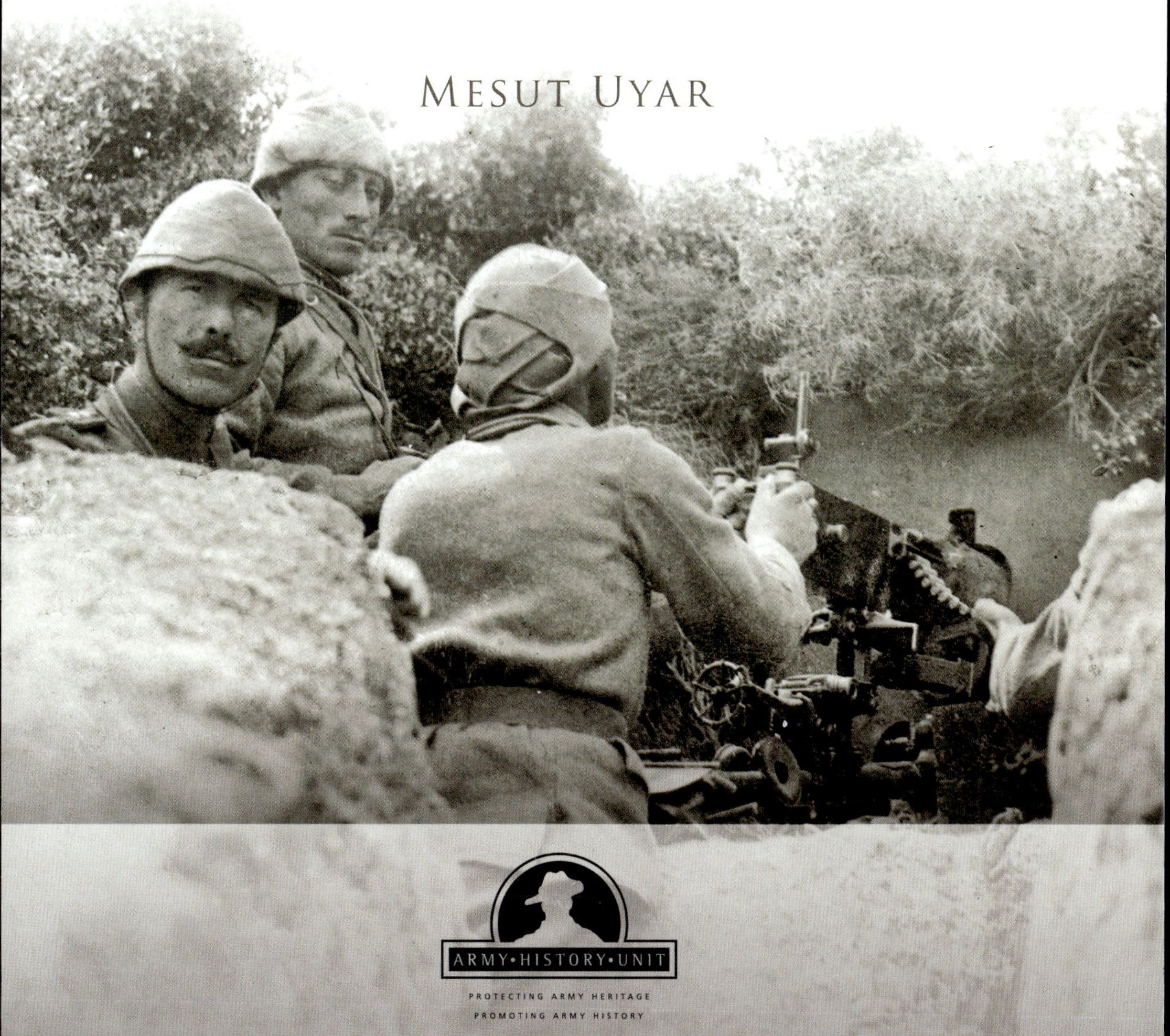

PROTECTING ARMY HERITAGE
PROMOTING ARMY HISTORY

©Copyright Army History Unit
Campbell Park Offices (CP2-5-166)
Canberra ACT 2600
AUSTRALIA
(02) 6266 4248
(02) 6266 4044 – fax
Copyright 2011 © Commonwealth of Australia

First published 2015

This book is copyright. Apart from any fair dealing for the purposes of private study, research, criticism or review as permitted under the Copyright Act, no part may be reproduced, stored in a retrieval system or transmitted in any form or by any means, electronic, mechanical, photocopying, recording or otherwise, without written permission.

See National Library of Australia for Cataloguing-in-Publication entry.

ISBN: 978-1-922132-99-4

Published by Big Sky Publishing, Sydney
Cover and typesetting by Think Productions, Melbourne
Printed in China through Asia Pacific Offset Limited

Front cover and title page: Machine-gun company commander (most probably the officer commanding the 125th Company) pose with a machine-gun crew somewhere near Lone Pine or Johnson's Jolly during the summer of 1915. Source: Author's private collection.
Back cover background: In a staged photo an infantry platoon prepares for an assault. (image courtesy of ATASE)
Back cover top right: Ottoman reinforcements march towards the front line. (image courtesy of Nejat Çuhadaroğlu)
Back cover bottom right: A logistic train carrying heavy equipment and tents for a field camp. (image courtesy of Nejat Çuhadaroğlu)

To my father the late Sergeant Major Tayyar Uyar, Signal Corps, Turkish Army, whom I still miss so much.

CONTENTS

Acknowledgements 5

A note on place names and terms 6

Preface 7

Chapter 1   Military reforms and the German Military Assistance Mission 10

Chapter 2   Early defensive strategies 38

Chapter 3   The initial defence on the coast 95

Epilogue   The day after 146

A note on Turkish sources 166

Selected bibliography 171

Index 175

ACKNOWLEDGEMENTS

In writing this book I have received enormous assistance from many people and organisations to whom I owe a significant debt of gratitude.

I would like to thank Dr Roger Lee and Dr Andrew Richardson of the Australian Army History Unit for offering me the opportunity to write the story of the Ottoman defence against the Anzac landings. Andrew also deserves special mention for his substantial efforts in proofreading the text and correcting my many English mistakes. Without his meticulous and tenacious editing I am afraid the book would be rather dull and also something of a challenge to read.

I have had the good fortune to discuss various aspects of the landing with Brigadier Chris Roberts (retd) who has written his own wonderful book on this topic from the perspective of the Australians and New Zealanders. Chris also provided extremely helpful comments on the final draft.

Nejat Çuhadaroğlu of the Hisart Museum and Yetkin İşçen generously allowed me to use valuable photographs from their private collections, while Serdar Ataksor and Hakan Akın kindly provided photographs and maps from their grandfathers' personal papers. The late Major Halis Ataksor's hand-marked mimeograph maps considerably enriched the book. I am also extremely grateful to Dr Phil Rutherford for his skilfully drawn illustrations.

The Turkish General Staff Military History Directorate (ATASE) Archive is an important resource centre for researching the history of the Ottoman military. I am grateful to Brigadier General Necdet Tuna, Colonel Özkan Ulutaş, Colonel Kemal Ellialtıoğlu, Colonel Suat Akgül (retd) and other ATASE staff for their valuable assistance.

The University of New South Wales, Canberra, provided me with wonderful working conditions and an academically stimulating environment for over two years. I would like to express my gratitude to the Rector, Professor Michael Frater, the ACSACS Director, Professor Tom Frame, and Professor Jeffrey Grey for their collegial friendship and assistance.

I am particularly grateful to Danny Neave from Big Sky Publishing for his patience and skill, particularly given the tight deadline in publishing this book in time for the centenary of the landing at Gallipoli in 2015. I would also like to thank Cathy McCullagh for editing and enriching the text.

Last but not least, I am very grateful for the understanding and support of my wife İlkay and my daughter Dilara. They stoically shouldered the burden of an absent husband/father who has spent much time away from his family to complete this book.

Naturally any errors of fact or interpretation are entirely my own responsibility. I note that the help provided by these organisations and individuals does not mean that they will necessarily agree with my conclusions.

A NOTE ON PLACE NAMES AND TERMS

Prior to the landing most of the topographical features at Anzac had not been named — at least not on military maps. The names that are now so familiar were generally devised during the battles that began on 25 April 1915. In most cases the names of officers, units and others inspired by the bloody nature of the conflict were given to the previously nameless features. Many features — particularly hills and other dominating terrain — were simply named for their height such as Hill 971 (Kocaçimentepe) which is marked in contemporary British maps as some 971 feet high. Geographical terms have also become names, including 'boyun' (literally 'saddle') where the original command post of the *8/2nd Company* was located prior to the landing. Likewise 'suyatağı' ('creek') later designated the location where Mustafa Kemal positioned the *5/3rd Mountain Artillery Battery*.

While the issue of naming the topographical features was more or less settled in the initial days following the landing, both sides struggled with the immense difficulty of identifying the myriad features of the rugged, broken landscape. Modern scholars still take time to develop a feel for the terrain and identify the places that saw actions fought or where units were located. It is worth remembering the singular difficulty presented by the topography of the campaign as the actions both prior to and following the Anzac landing are described in this narrative.

As a general rule, well-known English names have been employed throughout the text for the sake of clarity and simplicity, while the modern Turkish names have been provided in parentheses at their first appearance. In some cases, however, where the English spelling is problematic or confusing such as with the towns of Channakkale or Boghali, the modern Turkish spellings have been preferred: 'Çanakkale' and 'Bigalı' respectively.

Likewise, the term 'Ottoman' is preferred to 'Turk', 'Turkish' or 'Turkey'. 'Ottoman' is a more accurate name for the multi-ethnic, multi-religious and multi-cultural empire that once ruled a vast area well beyond the borders of modern-day Turkey.

PREFACE

With the enduring popularity of the Anzac legend and the build-up to commemorations for the centenary of the Gallipoli campaign, the publication of ever-increasing numbers of new books on various aspects of the campaign continues unabated in both Australia and Turkey. There is also a burgeoning interest on both sides in understanding the campaign from 'the other side of the hill'. This curiosity to learn more about the opposing side is stronger in Australia than in Turkey. However stereotypes, common mistakes and the remnants of wartime propaganda continue to obscure the true picture of the Ottoman Army. Irrespective of a book's aim, most readers are left with an image of a faceless army punctuated by the haunting visages of a few faded black and white photographs. Surprisingly, Turkish historiography contains little description of the respective unit commanders, officers and soldiers who shouldered the burden of war, with the important exception of the remarkable Mustafa Kemal Atatürk. Previous generations of Turkish historians preferred to look at the Gallipoli battles in a collective way and paid little attention to the contributions of individuals or to their perspectives on the conflict. Even in the highly detailed volumes of the Turkish *Official Military History*, it is difficult to find the names of the divisional and regimental commanders, let alone field and company-level officers, and any description of their contribution to the respective battles.

This book is an attempt to paint a portrait of the Ottoman officers and soldiers by focusing on a single battle on a single day, namely the defence against the Anzac landing on 25 April 1915. I specifically selected this day because of my belief that the fate of the entire Gallipoli campaign was actually decided on that one day. Despite the wealth of literature analysing the campaign and this day in particular, a number of riddles continue to dog the campaign literature, representing what Australian war correspondent and official historian Charles Bean termed a 'train of unsolved questions'. Bean conducted his own extensive research and analysis, seeking answers to these questions, but finally reached the conclusion that 'obviously the answers to some of these questions we could get only from the Turks, when, and if, they should ever supply us with them.' Indeed the documents held in the Turkish military archives and the wealth of published and unpublished personal war reminiscences are virtual treasure troves of valuable information on the Ottoman-Turkish perspective of the events of 25 April. Of itself, the information in many of these sources is insufficient to provide a complete picture and yield the answers to many of Bean's unanswered questions. However, documents such as these are invaluable when used in conjunction with other sources, in this case, those of the Australian participants.

In researching this volume I examined all the published Ottoman-Turkish *Official Military Histories*, including discussions relating to the publication of the first draft volume in 1916, through to the recent edition of the three-volume set in 2012. Contrary to common perception, there is not just one standard Turkish *Official Military History* (in three volumes) on the Gallipoli campaign, but rather at least *five* different sets of books. Thus I faced the daunting task of examining the development of the Turkish *Official History* perspective and the writing of all its volumes over a period of decades.

I also spent considerable time extensively researching the Turkish military archives —not just the relatively well known Turkish General Staff Military History Directorate (ATASE) Archive, but also the Ministry of Defence (MSB) Archive and some smaller archives such as the Turkish General Staff College Library. Fortunately, most of the war diaries and other official papers that relate to the Gallipoli campaign have survived. Indeed, the after-action reports of the key commanders proved extremely useful to my research.

My third task was to read all the personal narratives from the campaign that I could locate, both published and unpublished. Most of the veterans of the campaign added various reports and messages and also copied paragraphs or pages from the unit war diaries in order to verify their accounts or add to their recollection of an event. These verbatim reproductions of the official papers and personal insights into the battle provide a rare understanding of the sequence of events on 25 April and help fill a number of gaps in the archive holdings. I acquired printed and hand-drawn Ottoman military maps of the campaign and used these to plot the Ottoman accounts. These were extraordinarily valuable as they were the same maps used by the Ottoman commanders on 25 April 1915.

Having consumed all the available Turkish sources, I compared my findings with Australian, New Zealand and British documents and accounts. I focused in particular on the various riddles that have puzzled historians for the past 100 years (such as the presence or absence of machine-guns at the landing) and other questions concerning locations and timings. I often found myself returning to the Turkish sources to verify my emerging train of thought, or to find out who was where at a particular time. This was the most enjoyable part of writing the book as it was akin to finding the missing parts of a jigsaw puzzle from places other than the box in which they had come. I also discussed my findings and tested my ideas with various military historians and experts.

This book consists of an introduction, three main chapters and an epilogue. The first chapter describes the condition of the Ottoman Army in the aftermath of the Balkan Wars, the military's analysis of its performance, the far-reaching military reforms, the German Military Assistance Mission and the Ottoman Army's mobilisation and preparation for war. It is important to understand how an army which had soundly beaten a few years earlier took on a new lease of life and surprised friend and foe alike with its ability to fight. The Ottoman Army at Gallipoli proved that the Ottoman Empire was not the 'sick man of Europe' that so many European powers believed it to be in 1915. This chapter also identifies the true architects of this phoenix-like military rebirth.

The second chapter examines the Ottoman Army's planning and preparations for the defence of the Dardanelles. Special emphasis is placed on the army's battle experience, the adherence to fundamental defensive principles and the crucial roles of several individuals. Contrary to popular belief, the final defence doctrine and plan were born amid conflicting ideas and internal disputes that remained unresolved at the time of the landing and which poisoned relations between commanders during the crisis.

The third chapter represents the core of the book and examines the defence against the Anzac landing on 25 April 1915. The initial positions, reactions and movements of the Ottoman defenders are discussed in as much detail as possible with the provision of precise locations, timings and strength of the units and a detailed description of the various commanders. The reactions of operational and tactical-level commanders, the problems they faced, perceptions of a command void, the race for Third Ridge and the Ottoman counter-attacks have also been analysed in meticulous detail. In order to retain the focus on the main flow of events, some important issues and questions — such as the Ottoman use of machine-guns, artillery, the difficulties with Arab soldiers — and portraits of important Ottoman commanders are examined in the sidebars that accompany the text. Both modern and contemporary maps are used to illustrate the tactical developments on the ground. The hand-drawn lines and tactical symbols on the original Ottoman maps illustrate the way Ottoman officers understood the tactical picture that confronted them at a given moment on that first day. The book closes with the epilogue which describes the events of 26 April and explains the extraordinary significance of the first day of the campaign for the Ottoman Army.

In keeping with the general style of the Australian Army Campaign Series, footnotes and detailed bibliographies are not included. Instead, a note on Turkish sources and a selected bibliography are provided.

Special attention has been paid to sourcing previously unseen imagery of the Ottoman Army. With the assistance of the Turkish military archives, a number of Turkish collectors and the families of veterans, I have been able to acquire some extraordinary photos that have either never been published or have not been used effectively. These illustrations provide a valuable record of Ottoman uniforms, equipment and other aspects of the Ottoman soldier seldom evident in contemporary photos or accounts of the campaign.

As a last word, anyone with an interest in military history must not forget that wars are fought by at least two protagonists. Ultimately, to understand how and why that war was fought, it is necessary to see 'the other side of the hill'.

CHAPTER 1
MILITARY REFORMS AND THE GERMAN MILITARY ASSISTANCE MISSION

The Ottoman Army of 1913 retained few of the vestiges of its glorious past. It was a highly politicised polyglot army which had been defeated in detail in recent months by a coalition of small Balkan states. The only positives to emerge from the debacle were the stubborn defensive actions of three fortress cities, Edirne (Adrianople), Yanya (Janina) and İşkodra (Shoker), and the Çatalca line. For many Western observers of the war the Ottoman defeat confirmed the European belief in Ottoman decadence and elicited prophecies of the inevitable demise of the empire. The image of the 'sick man of Europe' loomed large once again. The Great Powers decided independently to hasten the demise of the dying empire. The Russians in particular were determined to follow the Italian example by launching a surprise invasion. The dire situation facing the Ottomans was exacerbated by internal conflict and a central government riven with strife and factionalism.

The Balkan defeats and the loss of almost all the empire's European provinces prompted a public outcry and demands for a complete overhaul of the military system to forestall the collapse of the empire. All the vested interests, including the officers themselves, blamed the officer corps for the apparent weakness of the army and its manifest inability to defend the empire. Partisan politics and infighting were widely cited as the real reason for the army's poor performance. Public derision and military defeat seriously eroded the morale of the officer corps, prompting open debate not only over their concerns for the fate of the empire, but the cause of their disastrous defeats in the Balkan Wars. Every new publication (particularly the memoirs of war veterans) instigated new discussions which delivered yet more publications. While most of these works pointed to political issues as the root cause, the debate was focussed primarily on problems within the Ottoman military and their possible solution. Ironically, the widespread and often vicious criticism and self-criticism reinforced the officers' sense of group identity and brotherhood and tightened the bonds forged in battle.

One important outcome of this debate was a sense of the urgent need for reform. The new Minister of War, Mahmud Şevket Pasha, planned to introduce a radical reform package with the assistance of a new German Military Advisory Mission. He also intended to purge the partisan officers led by Enver Bey before they could increase their influence, and planned to appoint the members of the German Military Mission to command positions, arming them with broad-ranging authority. The invitation to despatch a new military mission arrived in Berlin at a time when Germany was in the midst of a heated debate over its policy towards the Ottomans. The Balkan defeat had been greeted with surprise and dismay. The German General Staff claimed that the prestige of the German Army had suffered a heavy blow, while the Ministry of Foreign Affairs stridently declared that military investment in the Ottoman Empire was a waste of men and money. However there were those among the diplomats and military officers who did not share this pessimistic evaluation and regarded the Ottoman plight as a golden opportunity to further German interests in the empire. Chief among them was the German Ambassador to İstanbul, Hans von Wangenheim, who made it his mission to persuade Kaiser Wilhelm II and his military advisors to persevere with the Ottoman investment.

Mahmud Şevket Pasha did not live to see the results of his reform. He was assassinated on 11 June 1913 and replaced by the triumvirate (Lieutenant Colonel Enver, Colonel Cemal and Talat Bey) of the İttihad ve Terakki (the Committee of Union and Progress — CUP). The final agreement between Germany and the Ottoman Empire (for the duration of five years and with the option of an extension) was signed on 27 October 1913. This agreement handed responsibility for the implementation of all military reform packages and also, critically, direct command and control of many key units, to the German Military Mission. Moreover, the mission leader would become an essential part of all military decision-making processes including officer promotions and assignments. Kaiser Wilhelm chose a senior divisional commander from the Prussian Army, Major General Otto Liman von Sanders, as mission leader. It was an appointment that would be problematic from its inception. Liman von Sanders was an elderly general who would never have been promoted to the rank of corps commander in Germany and had now been elevated to lead a military mission with extraordinary powers, and to do so in a sensitive region. His selection suggested that the Kaiser and his advisors had not fully grasped the significance of the appointment, lacked a long-term perspective, and had simply opted for an easy solution.

The Russian leadership was dismayed by news of the Ottoman-German agreement and the establishment of a new German Military Mission. What concerned the Russians was not so much the new mission — despite its extended powers — but rather the fact that a German general was assuming command of the İstanbul garrison and the defence of the Bosphorus. Liman von Sanders arrived in İstanbul with a small group of mission members on 14 December 1913 amid a major political crisis over the mission's appointment. While von Sanders immediately assumed command of *I Army Corps*, the effects of the crisis delayed the despatch of the other members of the mission to their new posts.

The German mission faced enormous problems from the outset. The members arrived in December 1913 and had just nine months in which to reform the army before the Ottoman entry into the First World War. With the political crisis precipitated by their arrival, they were initially prevented from commencing work and lost two critical months. The delays were further compounded by the decision of the new Minister of War, Enver Pasha, von Sanders and his German advisors in Berlin to re-evaluate the assignments of the mission

LIMAN VON SANDERS

Otto Liman von Sanders wearing a Prussian major general's uniform. Von Sanders created a command void at the operational level by focusing solely on the Bolayır-Saros region and ignoring increasingly urgent reports from the units at Anzac on 25 April.

Otto Liman von Sanders was born in Stolp in Pomerania in 1855. He joined the military at an early age and worked his way up the ranks, albeit at a slower pace than his peers. He was not particularly bright and certainly no intellectual, but rather a typical line officer. It was only through sheer diligence, discipline and loyalty that he achieved the position of divisional commander. He was ennobled in 1913 and took his late wife's surname — von Sanders — as honorific.

In June 1913 when Kaiser Wilhelm II asked him to lead the military mission to the Ottoman Empire, he was one of the oldest divisional commanders in the Prussian Army. While not his first choice, von Sanders was one of the old school generals of whom the Kaiser was particularly fond. He had not previously served in the Ottoman Empire and had no foreign experience at all. It was an ill-judged appointment which saw an elderly general who would never have been promoted to the rank of corps commander in Germany chosen to lead a military mission with extraordinary powers, and to do so in a sensitive region.

Von Sanders arrived in İstanbul with a small group of mission members on 14 December 1913 in the middle of a major political crisis. The intense pressure on the Ottomans from Russia, Britain and France saw him promoted and appointed Chief Inspector-General and the other German officers assigned to key command and staff positions. Von Sanders was a difficult man to work with and a long way from the ideal soldier-diplomat needed to fill this sensitive position. Immediately after his arrival he became involved in disputes and clashes with almost all his Ottoman counterparts, the German Embassy and veteran German advisors. However Ambassador Hans von Wangenheim's efforts to secure his recall came to naught.

The declaration of mobilisation changed the situation dramatically and von Sanders was appointed commanding general of the *First Army* in İstanbul. He had finally received the field command he had long sought. However, at the same time, his authority as the commander of German officers in the Ottoman Army was eroded with the increase in personnel numbers and the despatch of various independent units to new locations. He remained in İstanbul and managed the reorganisation of the Ottoman Army until his next assignment as commanding general of the *Fifth Army* at Gallipoli on 24 March 1915.

Having conducted a brief inspection, von Sanders completely altered the defence doctrine and defensive plans for the Gallipoli Peninsula. While he did his best to reorganise and reinvigorate the units under his command, his harsh methods and stern nature aroused widespread animosity, even among the German officers. Von Sanders made the mistake of leaving units isolated and travelling to Bulair were he waited for an invasion to materialise for three days even as the first enemy landings occurred at Anzac, Helles and Kumkale. He was determined to destroy the enemy enclaves and launched a series of massive frontal attacks at Anzac and Helles between 27 April and 19 May. Having suffered heavy casualties without achieving any meaningful results, von Sanders came to the conclusion that the enemy could not be driven into the sea by frontal assaults and that a strong defence had to be mounted instead.

Von Sanders commanded with an iron fist and immediately dismissed any of his subordinates — Ottoman and German alike — who objected to orders or performed poorly in his opinion. Although there were few German officers under his command at the beginning of the campaign, von Sanders believed that he could exercise more effective authority with German officers in command or key staff positions in all his primary units. A number of his appointees, such as Hans Kannengiesser, performed well, but others did not, leading to open resentment in some units. In time, von Sanders became accustomed to working with

Ottoman officers and stopped giving preferential treatment to German officers.

While the August offensives caught von Sanders off guard, this time he reacted decisively by moving reserves and other units and organising them into temporary tactical groups to deal with the threat. He failed to anticipate the Allied evacuation of the Suvla-Anzac region and was powerless to prevent the withdrawal from Helles. With the termination of the campaign he was generously rewarded but, rather than receiving another combat assignment, he remained in the rear dealing with routine home guard duties.

On 19 February 1918 von Sanders was appointed commander of the *Yıldırım Army Group* (*Heeres Gruppen Kommando F*) in Palestine. He literally took over the wreckage of this formation. His predecessor, Erich von Falkenhayn, had not only wasted crucial operational opportunities but also destroyed relations between the Ottomans and Germans. The British Expeditionary Force had already captured Jerusalem and was attacking the Jordan River. Enver Pasha ordered von Sanders to defend Lebanon and Syria at all costs. Under these challenging circumstances, von Sanders discharged his duties with remarkable prudence, restraint, and loyalty, establishing a harmonious working relationship between the Ottomans and the Germans. He mobilised his troops to man a defensive line from the Mediterranean to the Dead Sea — an impossible mission. When the anticipated large-scale British assault began unexpectedly on 19 September 1918, the entire defensive line collapsed. In the subsequent battles, the army group lost half its personnel and a major proportion of its heavy weaponry. Although there was little possibility of halting the British advance before Aleppo and the Taurus Mountains, von Sanders decided to defend Damascus with what remained of the army group. It was a fatal decision. A large number of the soldiers who tried to retreat to Damascus were captured along the way. Von Sanders only just escaped, taking refuge in Adana where he was informed of the Armistice.

On 31 October von Sanders handed over the army group command to Mustafa Kemal Pasha and went to İstanbul. The new German government had tasked him with the evacuation of German troops which he managed until 24 January 1919. Von Sanders left İstanbul on 29 January but was interned by the British authorities in Malta to face accusations of war crimes against Greek civilians. He wrote his memoirs during his internment and was released without trial on 21 August. He retired from the army and died in 1929.

Von Sanders was an excellent field officer who enjoyed life in the field with his soldiers and keenly shared their hardships. A virtual workaholic, he worked extended hours and was given to micro-management, monitoring his subordinates relentlessly. However he was a stern disciplinarian who demanded absolute obedience and complete loyalty. He was also a poor communicator and an uninspiring leader. Understandably, von Sanders did not inspire affection or admiration from his men, but initially aroused animosity and fear. Interestingly, both von Sanders and his Ottoman subordinates eventually reached an understanding and were able to forge a strong relationship later in the war. In this sense his insistence on filling his staff with Ottoman officers was a very wise strategy. Having taken over from von Falkenhayn, he was compared favourably to his predecessor and enjoyed considerable popularity in 1918.

members. Ultimately, they opted to move some mission members to more crucial positions in the headquarters of the General Staff and Ministry of War. Thus a large number of officers were reappointed before they had even assumed their initial posts. Since none of them spoke Turkish, Ottoman officers trained in Germany and other officers fluent in foreign languages were hurriedly taken from their original posts and appointed as private interpreters to the German officers. Most of the German officers had never served overseas and the resulting handover process, adjustment to a new country and army, and the necessity to work through translators proved enormously time consuming. Moreover, von Sanders and most of his mission members were not officers of the calibre necessary to successfully discharge such a sensitive mission. With few exceptions, these were mediocre officers who lacked the necessary background or talent to perform their highly demanding jobs. Thus, contrary to popular belief, the German Military Mission was not the main factor behind the Ottoman revival and subsequent combat success.

NEW ORGANISATIONAL ARCHITECTURE

To a certain extent the Ottoman Army reflected the characteristics of Ottoman society. The empire was built on a medieval agrarian socio-economic structure with primitive internal communication and infrastructure, pronounced traditional ethnic and religious differences, highly localised communities and continuously dominated by internal strife and factionalism. While the German Army — and before it the Prussian — had long provided a source of inspiration and successive German military advisory missions had contributed significantly to the development of the Ottoman military system, the Ottoman Army had preserved its distinctive military culture. This distinctive culture was the product of a combination of emulation and large-scale adaptation and improvisation.

The European military system had been analysed and embraced by Ottoman officers long before the advent of the new mission. Hundreds of officers and technicians had been sent to Germany from 1885 on to serve in German Army units. Well before the arrival of the Sanders mission, these officers had already begun the process of transforming the Ottoman Army into a modern war machine using German military doctrine and war manuals. The mission members added momentum to a process already largely on track, provided further guidance and increased the influence of German-trained officers within the army. Indeed, as noted previously, the dominant motive for the establishment of a new German mission was the purging of politicised officers and the elimination of all the elements of partisan politics within the military. This purge had been affected by Enver Pasha who had acted unilaterally without informing von Sanders. In addition to partisan officers, most of the senior officers tainted with defeat were also purged, followed by old and incompetent regimental officers including the last remaining 'rankers' (*alaylı*). Even those rankers who demonstrated a measure of leadership potential and merit did not escape this radical purge. Enver Pasha and his advisers used this opportunity to shape an officer corps that was younger and more loyal. Older generations of general staff officers who were students of former German mission leader Colmar von der Goltz were assigned to positions well below their rank level or to

The number of German officers in the Ottoman Army

One of the most common stereotypes in the literature of the Gallipoli Campaign is the attribution of the Ottoman victory to German leadership. This is supported by a popular belief that German officers filled all key command or staff positions in the Ottoman forces at Gallipoli. The contemporary Anzac documents and personal accounts suggest there were several German officers at least on the battlefield on 25 April 1915. Their assumed presence is reflected in the names of terrain features such as 'German Officer's Trench' and 'German Officer's Spur'.

In fact no German officers fought against the Anzacs on the day of the landing and there were no German officers at either Anzac or Helles. Only the units of the *9th and 19th divisions* took part in the defence against the landings on the peninsula on 25 April and these formations did not have German officers in command, staff or other positions. Indeed there were no Germans on the staff of *III Corps*. The only Germans on the peninsula, other than those serving with the *Dardanelles Fortified Zone Command*, were Liman von Sanders, commanding general of the *Fifth Army*, his two aides-de-camp (Captain Erich R. Prigge and 1st Lieutenant Carl Mühlmann), and Major von Frese, the officer commanding *Headquarters Company, Fifth Army*. While the *5th Division* commander, Colonel Eduard von Sodenstern, was German, the division was positioned on the isthmus of the peninsula and did not take part in the fighting on 25 April. On 29 April von Sodenstern was appointed commander of the *Southern (Helles) Group*.

However there were German officers engaged against the French on the Asian side of the Dardanelles on 25 April. Colonel Arthur Nicolai, Commanding Officer of the *3rd Division*, was in charge of the Kumkale defence and his immediate superior was Brigadier General Erich Paul Weber, commanding general of *XV Corps*.

garrisons in distant regions. Most sought early retirement rather than suffer the humiliation of perceived demotion and thus provided new opportunities for a younger generation of General Staff officers to rise to senior command and staff positions. Only a small minority of the old guard managed to preserve their positions, largely thanks to their heroic conduct during the Balkan Wars.

In the same fashion, the largest military structural reform — the concept of the triangular division— was initiated in 1911, two years before the arrival of von Sanders. This concept was the brainchild of Ahmed İzzet Pasha, Chief of the General Staff at the time. The concept involved replacing the well-established square division structure (two brigades each with two regiments) with a division comprising three regiments each with three battalions, eliminating both brigade headquarters and a regiment. Although the number of regiments in a division was reduced, combat strength was preserved with the addition of an organic field artillery regiment, machine-gun companies and a more efficient command and control system. This was an innovative idea born of military intellectual discussions in Germany at the turn of the century, although the military conservatism that pervaded the German military prevented German officers adopting this concept until 1915. Interestingly, the new concept strongly influenced a number of Ottoman officers who were serving with German units at the time.

General Staff College officer cadets pose aboard a battleship in 1910. The Ottoman Army discovered the importance of joint operations following the 1909 reforms.

The introduction of triangular divisions sparked a chain reaction. Prior to this structural change, the Ottoman Army had no army corps echelon. The term 'army corps' had been used to denote two or three divisional groups without permanent standing corps staff and corps units. As a result, field armies were not only bulky and unwieldy, but also incapable of providing command, control, combat support and combat service support to their divisions. Army corps headquarters were eventually established (also triangular and each with three divisions and additional support units) on 8 January 1911 and took their personnel and corps units from disbanded brigade echelon and field armies.

Prior to the mobilisation of August 1914, an army inspectorate was the highest field command that existed within the command architecture. On mobilisation four field army commands were activated: the *First Army* in İstanbul, the *Second Army* in Edirne, the *Third Army* in Erzincan and the *Fourth Army* in Damascus. Each of these usually commanded three numbered army corps and a total of 34 numbered divisions. There was one independent army corps (*VII Corps* with two divisions) in Yemen and two independent divisions (*21st* and *22nd Division*) in Asir (north of Yemen) and Hejaz respectively. In addition, two regions (Bosphorus and Dardanelles Straits) and two cities (Edirne and Erzurum) had been designated fortified zones and placed under the control of the fortress artillery inspectorate-general.

As part of its program to establish a new army organisational system, the General Staff first had to manage the detritus of the Balkan defeats. Army corps headquarters and divisions that were deployed around the Çatalca Fortified Zone had to be sent to their old or new garrisons, thousands of prisoners of war and detainees returning from captivity had to be reintegrated into their new units, and civil disturbances in several provinces had to be quelled. The confusion created by the reorganisation was so immense that some headquarters and units moved forward and then backwards, passing through several transformations and reorganisations. These transformations and movements took time to effect and many units were caught in the middle of their transformation when mobilisation was declared on 2 August 1914.

MILITARY EDUCATION AND TRAINING

For its supply of young officers, the Ottoman Army relied on the Imperial Military Academy (*Mekteb-i Fünun-u Harbiye-i Şahane*), founded in 1834, and the Imperial Engineering School (*Mühendishane-i Berri-i Hümayun*), founded in 1795, both of which were located in İstanbul. The Engineering School trained the 'scientific' branches of the army — artillery and engineering officers — while the Academy produced infantry and cavalry officers. With the closure of the military section of the Engineering School in 1909, the Academy assumed responsibility for training artillery officers and engineers. The combat service support branches, traditionally regarded as non-military and administrative, had separate vocational schools.

In the Military Academy, commonly and affectionately known as *Harbiye*, cadets took combined military training and academic courses over a three-year period. The Ottoman administration viewed the officer training process not simply as a form of military training, but also as an important element of the modernisation of the empire. Consequently, academic courses constituted the core of the curriculum and consumed the majority of the available time.

General Staff College officer cadets posing in Çanakkale in 1910. The Dardanelles was an indispensable part of college staff rides.

The General Staff College (*Erkân-ı Harbiye Mektebi*) course, which was also three years long, was founded in 1846 and followed the French model. Until 1909 it took its officer cadets directly from the Military Academy. However, in the aftermath of the 1909 military reforms, admission to the college was drastically altered to align it with the German system. Instead of directly enrolling the top cadets of the Military Academy, candidates were selected from young officers with a minimum service of six years in units who then sat a highly competitive examination. Candidates required outstanding performance evaluation reports from their superiors to qualify for ever more rigorously competitive entrance examinations. The college was small, with fewer than 200 cadets at any given time, and was located within the Military Academy barracks. However it was highly prestigious and graduation from this hallowed institution was regarded as the single most important, if not the only key to a successful military career.

One major criticism frequently levelled at the military education system concerned its heavy emphasis on theory which left little time for military application. The cadets spent most of their time learning the principles and theories of various sciences including civil and mechanical engineering, ballistics and geography, while insufficient time was allocated to the military application of these courses. The cadets were commissioned without field experience and having had no opportunity to learn practical leadership. Critics of the Academy course argued that officers required a more thorough understanding of warfare and leadership and that this could only be obtained by completing military subjects while serving with units in the field wherever possible. They advocated the abolition of the old French-style semi-engineering curriculum and its replacement with a modern German system based on military application and frequent regimental tours. The German military advisors, starting with von der Goltz in 1883, recommended and preached this change relentlessly. They finally achieved their aim in 1913, although the outbreak of war effectively stymied any opportunity to introduce a new curriculum.

Gendarmerie NCOs completing infantry basic training pose for journalists at Pangaltı Barracks during the first weeks of the mobilisation in August 1914. The Ministry of Defence used the gendarmerie to raise line infantry units.

Prior to the 1909 reforms, the Ottoman Army did not possess a professional non-commissioned officer (NCO) corps. The military reformers simply ignored the importance of an NCO corps, regarding the foundation and extension of an academically trained officer corps as the sole solution to the army's military leadership problems. This lapse was perhaps initially excusable given the enormous difficulties the administration faced finding suitable officer candidates, let alone NCOs. The lack of systematised NCO selection and training was somewhat ameliorated by the fact that the ten to 15-year compulsory service period created sufficient opportunities for units to select and train their own NCOs. However no attempt was made to create a professional NCO corps following the foundation of an effective professional military educational system for officers and a drastic reduction in compulsory military service. Consequently, units were once again left to their own devices to train and raise NCOs from soldiers over a far shorter compulsory service period.

Chapter 1

A Maxim MG99 positioned on the Galata Bridge in İstanbul during the counter-revolutionary uprising in April 1909. The Ottoman army had purchased various types of machine-guns before the 7.65 mm Maxim MG 09 became the standard gun in 1909.

The Ottoman military had long been accustomed to sourcing NCOs and officers from the ranks. Almost all NCOs acquired their skills and learnt their trade through practical experience in units and on campaign without any systematic or organised training. Provided they completed compulsory active service, and with the consent of the company and battalion commanders, recruits could usually secure a re-engagement to continue in the service. However finding suitable volunteers or aspirants from among the recruits was a perennial problem due in large part to the low salary and the insecure tenure of NCOs. An effective NCO corps could only be established with the security of a long-term tenure and the lure of a good salary. In the past the rapid demobilisation and turnover of personnel immediately after each war had prevented the army retaining its best and most experienced soldiers as NCOs. Equally, NCOs were unable to gain a permanent and respected place within the command structure and were similarly unable to build a group identity and mentality. Under these conditions the attrition rates were understandably high. For most NCOs, military service was simply a brief interval that disrupted their lives for a given period before they were released to return to their civilian professions. It was also common for NCOs to pursue a variety of economic activities to supplement their meagre salary. Not surprisingly, corruption and embezzlement were rife. The only incentive for NCOs to commit to permanent military careers was commissioning from the ranks, and loyalty and seniority were generally rewarded in the Ottoman Army. Any NCO who was patient and sufficiently robust to endure the harsh military life for a reasonable period of time was sure to be rewarded with a commission.

The 1909 military reforms radically altered the military system for NCOs by establishing three-year secondary-level military schools, similar to a military secondary college, in every field army region. The establishment of the first school was celebrated with lavish ceremonies in İstanbul in 1909 and ten others were opened simultaneously in the provinces. While the establishment of schools for NCOs placed the corps on a more secure and respectable footing, other reforms in the same package were instrumental in destroying age-old traditions and privileges. With the abolition of the *alaylı* category and the purge of *alaylı* officers from the military, commissioning from the ranks effectively disappeared and there was no incentive for conscripts and current NCOs to commit to a military career.

One of the legacies of the Balkan Wars however, was the recognition by officers and soldiers alike of the value of NCOs, who had proven their worth, rallying and leading their troops even in the aftermath of humiliating defeats. The opportunity had now arrived to firmly establish NCOs in the army institution. It was an opportunity that was destined to be lost. During the mobilisation period, the military leadership decided on the wholesale commissioning of the school-trained NCOs to compensate for the acute shortage of officers. In doing so they seriously damaged the army's ability to create a viable NCO corps. This misguided decision saw the Ottoman Army enter the war without an effective NCO corps and suffer heavily as a result. Consequently, junior career officers and reserve officers found themselves assuming NCO responsibilities for the first two years of the war, managing every aspect of soldiering from leading their men in combat actions to ensuring a fair division of food, the training of conscripts to supervising sanitation and hygiene.

An inspection of musketry during the early years of the 1900s. The soldiers are using obsolete Martini-Peabody rifles. Combat training and musketry were serious weaknesses in the Hamidian military.

One of the most significant problems confronting the new Ottoman leadership concerned individual and unit training in the army. The previous sultan, Abdülhamid II (1876–1909), had harboured grave suspicions over the loyalty of his army and had confined the units to their barracks. Basic training for soldiers was strictly limited to close-order drill and parades. Soldiers were not permitted to fire their rifles and musketry was an almost unknown trade. Officers seldom attended training and sent NCOs to conduct interminably tedious and repetitive drills. A few highly enthusiastic and dedicated officers tried various methods, sometimes pushing the boundaries of legality, to conduct realistic training. Some went to extraordinary lengths, manufacturing fictitious incidents including firefights with bandits in order to obtain ammunition for musketry training.

An 87mm Krupp field battery during a field exercise prior to 1908. Note the mantle on the barrel and the limber behind. Field exercises were very rare and something of a novelty during the reign of Abdülhamid II. The Ottoman Army learnt their importance the hard way during the Balkan Wars.

The Balkan Wars provided a tragic expose of the sorry state of individual soldier training and the question of military training became the subject of close study and intense discussion following the war. The entire system of training institutions and establishments was found to be seriously flawed, underdeveloped and lacking coordination. As a result, a single, overarching training scheme was introduced, based on yearly cycles. To ensure uniformity of training throughout the army, each training year commenced in October, the year divided into four according to the seasons. The conscripts passed through basic individual and squad training in winter followed by platoon and company training in spring, battalion and regimental training in summer and divisional or army corps manoeuvres in autumn.

A group of soldiers wash their clothes near a small stream. Although the Ottoman military authorities were aware of the importance of hygiene they had limited means to provide units with modern equipment for sanitation purposes (image courtesy of Nejat Çuhadaroğlu).

But the Ottoman Army had little time to practise its new training system, the July crisis and the August mobilisation cutting it abruptly short. Waves of new conscripts flooded divisions and there was no alternative but to train them in the units. Only after the units had reached war footing did permanent depot regiments commence operation. Regulations tasked each division with raising and operating a depot regiment to train new conscripts. Following the initial hectic days of mobilisation, the depot regiments began to function smoothly, particularly those in the western regions of the empire. However the declaration of war and the outbreak of hostilities crippled the newly founded depot training system as the General Staff reacted by using the depot regiments as a stop-gap measure during the initial emergency. *III Corps*, for example, was ordered to send the *8th Division* to Syria and raise a completely new division, the *19th Division*, from depot regiments. Thus *III Corps* lost its three depot regiments for a period of time and raised only one, some months later. The General Staff ultimately used depot regiments for a variety of tasks — all different to their intended purpose — including raising new divisions, replacing lost regiments, providing coastal or area security and occasionally as counterinsurgency forces.

In an army in which the basic training issue remained unresolved, the training of higher formations and the exercise of those formations was something of a luxury. Thus the quality and intensity of unit training varied from unit to unit depending on the character and capacity of individual commanders in an officers' army like that of the Ottomans. Even the most ardent supporters of unit training did not appreciate its crucial fundamentals such as continuous unit preparedness training at all organisational levels, all-arms combined training, realistic enemy intelligence estimates and scenario-based training. Very few units, among them the elite *III Corps*, practised these forms of training with any intensity prior to the war.

Chapter 1

A field artillery battery (armed with 75mm Krupp *feldkanone* L/30 M1903) during a large military parade in 1910. The end of the Abdülhamid reign gave new life to the military and the Ottoman public marvelled at its new military achievements. However the Balkan Wars brutally revealed the serious weakness behind the façade.

THE MOBILISATION FOR WAR

Enver Pasha, the new Minister of War and Chief of the General Staff, was convinced that the coming war would be a young man's war. As described, many high-ranking officers were (justly or unjustly) purged from the military under the pretext of incompetence or old age. Others were assigned to 'prestigious' positions essentially removed from military influence. The transformed younger and leaner officer corps was fiercely determined to cleanse the stain of the Balkan defeats from its reputation. Although most officers were keen for a long period of peace so as to complete the reform and reorganisation process they were not intimidated by the prospect of war, regarding it as a welcome opportunity, if a little earlier than they had hoped. The majority of officers lobbied for active service in preference to the less glamorous but essential administrative and logistics appointments.

The new Ottoman leadership viewed the outbreak of war as a threat to the very existence of the empire. The security of the empire depended on the broadest possible extension of military service to all groups and provinces. More rigid and tougher legislation was introduced to which there would be few exceptions. The Military Service Law of 1914 was a product of this new approach. Like its predecessors, it was enacted under the provisions of the 1876 constitution which required all citizens of the empire to serve in the defence of the state. Military service was once again proclaimed compulsory for all able-bodied males between the ages of 21 and 46. The term of active service began in the year following that in which a man celebrated his 20th birthday. The new period of service comprised 25 years in the infantry and transport corps, including two years' continuous active service, while the remaining 23 years were served in the reserves. For other army branches and the gendarmerie the period was 20 years, divided into three years' active service and 17 years in the reserves. However, in time of war, the Ministry of War had the power to delay the final release of men who had completed their term of service. The ministry could also call up entire new cohorts of conscripts prior to the normal date of enlistment and was empowered to extend liability.

An infantry company during a roll call, most likely in İstanbul. The combat strength of an Ottoman company was around 300 men at the beginning of the war (image courtesy of Nejat Çuhadaroğlu).

In order to cement peacetime conscription and to ensure smooth and rapid wartime mobilisation, the empire, with the exception of the Arabian Peninsula, was divided into 12 regions with an army corps stationed in each region. The regions were then divided into sub-regions to supply conscripts to specific divisions of the corps. The geographic size of sub-regions was measured according to the density of the respective populations. Each was tasked with raising the yearly allocated number of conscripts for its division during peacetime. In time of war the sub-regions were expected to provide sufficient conscripts and reservists to bring the divisions up to war strength and were also expected to produce additional depot regiments for each division. The Ministry of War provided recruits for the navy, gendarmerie, border guards and the independent *VII Yemen Corps*, the *21st Asir* and *22nd Hejaz divisions* from the combined pool of 12 army corps conscription regions. Coastal provinces traditionally provided the majority of naval conscripts while the other formations received their allocation from the more populous provinces. Navy and gendarmerie representatives in sub-region conscription committees were entitled to select conscripts for their services. This privilege was not extended to the independent formations which had no choice but to take what was left in the pool.

The Ottoman General Staff faced a particular set of constraints and dilemmas in mobilising its resources. The empire remained vast, even after losing its European territories. However its population was thinly dispersed with poor and underdeveloped transportation and communications infrastructure. Given these constraints the mobilisation of personnel proceeded surprisingly smoothly, particularly in parts of the west region of Anatolia. Thousands of men flooded the recruitment centres on cue — at least a quarter of whom were sent home owing to serious shortages of food, clothing and equipment. However this was not the case in eastern parts of Anatolia and in the predominantly Arab populated provinces to the south. But there remained an enormous difference between the expectations of the General Staff and the popular understanding of the universal military obligation. This was compounded by the attitude of sections of the population such as non-Muslim religious groups who had virtually no tradition of conscription and the majority of nomadic and mountain tribes who tried their best to evade the call-up.

The situation in terms of weapons, equipment and ammunition was universally dire. The Ottoman Army had lost more than half its heavy equipment and weapons during the humiliating retreats and surrenders of the Balkan Wars. As a result, the quality of weapons and equipment varied greatly between the units and the army simply did not have the means to provide for its considerably expanded numbers. The logistical problems of mobilisation were compounded by corruption, incompetence and even outright treason. Against all expectations, the new alliance with Germany did not immediately rectify critical shortages because of the lack of direct railway connections for the shipping of materiel and armaments. All transportation between Germany and the Ottoman Empire was at the mercy of Romania and Bulgaria and only a fraction of the promised supplies arrived from Germany.

The massive expansion of the Ottoman Army following mobilisation required a correspondingly huge influx of new officers. The mobilisation clearly demonstrated the dangerously fragile state of the officer corps. The mobilised personnel strength of the military was enormous: more than a million men with a combat strength of 820,000. However the strength of the regular officer corps was just 12,469; for every 100 combat soldiers, the administration provided only 1.5 officers. Neither the Ministry of War nor the General Staff appeared to have seriously considered the dearth of officers prior to mobilisation. To address this critical shortage, the administration took the drastic action of recalling recently purged officers and tapping the reservoir of retired officers (known as 'dugouts'). The recent products of NCO schools were commissioned wholesale and Military Academy cadets were graduated early. However these last-minute measures did little to alleviate the difficulties confronting the Ottoman Army.

THE OTTOMAN DEFENCE AGAINST THE ANZAC LANDING: 25 April 1915

A studio photograph of a battalion commander issuing an operational order to his company commanders. The battalion commander and his two senior company commanders are captains and the junior company commanders are 1st lieutenants. The average age and rank of the Ottoman officer corps dropped dramatically following the wide-scale purges in 1913 and 1914. It was common to find lieutenants commanding companies, captains battalions, majors regiments and lieutenant colonels divisions (image courtesy of Nejat Çuhadaroğlu).

The military leadership eventually realised that it had little alternative but to commission suitable candidates from the pool of reserves and conscripts. This presented enormous problems. The Ottoman military did not have a reserve officer system — this was a concept that was largely unknown at the time. While the first reserve officer training corps was founded on 1 August 1910 and managed to graduate two classes just prior to the Balkan Wars, it was closed down during the war and did not reopen. Apparently it left no legacy of any value as the İstanbul Reserve Officer Training Corps (İhtiyat Zabit Talimgâhı) was founded hurriedly almost from scratch a few days after the mobilisation on 9 August 1914.

The İstanbul Reserve Officer Training Corps during the early days of its foundation. Hundreds of reserve officer candidates rushed to training centres immediately following the declaration of mobilisation. For almost a month the authorities faced huge problems supplying them with uniforms and weapons.

The lack of any clause relating to reserve officers in the mobilisation decree caused chaos at the beginning of the process. The Ministry of War hurriedly sent amendments to recruitment centres which directed them to send university graduates and students to İstanbul. Wisely, the administration did not allow religion or ethnic identity to bar eligible conscripts from joining the reserve officer corps. In contrast to its European counterparts, the Ottoman Army made no distinction based on race, religion or class. Thus the training centre became a mirror of Ottoman society. Old and young graduates and students flooded the Officer Training Corps, overwhelming its capacity to clothe, arm, feed and accommodate its new recruits. As the initial wave of reserves began training, the administration added religious high school graduates and students, creating another enormous wave of reserves. At the same time, planning and policy on the management of the various civil services, schools, factories and even government bureaucracy remained in abeyance; thus, in the early months of the mobilisation, the whole country came to a standstill.

At the time of the reserve mobilisation most of the military instructors at the Military Academy had left to assume their war postings while all the cadets had been commissioned and sent to combat units. The Training Corps Commander, Major Naci (Eldeniz), managed to retain some of the instructors and cadets and establish an instructional core for the resumption of training. His aim was to quickly teach basic recruit drill and infantry skills such as marching, musketry, entrenching, patrolling and map-reading, as well as those skills deemed necessary for a company grade officer. There was no established program and the rush of thousands of reserves overwhelmed the meagre cadre. Problems and obstacles were overcome through improvisation and sheer ingenuity. Given the lack of experienced NCOs, junior military academy cadets or cadets from middle level military schools had to act as drill sergeants. They would remain in these positions for well over a year until invalid reserve officers with some combat experience took over these duties.

In an effort to organise and standardise training, German Colonel Hans Rabe was assigned as the overall commander of the reserve officer training centres. He brought his team of experienced instructors and drill masters and attempted to introduce elements of the German *Offizier-Aspiranten-Kursus*. However the Ottoman reserve officer training system, which had already forged its own character from lessons learned during the hectic weeks of mobilisation, remained resilient. Consequently, Rabe found himself juggling German theory and Ottoman practice. He fixed the term of the course at between six and eight months. More training centres and units were opened in order to spread the burden and provide more efficient and realistic training. For example, cadets selected for the artillery branch were initially sent to artillery units for on-the-job training. Later a special artillery training and gunnery centre was established to provide short 'crash courses' on rudimentary ballistics, registration, range tables, correction and gunnery. Infantry cadets were divided into battalions and sent to satellite camps in and around İstanbul. The training was rigorous, intensive and repetitive. Leave was rarely granted. Even at this stage the relative success of the training corps was due in large part to the enthusiasm and genuine willingness of the cadets to learn.

The Ottoman military leadership harboured serious concerns over the ability of its reserve officers. The lack of reserve officer tradition in the army and the weakness of the training corps were instrumental in reinforcing the military leadership's professional bias. Ultimately the leadership decided not to commission cadets at the end of the course but following an additional six-month probation in a unit. Under a hastily prepared and introduced regulation, based roughly on a similar German regulation, cadets were graduated as *ihtiyat zabit namzeti* (reserve officer candidates or *offizierstellvertreter*) with corporal rank tabs and assigned as squad leaders. They were automatically promoted sergeant after three months and reassigned as platoon sergeants. At the end of the probation period, battalion and company commanders evaluated the performance of individual candidates. The successful candidates were commissioned as *zabit vekili* (literally 'deputy officer', similar to German *feldwebelleutant* rank). This was a completely new rank which clearly reflected the level of distrust of reserve officers. Those who had failed the final evaluation would continue as NCOs with an opportunity for reconsideration at a later date.

Reserve officer candidates pose near the coastline. Regulations stipulated they complete a six-month probationary period before being commissioned and assigned as platoon leaders. In practice, however, most of them took over platoons without having officer status.

This relatively complex probation and rank status created a series of problems, at least for the first year of the war. First, the policy upset every reserve officer and, in some cases, prompted insubordination. Older, more mature men who had often held positions of greater prestige and who already felt humiliated by their treatment at the training corps, rebelled against this rank and probation system. Most of them gained exemptions from military service to return to their civilian jobs or were transferred to rear service positions. Thus this valuable group of potential leaders was lost, more or less permanently. Second, career officers, who had regarded themselves as a close-knit family, were initially unhappy at the inclusion of reserve officers in the officer corps and at the prospect of working side by side with them. The unrewarding and complex probation system appeared to confirm their concept of reserve stereotypes and their prejudices. The reserve officer candidates generally did not receive a warm welcome and were forced to endure punishing weeks before gaining a place.

Reserve officer candidates undergoing basic training at the İstanbul *Reserve Officer Corps*. Notice the difference in uniforms. Candidates with the financial means purchased tailor-made uniforms while the others wore whatever was left in the depots (image courtesy of Nejat Çuhadaroğlu).

It is difficult to overstate the problems confronting the reserve officer candidates who often found themselves commanding a platoon (sometimes even a company) without the support of an experienced NCO. The NCOs, if there were any available, were unhappy with this arrangement for obvious reasons. Candidates also had enormous difficulty establishing their credibility with their soldiers who were accustomed to strong leadership. The system worked only in units that were still in their peacetime garrisons with sufficient officers to conduct proper probation and orientation. The massive casualties suffered during the first combat actions forced the career officers to accept reserve officers, although prejudice and resentment never entirely vanished. The reserve officers felt disempowered and isolated in the face of apparently arbitrary and often coercive authority at the battalion and company level and they frequently took a long time to settle in. Most of the reserve officers had to learn their trade on the job, teaching themselves using various methods, while enduring harsh conditions on the front line, often in isolation. Many gained their military knowledge by imitating their fellow junior career officers, some from the study of military manuals and others, who were more fortunate, from experienced NCOs.

Surprisingly, commissioning from the ranks was not regarded as a proper source of officers due to the widespread belief that officer-like qualities could only be gained through higher education. Even meritorious soldiers with some education were not considered for commissioning during the war. Thus not only did a valuable source remain untapped, but this policy also created enormous uneasiness among the soldiers. On the other hand, during the initial operations, most 'dugout' officers appeared to cause more trouble than they were worth. Consequently most of them were transferred to rear echelon logistic and administrative units or were discharged from the army altogether.

STRATEGY AND CONCENTRATION

When the German Army stormed into Belgium the Ottoman military was caught largely unprepared. German Colonel Friedrich Bronsart von Schellendorf had been at the helm of the Ottoman General Staff for less than a year. Officially, Enver Pasha was Chief of the General Staff in addition to filling his position as the Minister of War, with von Schellendorf his first assistant chief. However, Enver Pasha had neither the necessary experience nor background to handle the highly technical and demanding general staff duties — nor did he enjoy the burden of staff work. Instead, he preferred to deal with grand issues at the strategic level and then in only cursory fashion. As a result, von Schellendorf quickly became the de facto Chief of the General Staff. He immediately began reorganising the General Staff, shaping it to become a mirror image of the German General Staff. German General Staff officers were assigned as branch chiefs and young, talented Ottoman General Staff officers, most of whom were also German trained, became their deputies. Under von Schellendorf's command, the staff amended the strategic mobilisation and concentration plan and rewrote most of the future campaign plans.

While the General Staff was dealing with the problems of mobilisation, the Ottoman leadership failed to develop an effective strategy that could achieve its political aims. First, the Ottoman leaders were effectively divided into two camps in terms of their attitude to entry into the war and their preference for an alliance. Enver Pasha, Cemal Pasha and Talat Bey — the triumvirate of the governing CUP — either converted or sidelined the opposition to a German alliance. However their methods were instrumental in causing ill-feeling and further opposition. Second, Grand Vizier Said Halim Pasha and the civilian members of the leadership did not fully understand the extraordinary demands on the empire of waging war. They had only a limited understanding of the fundamental decisions that would govern the nature, scope, length, economic and human cost of the war. They also lacked the courage to face the likely consequences of war. The limitations of the civilian leadership effectively saw them sidelined by the CUP triumvirate. Third, Enver Pasha and the inner circle of the CUP believed in the superiority of German military thinking and in the imminence of victory. They were convinced that the Ottoman military's role was to divert as many Entente troops as possible to assist the Germans to win decisive victories on the main fronts. This attitude was welcomed by the German General Staff, which regarded the Ottoman military as a useful tool to divert attention and force the enemy to allocate more troops to the 'Oriental sideshows'. Nevertheless, this attitude ignored the need to defend the empire's borders and territories and presented the leadership with a dilemma it was unable to solve.

With the apparent failure of the Ottoman leadership, German-led General Staff quickly filled the vacuum and became more or less the main actors in developing an effective war strategy. Only Enver Pasha and, to a certain extent, Cemal Pasha, were able to influence the formulation of strategy. Their joint assessment was that the most vulnerable parts of the empire were its capital, İstanbul, and the Dardanelles Straits. Previous conflicts and crises had clearly established a pattern in which the enemies of the empire had tried to force the Straits in order to dictate their terms to the Ottoman government. Moreover, against all expectations and despite prolonged negotiations, Bulgaria and Romania continued to maintain their neutrality. Under these conditions the European borders and the fortress city of Edirne (Adrianople) had to be protected against a possible attack. Thus a defensive strategy in the west became the inevitable choice.

The Ottoman leadership and General Staff spent considerable time agreeing a strategy to meet the Russian threat at the Caucasus border. Historically, the Ottomans had generally failed to halt Russian incursions over the border. Indeed in 1829 and again in 1877 the Russian Army had penetrated deep into eastern Anatolia and captured Erzurum. In a spirit of pessimism a strategic defence was considered the best possible strategy, but no final decision was made as to where to establish the main defensive line. Interestingly, the southern borders and regions of the empire were ignored at this stage. There was no threat assessment or discussion of Mesopotamia, Yemen and Hejaz and only vague speculation on the defence of Palestine, Lebanon and Syria. Instead, units that were stationed or mobilised in the south were regarded as suitable for deployment to the Straits or Thrace. The problem of interior security was similarly ignored. To create more mobile tactical units for the army, the gendarmerie was reorganised according to conventional military needs and to establish line infantry divisions and regiments. Consequently, even the most volatile provinces would be left without adequate security. Governors were later forced to use elderly or unfit ex-servicemen and the routinely problematic village guards in an attempt to maintain order.

This image of Gendarmerie NCOs at Pangaltı barracks during the early weeks of the mobilisation illustrates the difficulties they experienced with their new combat equipment.

Even after ignoring the possibility of a threat from the south, the threat assessment clearly reinforced the importance of strategic defence. However, at the same time, the prevalent European 'cult of the offensive' significantly influenced the Ottoman military leadership. Like their European counterparts, they believed that modern wars would be brief and the outcome decided by massive offensive operations. The Russo-Japanese War and the Balkan defeats clearly reinforced this offensive spirit. In addition, a protracted war was regarded as highly likely to destroy the fragile socio-political framework of the empire. For this reason, the Ottoman leadership reassessed defensive strategies as likely to lead to defeat. They were also convinced that the Ottoman military had to contribute directly to the main theatres of operations in Europe before the final German victory in order to secure an honourable place at the peace negotiations. Liman von Sanders and Colmar von der Goltz suggested opening a new front either with Romania or in Odessa, using the divisions that had been concentrated in and around the Straits. This suggestion was welcomed by both Enver Pasha and the German General Staff. However the main obstacle remained Bulgarian and Romanian neutrality.

THE OTTOMAN DEFENCE AGAINST THE ANZAC LANDING: 25 April 1915

Colmar von der Goltz was highly popular within the Ottoman Army but Enver Pasha and the German Embassy staff in İstanbul simply hated him. However they later welcomed his return as a means of weakening the authority of von Sanders.

Under this strategy the Ottoman General Staff prepared a single mobilisation and concentration plan (the so-called Plan Number One) in which most of the army corps and divisions (a total of 26 divisions from 38 numbered divisions) would be concentrated around İstanbul and the Dardanelles Straits to respond to possible threats. They also planned to use two army corps against Russia (either at the Romanian border or around Odessa) in order to reduce the burden on the Habsburg military. As a result, one army corps from the *Third Army*, two army corps headquarters and three divisions from the *Iraq Regional Command* (leaving only one division there) and almost all the divisions of the *Fourth Army* were deployed to Thrace. However, due to conflicting messages from the German political and military leadership, the Ottoman military soon began to make radical changes to these plans. Two army corps, each with two divisions, were reallocated to the *Fourth Army* to launch a surprise attack on the Suez Canal. *X Army Corps* was returned to its mother unit, the *Third Army*, with the changing strategic concept involving Russia. These sudden changes created havoc within the units, which had to march first forward to a new location and then back to their original positions.

By autumn 1914, most Ottoman officers had reached the conclusion that their country's continuing neutrality was no longer feasible and that the empire would eventually be drawn into the war one way or another. The general view was that, in order to prevail, the empire had to join the war on the side of Germany. Nevertheless, the Ottoman officers insisted that the Ottoman Empire's entry into the war be postponed by two years, particularly following the Austro-Hungarian Army's crushing defeat at the hands of Serbia and Russia and the deadlock on the Western Front. The officers strongly believed that addressing and remedying the Ottoman Army's deficiencies was an essential precursor to its entry into the war. Despite this belief, three months of vacillation and diplomatic manoeuvring would see the Ottoman Empire drawn into the war on the side of Germany.

CHAPTER 2
EARLY DEFENSIVE STRATEGIES

The Dardanelles Straits and Gallipoli Peninsula had been part of an organised fortress command from very early times that had seen fortresses and other fortifications built, enlarged and rebuilt during the reign of several Ottoman sultans. Throughout this period, defence of the area remained largely the responsibility of the Ottoman artillery corps. In fact, almost every artillery officer, particularly the heavy artillery branch, served at least one term in the *Dardanelles Fortified Zone Command* (Çanakkale Müstahkem Mevki Kumandanlığı) prior to 1914. From time to time responsibility for the area's defence was handed off to other operational commands, most recently the *Composite Gallipoli Corps* during the Balkan Wars. However the *Fortified Zone Command* had continued to retain authority for the defensive system itself.

The first serious danger to the Dardanelles in modern times occurred during the Ottoman-Italian War of 1911–12. The Italian leadership was keen to demonstrate the might of the recently united Italy and build a colonial empire. To this end, the Italians had been plotting to annex Libya for some time. On 29 September 1911 they finally struck, declaring war on the Ottoman Empire. In contrast to their expectation of an easy victory, the Italian expeditionary force faced a determined defence and, their initial invasion repelled, took refuge in coastal enclaves. After several bloody defeats the Italian leadership reached the realisation that the expeditionary force would not be able to defeat the Ottoman defenders and conquer the Libyan interior. Instead the Italians decided to shift the war to the core regions of the empire in order to force the Ottoman political leadership to relinquish Libya. They could not risk another land confrontation with the Ottoman military so decided to use their navy acting in isolation. From February to April 1912, the Italian Navy employed various tactics including naval demonstrations and limited shelling of the Red Sea, Albanian, Syrian and Aegean coastlines. Ignoring the protests of the Great Powers, Italy decided to escalate the confrontation by blockading and attacking the Straits.

At the start of the war the Ottoman Ministry of Defence and the General Staff carefully evaluated the Italian war aims and strategy and their evaluation told them to expect an attack on the Dardanelles Straits. Although the Italians had a limited capacity to launch an amphibious landing, the Ottoman leadership decided to activate a field army with six divisions to take over the land defence from the *Fortified Zone Command*. The Çanakkale (Dardanelles) Provisional Army was activated under the command of Ali Rıza Pasha in October 1911. *II Corps* (*5th*, *9th* and İzmit divisions) and *III Corps* (*Bursa*, Çanakkale and *Edremit divisions*) were placed under command of this new field army.

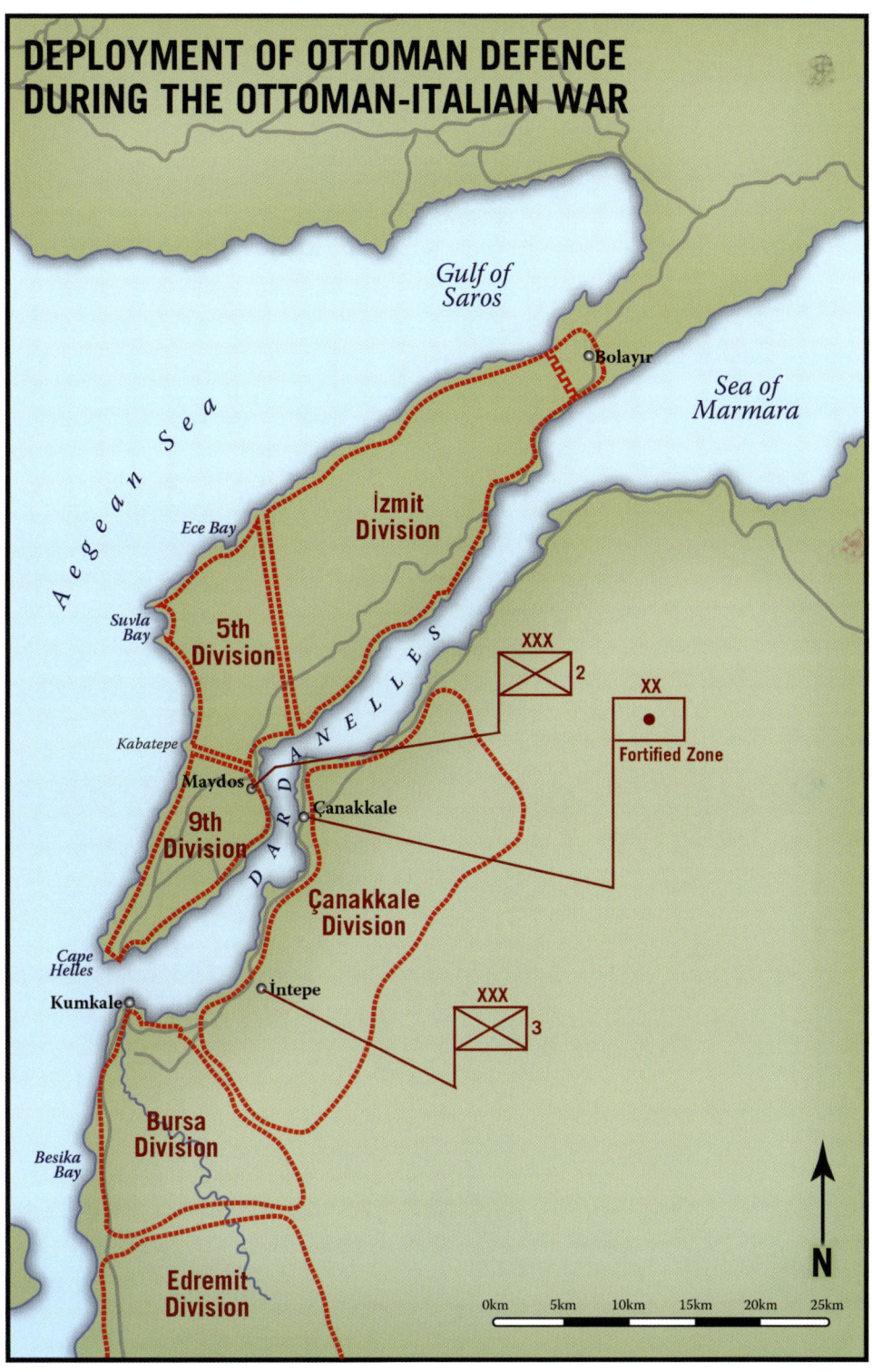

Deployment of Ottoman Defence during the Ottoman-Italian War

THE OTTOMAN DEFENCE AGAINST THE ANZAC LANDING: 25 April 1915

Ali Rıza Pasha was appointed commander of the entire defence — albeit in name only. Minister of Defence Mahmud Şevket Pasha cautioned him not to interfere with the *Fortified Zone Command* and the defence against the naval attack. However this effectively created a dual command, with each commander more or less independent of the other. For obvious reasons Rüşdü Pasha, the *Fortified Zone* commander, was not happy with this arrangement. He persuaded Ali Rıza Pasha and the *Fortified Zone* staff to prepare a joint plan for the defence against an enemy landing. Accordingly, Ali Rıza Pasha tasked *II Corps* with the defence of the Gallipoli Peninsula and *III Corps* with safeguarding the Anatolian side of the Straits. The Seddülbahir (Helles), Kabatepe (Gaba Tepe) and Kumkale regions were identified as possible main landings sites. Two regular divisions and a first rate reserve division, *Bursa*, were assigned to the defence of these key regions.

The *Dardanelles Fortified Zone Command* staff in April 1912 during the Ottoman-Italian War. From left to right: Galib Pasha (the fortress artillery commander), Rüşdü Pasha (Fortified Zone commander) and Mustafa (Chief of Staff).

Rüşdü Pasha and his staff also recognised the limitations of the fortifications and fixed coastal heavy artillery. More than half of these guns had little capacity to counter an attack by modern battleships due to limitations of range and slow-firing mechanisms. They also knew that they could expect minimal support from the Ottoman naval fleet. Plans to use some battleships as coastal floating batteries came to naught. There was only one way to reinforce the current defensive system — sea mines. They proposed to close the Strait with five belts of contact mines. Mahmud Şevket Pasha considered this proposition, noting its possibilities, and immediately arranged the import of modern mines from Germany and other sources. *Fortified Zone Command* anxiously awaited the delivery of the first batch of mines in February. Meanwhile Ali Rıza Pasha tried his best to erect defensive lines around key landing sites despite lacking the essential elements: barbed wire, cement and other materials to build fortifications. Units resorted to digging trenches, gun positions and earthen fortifications. With limited means of transportation and communication, Ali Rıza Pasha concentrated all his divisions on the coast and maintained regimental-size reserves. The first roads connecting key locations were constructed during this crisis.

Staff of Orhaniye Fort, April 1912.

Fortunately for Ali Rıza Pasha, the Italians had never planned to test Ottoman land defences. The Italian Navy finally appeared in front of the outer Straits fortifications on 18 April after much delay. The Italian Vice Admiral, Leone Viale, planned to bombard four of the outer forts in an attempt to lure the Ottoman fleet into committing to a naval engagement. Four Italian battleships bombarded the Anatolian forts of Orhaniye and Kumkale while three battleships bombarded the European forts Seddülbahir and Ertuğrul. The bombardment lasted three hours and achieved little. Only one building at Orhaniye was damaged and a soldier killed at Kumkale. Viale's ships were plagued with problems and many damaged in accidents and he decided not to renew the attack, finally launching a failed torpedo boat raid on the night of 18/19 July 1912 as a futile last resort.

The Italian cruiser *Vittorio Emanuele* bombards the Kumkale fort on 18 April 1912. The Italian fleet were plagued with problems during the three-hour bombardment. Vice-Admiral Leone Viale did not renew the attack.

The second big test of the Dardanelles defence system took place six months later with the outbreak of the Balkan Wars on 8 October 1912. The Ottoman administration was determined to fight for every inch of the empire's territory. Overconfident General Staff officers insisted on acting offensively at the operational level while conducting defensive operations at the strategic level — a key element of the newly introduced German doctrine. They naively hoped that the small militaries of the Balkan states would not have the means to launch coordinated assaults, allowing the Ottoman units the opportunity to defeat them individually. As a consequence, the General Staff initially did not allocate units for the defence of the Dardanelles other than *Fortified Zone Command*'s organic fortress artillery regiments and some second rate reserve territorial defence units. The only regular formation at the Dardanelles, the *5th Division*, was assigned to the Bulgarian frontier close to Kırkkilise. Nevertheless, at the last minute, the General Staff planners wavered and *XV Provisional Army Corps* (Çanakkale and *Edremit divisions*) was tasked with defending the Dardanelles against enemy landings given the continuing Italian threat and the added possibility of attacks by Greek forces.

On 18 April 1912 the Italian fleet fired more than 400 shells but managed to hit only this building in Orhaniye Fort.

In 1912 the Bulgarian Army launched a lighting campaign and defeated the Ottoman *Eastern Army* in two separate battles in Kırkkilise (22–23 October) and Lüleburgaz (29 October–2 November). Several detachments retreated to the Gallipoli Peninsula while most of the units of the *Eastern Army* took refuge behind the Çatalca defensive line in front of İstanbul. In similar fashion, the *Western Army* in Macedonia was also defeated in several battles and disintegrated. Suddenly the possibility of a Greek naval attack against the Dardanelles loomed large. New regular (*27th* and *Composite divisions*) and reserve units (*Afyon*) were rushed to the Dardanelles. *XV Corps* was disbanded and a new formation, the *Composite Gallipoli Army Corps*, was activated under the command of Çolak Fahri Pasha.

THE OTTOMAN DEFENCE AGAINST THE ANZAC LANDING: 25 April 1915

A group photo of the *Composite Division* officers in Atıf Bey Çiftliği on the Gallipoli Peninsula during the Balkan Wars. The *Composite Division* bore the brunt of the Bolayır assault on 8 February 1913 (image courtesy of Nejat Çuhadaroğlu).

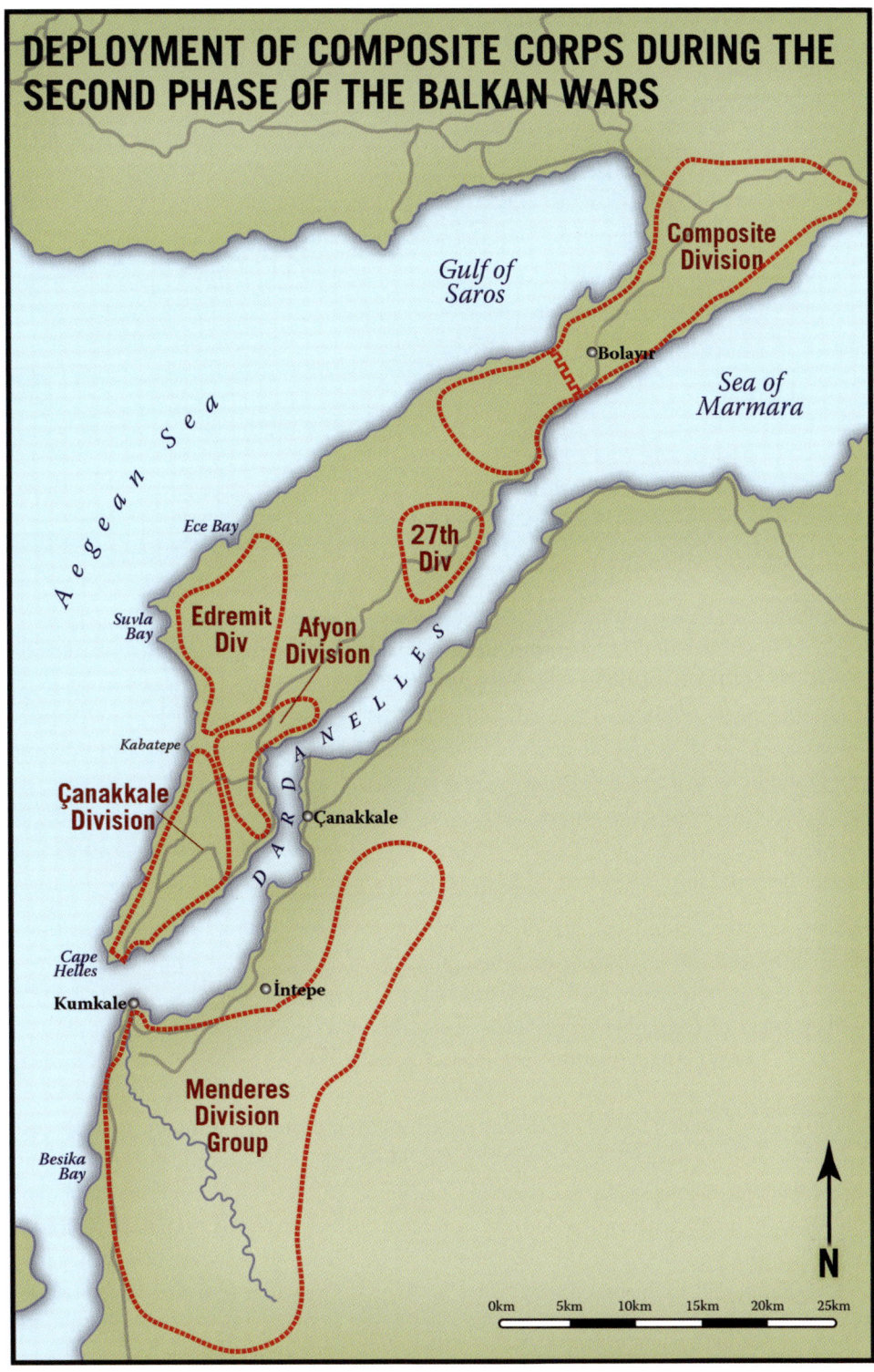

Deployment of Composite Corps during the second phase of the Balkan Wars just before the Bulgarian offensive

A 355mm Krupp L/35 fortress gun and its crew during the Balkan Wars, most likely in Anadolu Hamidiye Fort. The expected naval attack did not take place but it provided an excellent opportunity to prepare and practise defensive plans (image courtesy of ATASE).

Fahri Pasha faced a very difficult mission. He not only needed to reorganise and train his largely demoralised soldiers, but also make the necessary preparations to repel possible landings. Fahri Pasha wisely left the *Fortified Zone Command* to deal with any naval attack against the Straits and instead focused on the land defence system. He quickly implemented the old defensive plans, modifying them slightly. Instead of holding the Anatolian side with two divisions, he activated the *Menderes Divisional Group* and tasked it with the defence. He kept his best two divisions in reserve and manned the southern side of the peninsula with two reserve divisions. He allocated most of his firepower to the aging Crimean War-era Bolayır (Bulair) defensive line. Units once again raced to repair and improve old defensive positions.

Against all expectations, instead of a naval attack or amphibious landing, the threat materialised from the land. Following their failure to breach the Çatalca line, the Bulgarian military leadership decided to force Gallipoli and activated the Bulgarian Fourth Army at the beginning of December. Fortunately a ceasefire was agreed a few days later and the Bulgarians had no opportunity to attempt to force the Bolayır line. Instead the Ottoman General Staff took the initiative. An amphibious operation was planned against the Fourth Bulgarian Army, with a landing at Şarköy aimed to save Edirne by hitting the concentrated Bulgarian forces opposite Çatalca from the rear. However a series of unfortunate incidents and developments involving the weather, technical failures, and communication and coordination problems handicapped the operation. The first leg of the attack, a frontal assault by the *Composite Corps* at Bolayır, stalled under the fire of well-entrenched Bulgarian infantry supported by massive coordinated artillery and machine-gun fire on 8 February 1913. While the Şarköy amphibious landing succeeded in establishing beachheads, the recently reinforced Bulgarian divisions launched uncoordinated but effective assaults forcing the operation to be abandoned two days later on 10 February.

Following this failure the *Composite Corps* remained in defence during subsequent operations and throughout the second ceasefire period. With the start of the Second Balkan War between the former Balkan allies, however, the Ottoman Army seized the opportunity to recapture Eastern Thrace and Edirne. The *Composite Corps* raced to reach Edirne but was outrun by *X Corps*.

Both of these limited attacks provided the Ottoman defenders a valuable opportunity to test their defensive system and practise various tactics and techniques. These experiences also highlighted some of the requirements and limitations of the army's basic defensive principles. Although the peninsula defence system was in its infancy, it provided a useful opportunity for staff and artillery officers to analyse and practise defensive tactics against amphibious operations. The *Fortified Zone Command*, for example, discovered not only the serious limitations of the current Straits defence and how to deal with these, but also the necessity to prepare and coordinate a defence against landings. A defensive system to counter landings based on a provisional army or army corps with six divisions was also devised during this crisis.

Mustafa Kemal (Atatürk) with his good friend Lieutenant Commander Rauf (Orbay) at Gallipoli during the Balkan Wars. As the Chief of Operations of the *Dardanelles Composite Corps*, Mustafa Kemal gained valuable experience of the region and its defence system.

THE OTTOMAN DEFENCE AGAINST THE ANZAC LANDING: 25 April 1915

Some of the Ottoman Army's key military leaders and units gained first-hand battle experience during these wars. Mustafa Kemal (Atatürk) was the Chief of Operations Branch of the *Composite Corps* and was one of the key planners of the Şarköy-Bolayır amphibious operation. He witnessed the deadly combination of fortification, machine-guns and artillery in defence. Infantry regiments from the *27th* and *Composite divisions* were literally annihilated in front of the Bulgarian trenches by enfilading machine-gun fire and artillery barrages during a daylight attack on 8 February 1913. Likewise, most of the future soldiers of the *9th* and *19th divisions* learned their trade during these crises and wars. These men were mostly from the Dardanelles or neighbouring regions and knew the terrain intimately. These recent rehearsals ensured that they learned the basics of entrenchment, musketry in the field and independent small unit actions.

ESAD PASHA AND *III ARMY CORPS*

Given the critical role of Esad (Bülkat) Pasha and *III Corps* during the 25 April landings, it is important to understand how *III Corps* trained and prepared for war under his command. *III Corps* was the only corps that emerged from the Balkan Wars more or less intact, its reputation forged in battle. But Esad Pasha was quick to discover that *III Corps* also had its problems. As commander of the corps prior to the war, he knew the corps and its area of responsibility well. Esad Pasha was aware that he needed to rectify numerous weaknesses before his corps could become an effective fighting force, first and foremost concerning his staff which was largely ineffective and dysfunctional. His Chief of Staff, German Lieutenant Colonel Perrinet von Thauvenay, was not a particularly competent staff officer and nor was he gifted with great intelligence. Moreover his relations with his Ottoman colleagues were strained at best and his tendency towards alcoholism caused embarrassment within the German Military Mission. However Esad Pasha tried his best to find a use for him and other problematic staff officers. While he was a demanding commander, he had a kindly and forgiving disposition and believed in the virtue of a second chance. Unfortunately his kindness proved misplaced and, by September 1914, all the officers to whom he had shown such latitude had been relieved of their duties. His new Chief of Staff, Lieutenant Colonel Fahreddin, was also not a particularly bright staff officer, but he was loyal and hard working and, most importantly for Esad Pasha, he maintained excellent relations with almost all the divisional and regimental commanders, most of whom were his classmates or acquaintances.

Esad Pasha brought personal qualities to the role of corps commander which made him popular with his officers and with the rank and file soldiers. His style of command was very different to that of other commanders. He considered himself first and foremost a leader and trainer and regarded his job as to lead and train, rather than push and punish his men. Although no general of any of the fighting nations was prepared for the tactical realities of the First World War, Esad Pasha certainly had the necessary experience. As the heroic defender of Janina (Yanya) he learnt by experience the deadly effects of modern weapons used from fortified positions against attacking infantry in the open. He quickly realised that the old style massive infantry frontal attacks were futile against prepared defensive lines and could only lead to unnecessary mass casualties which were harmful to morale.

Esad Pasha with his staff officers: on his left is Chief of Staff Fahreddin (Altay) and on his right, Chief of Operations Ohrili Kemal. Esad Pasha successfully trained and prepared his corps for war. But his performance on 25 April was less than inspiring (image courtesy of ATASE).

THE OTTOMAN DEFENCE AGAINST THE ANZAC LANDING: 25 April 1915

Esad (Bülkat) Pasha

The portrait of Esad (Bülkat) Pasha painted by Austrian artist Wilhelm Victor Krausz (image courtesy of Yetkin İşcen).

Chapter 2

Esad Pasha was born in Janina (Yanya) in 1862. He graduated at the top of his class from the Imperial Military Academy in İstanbul in 1887. He continued his military education at the General Staff College and again graduated at the top his class in 1890. He was selected for military training in Germany and spent four years in different Alsatian and Prussian units and headquarters in Strasbourg and Berlin.

Esad returned to the Ottoman Empire in 1894 and was initially assigned to the General Staff Intelligence Division. He did not like working with the General Staff and happily transferred to a less prestigious professorship at the Imperial Military Academy the following year. He was soon appointed Dean of Academics and remained in this position, except for a brief interval, until 1906. He excelled in this demanding but essentially dead-end job and gained the honorific title of 'teacher of the teachers'. It is worth noting that most of the high and medium-ranking officers of the First World War were his former students.

Esad served as the Chief of Staff of the 1st Infantry Division during the Ottoman-Greek War of 1897. His achievements in military education and his outstanding loyalty saw him promoted to major general in 1901 and lieutenant general in 1906. One year later he was appointed Acting Commander of the *Third Field Army* in Salonika. Esat Pasha remained aloof from government efforts to combat and prosecute partisan officers, most of whom were his former students. Not surprisingly, he was sacked from his position and placed under surveillance a year later. While the rebellion succeeded, with the Sultan forced to accept the resultant demands, Esat Pasha gained no benefit from the new order. He was treated as a functionary of the old regime and was unfairly demoted to the rank of brigadier general. For two years he was assigned one idiosyncratic staff job after another. His stoicism and unquestioning loyalty finally paid off and he was first appointed commanding general of the *5th Division* at Gallipoli in December 1910 and then commanding general of *II Army Corps* in Tekirdağ (Rodosto) three months later. He spent barely a year in this position before he was assigned to his hometown, Janina, as commanding general of the *23rd Division*. Interestingly, all these assignments were instrumental in providing much-needed military expertise concerning Gallipoli and the surrounding area.

Following the mobilisation decree in 1912, Esat Pasha was appointed commanding general of the newly activated independent *Janina Army Corps* with orders to defend Janina province at all costs. He organised his limited forces and sources efficiently and, instead of waiting for the enemy at the fortress, he devised an active defence plan which capitalised on the local geography. He kept the Greek Epirus Army at bay for three months with constant counter-attacks and then effected a remarkable fighting retreat towards the fortifications of Janina. With no hope of further relief and increasing unrest within the local population, he withstood Greek attacks for a further three months behind the fortifications of Janina. He surrendered on 6 March 1913.

Esad Pasha returned from captivity in December 1913. Not only did he receive no credit for his heroic defence of Janina, he barely escaped the large-scale purge. He was then appointed commanding general of *III Army Corps*. As a well-known army trainer, he initiated an extensive training program and addressed most of the problems born of the Balkan defeat. Largely due to his efforts, *III Corps* became the only corps that fulfilled its mobilisation requirements on time. The main duty of the corps was to reinforce the Gallipoli Peninsula and the Asiatic coastal defence against possible enemy landings. He achieved a remarkable degree of coordination with the *Fortified Zone Command* but this lasted just a few months. Liman von Sanders was appointed *Fifth Army* commander and tasked with the land defence of the Dardanelles region on 26 March 1915.

Without complaint, Esad Pasha turned his efforts to working harmoniously with von Sanders. Although he did not handle the command crisis on 25 April well, as the commander in charge of the northern sector of the Gallipoli Peninsula he played an important role in conducting the defence throughout the campaign. While his photo frequently appeared in newspapers and magazines and he once again became a household name during the war, Enver Pasha did not assign him to active combat command positions following the end of the campaign. He was appointed commanding general of the *First Army* in İstanbul and performed largely protocol duties such as general in charge of official visits and supervised the training of cohorts of recruits for other field armies. He was awarded multiple decorations and sent to Germany as a guest of honour but, until the summer of 1918, he remained serving in İstanbul. At the beginning of June 1918 he was appointed *Third Army* commander at the Caucasus front. The timing of his appointment meant that he took little part in operations prior to the end of war. He retired from the military during the Armistice period, having become convinced that he would never again be appointed to positions of influence.

Esad Pasha was very bitter at his treatment, shunning politics and dedicating himself to his family, writing his memoirs during his long retirement. His unpublished account is characterised by detailed personal insight and analysis and includes a large number of documents which provide a rare insight into the Ottoman Army corps system. However the section that describes the events of 25 April is brief in comparison with the others. He basically glosses over the unpleasant parts of the day and highlights evidence of his positive role. He died peacefully and privately in 1952. It is unfortunate that the life of Esat Pasha has received little recognition or has yet to attract serious study.

Esad Pasha took every opportunity to share the lessons he had learned from the Balkan Wars with his officers and soldiers who were keen and anxious to learn. Above all, he was an excellent judge of men. He invested time in identifying, encouraging and promoting capable officers. Similarly, he dismissed those who did not perform. At the same time he had to improvise extensively given the acute shortages of essential equipment that plagued the Ottoman Army. He paid special attention to the ever-problematic logistical and administrative issues. He conducted frequent inspections, literally popping up in unexpected places at odd times. He was convinced that personal example was the key to leadership and he achieved remarkable results.

Yet Esad Pasha's success was eventually to prove his downfall. The General Staff had a tendency to use *III Corps* as a form of depot for rapid reaction forces or to provide stop-gap measures in a crisis. When Ibn Suud of Najd began to threaten local security in Basra province, a crack battalion from the *26th Regiment* was hurriedly despatched to take control of the situation. While this was supposed to be a temporary mission, the battalion never returned. Most damagingly, during the early days of the mobilisation, the *8th Division* and all its units were reassigned to Syria. Esad Pasha responded by activating the *19th Division* from the depot regiments in record time, bolstering it with companies from other units. He convinced the Ministry of War to assign bright young General Staff officers to this division including Mustafa Kemal [Atatürk]. But the General Staff once again intervened and exchanged two regiments (*55th* and *56th*) from this brand new division with two from Syria (*72nd* and *77th regiments*). Esad Pasha stoically accepted these orders and duly raised new units from scratch.

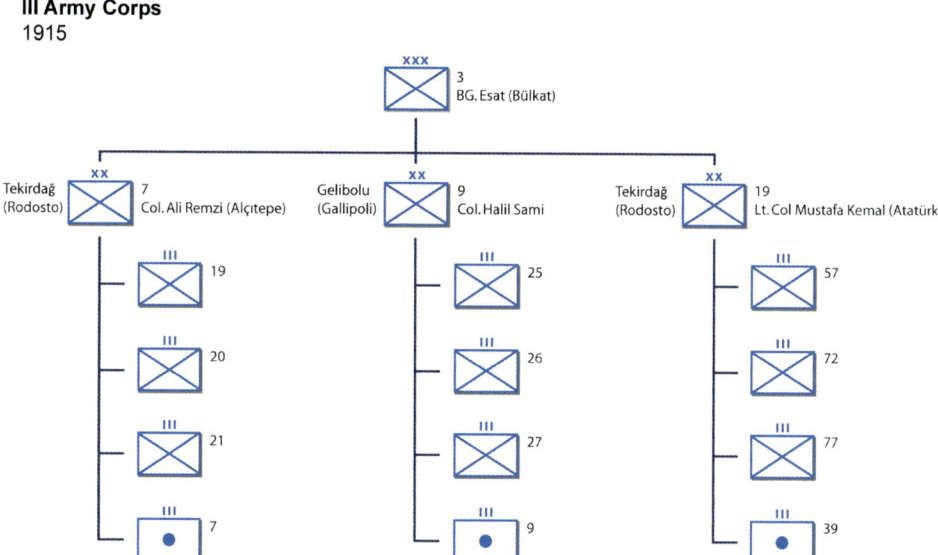

Under the new unit architecture and system, the standing army provided a framework which its units would bring up to war strength using the mobilised reservists and conscripts. No new manoeuvre units higher than company level were envisaged and the only new larger formations were logistical and administrative. Thus the mobilisation appeared straightforward and easy to accomplish — at least on paper. The July crisis and the war in Europe that followed severely tested this 'simple' personnel mobilisation system. The Balkan Wars had left the army exhausted, demoralised and in need of urgent re-equipping and refurbishment. Most of the corps and divisional headquarters were still sited some distance from their peacetime garrisons in their Balkan Wars concentrations. To further complicate matters, some of the original conscription regions of a number of corps and divisions had been annexed by the Balkan states and these formations now had to move to completely new regions. The organisational architecture was still new and a series of hasty amendments designed to assist in its implementation simply created chaos. Amid the confusion the Ottoman administration declared mobilisation on 2 August 1914.

Two infantry squads pose for journalist in front of the İstanbul walls during the first weeks of the mobilisation in August 1914. The army's uniforms and equipment remained more or less the same throughout the war (image courtesy of Nejat Çuhadaroğlu).

Despite the turmoil, the drastic changes had clearly borne fruit. For the first time, the empire as a whole had been forced to mobilise. There were no impressive patriotic demonstrations like those that had characterised the previous mobilisation. Thousands of men flooded the conscription centres in western Anatolia as required, although as previously described, at least a quarter of these were sent home because of serious shortages of food, clothing and equipment. In other areas the mobilisation proceeded slowly because of the serious limitations of local committees, drastic changes in the structure of the military organisation and a pervasive air of uncertainty in some of the conscription sub-regions. It quickly became clear that an intimate knowledge of the local population and conditions was essential for the success of the mobilisation and most of the conscription centres lacked staff with this qualification. With the exception of *III Corps* and *VII Corps* (which was excluded from the mobilisation), none of the 12 corps completed its mobilisation on time. Indeed *I Corps* took over a month, while most of the other corps spent at least an extra two or three weeks completing their mobilisation. Nonetheless, the army eventually exceeded the authorised war strength, reaching an imposing total of over a million men, translating to a combat strength of 820,000. The Ottoman Army of 1914 was also far most representative of the empire's population than that of any other period.

Esad Pasha's extraordinary record in preparing his corps for war is all the more remarkable when compared to the performance of other units. Not only was *III Corps* the only corps that completed its mobilisation on time, it was also the only corps that successfully activated its combat service support units, including supply trains. However it was beset by a range of problems common to the armed forces as a whole. One of its most serious difficulties only emerged with the completion of personnel mobilisation. Under the relevant regulations, once the units reached their war strength and moved to their concentration places or fronts, the corps and divisional commanders were to hand over their regional responsibilities to conscription region and sub-region chiefs. These chiefs were tasked to maintain the constant flow of soldiers to the corps and also to complete their basic and refresher training. The Balkan Wars clearly demonstrated that reservists needed at least a modicum of training to be of any use in war. A cadre of career officers and — importantly —well-trained NCOs as drill sergeants was required to implement this training. However the Ottoman Army simply did not have surplus officers or NCOs to man depot regiments at the conscription centres.

The Ottoman political and military leadership, like other European military leaderships, was not expecting to fight a long war of attrition. Consequently the Ottoman conscription system was designed to suit a short, regional war. It was certainly not tailored to the requirements of a protracted world war and the rapid expansion necessary to sustain this. The opening months of the war provided clear evidence of the catastrophic casualty figures that resulted from the modern way of warfare and also prompted alarm over the accompanying problem of mass casualty replacement. The *Third Army* at the Caucasus front lost more than 70% of its combat strength in less than three months while the single division on the Mesopotamian front surrendered on 9 December 1914 having suffered several humiliating defeats. The toll of casualties surprised even the most confirmed pessimists and horrified the public. Only the enormous numbers of conscripts and the distraction of the enemy threat against the Straits alleviated this initial crisis.

In accordance with the mobilisation and concentration plan, *III Corps* was tasked to reinforce the Gallipoli Peninsula and Asian coastline defence against a possible enemy landing. The *Dardanelles Fortified Zone Command* was in charge of the naval defence and necessary defensive preparations to repel enemy landings and initially only the *9th Division* was placed under its command. *III Corps* remained on high alert to reinforce the defence at Tekirdağ until the proclamation of war. On 2 November Esad Pasha moved his headquarters and remaining units to the Dardanelles.

Crew of a 240mm Krupp L/35 fortress gun, most probably in Rumeli Mecidiye Fort. Note the presence of Germans (image courtesy of Nejat Çuhadaroğlu).

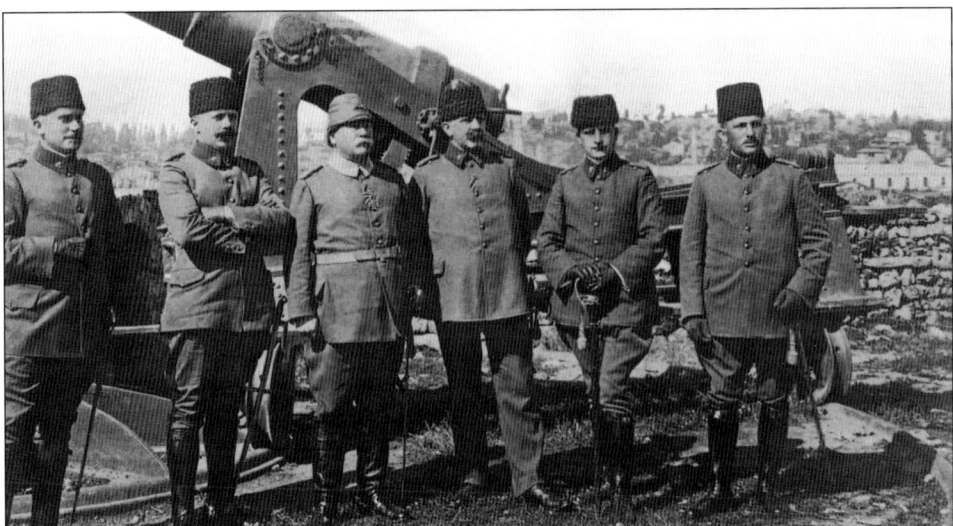

German artillery experts pose in front of an obsolete 150mm Krupp L/26 fortress howitzer. While the German experts made an important contribution to the Straits defence, in contrast to common perception, there were no Germans at Anzac and Helles on 25 April (image courtesy of Nejat Çuhadaroğlu).

His new assignment was to represent his greatest professional challenge. Nevertheless he enthusiastically began to plan. Cevad (Çobanlı), Commanding Officer of the *Fortified Zone Command*, and his staff were unhappy at the prospect of relinquishing control of the defence against the landings. They regarded the new division of responsibility as detrimental to the integrity of the defensive plan. The Dardanelles region had been under the control of the fortress artillery for a more than a century. Unsurprisingly, the *Fortified Zone Command* regarded itself as the rightful military guardian of the Dardanelles defence. Esad Pasha approached the problem diplomatically, wary of offending the command staff. After several meetings, he approved the existing defence plans and allowed the command staff to resume their traditional role.

The *Dardanelles Fortified Zone* Commander Cevad (Çobanlı) Pasha and his staff in front of his tactical command post at Hacıpaşa Çiftliği. The fortress artillery advisor, Colonel Heinrich Wehrle, is the second officer on his left. The *Fortified Zone Command* was in charge of the whole defence and prepared defensive plans prior to the arrival of von Sanders (image courtesy of ATASE).

THE OTTOMAN DEFENCE AGAINST THE ANZAC LANDING: 25 April 1915

As in previous war plans and deployments, the *Fortified Zone Command* expected the main landings to occur at the southern tip of the peninsula (Seddülbahir-Cape Helles region) and the Kabatepe region, as these two areas offered the shortest avenues of approach to overcome the Straits defences on the peninsula. Consequently, most of the available troops were allocated to these areas while the other suitable landing sites at Bolayır-Saros, Kumkale and Beşika were covered by a weak screening force on the coastline and some mobile reserves positioned behind. The main problem at this stage was the lack of troops to perform this immense defensive task. The Ottoman General Staff initially assigned only the *9th Division* and four local gendarmerie battalions. *III Corps* headquarters and the *7th Division* joined them later. This was a serious limitation. Previous experience told them that at least six divisions were required to prepare and conduct the defence. The additional divisions were finally allocated at the end of March following the arrival of Liman von Sanders.

The Ottoman artillery experts argued the case for destroying the enemy landing forces on the coast using mutually supporting prepared positions without giving them a chance to establish beachheads. They knew from previous campaigns that naval artillery fire, with its flat trajectory, posed little serious threat to entrenched infantry. The lack of paved roads on the peninsula and the limited mobility of the infantry regiments also influenced their thinking. As a result the main defensive body was sited in forward defensive positions close to the possible landing sites while small reserves were retained in the interior. Thus a division would entrench 12 companies on the coast, four companies as immediate reserves, eight companies as the regimental reserve with half an hour's reaction time, and the remaining 12 companies as the divisional reserve with a reaction time of one and a half hours. Local units were tasked to conduct counter-attacks whenever possible.

A group of Ottoman officers and soldiers pose at Merkez Fort in the Bolayır line. Esad Pasha organised the artillery units into a fortress artillery battalion.

The *7th Division* Commander, Ali Remzi (Alçıtepe), and his staff pose after the evacuation of Suvla. The *7th Division* was at Bolayır during the initial landings and joined the battle two days later because of von Sanders' expectation of a main landing against the Bolayır-Saros region (image courtesy of ATASE).

An artillery forward observation post reports corrections during a field exercise near İstanbul in August 1914. The Ottoman officers learnt tough lessons on the importance of field exercises and manoeuvres during the Balkan Wars.

In addition, most of the mobile artillery batteries and machine-guns were sited close to the coast in covered firing positions. The key principle of the defensive concept was to anchor battalion and regiment-level defensive positions around selected fortified points. Zığındere, Kumtepe, Kabatepe and three other locations (Teke, Eskihisarlık and Seddülbahir) at Helles were selected as critical positions to be fortified. The fortification and improvement of defensive positions overlooking possible landing sites was commenced early but the shortage of barbed wire and other entrenching material slowed progress. By the end of March only some sections of Seddülbahir and Kabatepe had been fortified.

Soldiers of the *9th Division* digging trenches near the coast. The pre-Sanders Ottoman defence concept placed more emphasis on keeping the coastal defences strong. Ottoman soldiers spent months preparing defensive positions without entrenching tools and suitable materials. As a result the trenches were rudimentary and lacked even basic fortification.

In the meantime the *Fortified Zone Command* decided to assign permanent fire support units from its reserve personnel to fortified points to compensate for the constant rotation of the infantry units. While it was easy to allocate personnel from reserves, it was far more difficult to arm them. Eventually, a motley collection of antiquated weapons discarded by active army and navy units and others purloined from surplus stocks were given to these new units. Among these, ex-Navy 1-inch (three or four-barrelled) Nordenfelt and 37mm Maxim-Nordenfelt (known as a 'pom-pom') rapid fire guns were organised into platoons (two or three guns) and companies (12 or 13 guns) and assigned to fortified positions. Similarly, some of the surplus 87mm Krupp L/24 M1885 field guns from the *Fortified Zone Command* inventory were also distributed in two-gun platoons. This was a desperate measure as most of these weapons were too old to be reliable and prone to break down. They had no spare parts and limited stocks of ammunition. In spite of these problems the *Fortified Zone Command*, with the help of *III Corps* units, began its slow preparation for the amphibious landings that it knew must come.

British 1-inch four-barrel Nordenfelt rapid fire gun. The *Fortified Zone Command* positioned 11 Nordenfelt guns (mostly decommissioned from the navy) in fortified places on the Gallipoli Peninsula.

British 37mm Maxim-Nordenfelt (better known as the 'pom-pom' or 1-pounder) rapid fire gun. The *Fortified Zone Command* positioned four of these near Seddülbahir.

ŞEFIK AND THE *27TH REGIMENT*

The *27th Regiment* was the home regiment of the Gallipoli Peninsula. Most of its conscripts and NCOs were Gallipoli locals or came from neighbouring provinces. The regiment's ethnic composition was characteristically diverse. At that time Gallipoli was a very cosmopolitan region. Its villages boasted a sizable Greek population, there was a strong Jewish presence in the towns and there were also Armenians living on the peninsula. However the Ottoman Army had been badly let down by its non-Muslim soldiers during the last war. During the mobilisation for the Balkan Wars, large numbers of non-Muslims had either evaded mobilisation orders or deserted at the first opportunity. With the exception of the Jewish conscripts, very few of them had been willing to fight for the empire. Many, in fact, had fled or surrendered during combat actions. The Ottoman administration was highly suspicious of the dubious loyalty of Greeks and Armenians and assigned most to combat service support units or labour battalions. Unlike the others, Jews were not singled out and were assigned to combat and non-combat units according to age, physical ability and profession like their Muslim comrades. Thus most of the combat soldiers of the regiment were local Muslims, while half of the combat service support and other auxiliary units supporting the regiment comprised non-Muslims.

Lieutenant Colonel İrfan was the Commanding Officer of the *27th Regiment* when the Ottoman administration declared mobilisation on 2 August 1914. With the mobilisation order the *27th Regiment*, along with the other regiments of the *9th Division*, came under the tactical command of the *Dardanelles Fortified Zone*. İrfan immediately assigned detachments to the coast to act as an observation and screening force. The mobilisation proceeded quickly and smoothly and the regiment began unit combat training and manoeuvres on 16 August. At the same time İrfan was assigned as the regional commander of Gallipoli and several units were placed under his command including the *Gallipoli Gendarmerie Battalion*, the *2/9th Field Artillery Battalion* and the *Bolayır Heavy Fortress Artillery Battalion*.

While the continuous coastal surveillance represented a serious drain on resources, the *27th Regiment* was in a fortunate position compared to other regiments. It remained in its home garrison and experienced no serious logistic or administrative problems during the mobilisation and afterwards. Most of the soldiers were tough combat veterans, highly motivated at the prospect of protecting their own villages and towns. Moreover individual and unit training was conducted efficiently and according to a defined timetable, thus providing ample opportunity to train and integrate raw recruits.

Despite the fact that the Ottoman Empire remained neutral until the end of October, tensions remained high, particularly with the passage of the German battleships *Göben* and *Breslau* on 10 August, and all the units in the Dardanelles region remained on a war footing, as if war had been declared. After three tense months, and with the proclamation of war on 2 November, the *27th Regiment* received orders for a full deployment to the coast. The regiment initially covered the entire western coast of the peninsula, its units dispersed some distance from one another. However on 6 November *III Corps* arrived to assume responsibility for the land defence and the regiment was tasked to cover only the southern region (including Suvla, Kabatepe and Helles). With this change in responsibility the command post moved to Maydos.

The most important change from the perspective of this study took place on 10 November. İrfan was appointed to command the *Menderes Detachment* which had been tasked to defend the Asiatic shore and Major Mehmed Şefik (Aker) took over command of the *27th*. Şefik had previously commanded the *3/25th Battalion* and was a well-known and respected officer. But he was also known as a difficult subordinate with a tendency to be uncompromising. He assumed his new command with his characteristic energy and his officers and other ranks quickly learned that he was a serious commander with little tolerance for inefficiency.

Chapter 2

MEHMED ŞEFIK (AKER)

Mehmed Şefik (Aker) was born in Monastir (Manastır) in 1877 and graduated from the Imperial Military Academy in İstanbul in 1894. He was a successful student, albeit not a high achiever, and was not selected to attend General Staff College. His first appointment was to a platoon leadership position in Debre in Albania. The Ottoman-Greek War of 1897 gave him an opportunity to learn his trade in the hard school of war. He served with distinction and was selected as a staff officer at the headquarters of the *28th Brigade* in İstanbul. However Şefik was a man of action and did not remain long in this position, volunteering for the *Yemen Expeditionary Force* on 8 March 1900, although he did not receive the combat command position he sought. For two years he served on the staff of the *14th Division*, including a brief period as the Chief of Staff. Conditions in Yemen were harsh and the counterinsurgency campaign was brutal. Şefik fell seriously ill and returned to İstanbul in 1902.

Between 1903 and 1911 Şefik served in company and battalion command positions in the North Aegean region. When the Ottoman-Italian War broke out in 1911, he once again volunteered for a combat command. He commanded local volunteers and valiantly fought against the Italians but received no credit for his success. He sought service with his former unit during the Balkan Wars but his posting did not eventuate until the final stages of the war. As Commanding Officer of the *Ezine Reserve Battalion* he was assigned to the Suvla region, an assignment that would prove fortuitous, allowing him to gain first-hand experience of the region and the soldiers he would command during the Gallipoli Campaign.

The disastrous defeats and radical reforms in the aftermath of the Balkan Wars dramatically altered the structure of the Ottoman Army. Thousands of officers were purged and the remainder scattered throughout the empire. Şefik was fortunate to remain in the Dardanelles where he was appointed Commanding Officer of the *3/25th Battalion*. He worked hard to reorganise and train his battalion although he remained bitter that his brilliant war record had been ignored. The turning point in his military career was his appointment —initially temporarily — as Commanding Officer of the *27th Regiment* in Maydos. This was one the most battle-hardened regiments in the army. Şefik immediately identified the Arıburnu region as the key to the defence of the northern region in contrast to the opinion of his commanding officers and colleagues. With no engineering support, he pushed his soldiers to the limit digging trenches, gun positions and other earthen fortifications.

The Anzac landings on 25 April proved that his conviction was well founded. He was the best regimental officer in the Ottoman Army and his exceptional and driving leadership turned the battle. He continued to play important roles in subsequent battles, but swiftly became disillusioned with the poorly planned and led mass attacks that cost the Ottoman Army so dearly. Despite Şefik's vocal criticism of poor tactics and leadership his combat successes was recognised and he was highly decorated and appointed Commanding Officer of the *19th Division* on 8 August 1915.

THE OTTOMAN DEFENCE AGAINST THE ANZAC LANDING: 25 April 1915

A studio photograph of Şefik (Aker) and his aide-de-camp in İzmir (Smyrna), probably taken in 1917. Şefik was a talented, intelligent and inspiring leader but he was also a difficult subordinate (image courtesy of Yetkin İşcen).

With the end of the Gallipoli campaign, the *19th Division* was selected to reinforce the Austro-Hungarian Army in Galicia-Poland. Şefik, a renowned army trainer, took just seven months to transform his division into the best in the entire army. The division finished its deployment to Galicia as part of *XV Corps* in August 1916. The Austro-Hungarian Army was in an appalling state and the front line could only be held with the assistance of the Germans. The soldiers of the *Ottoman Expeditionary Force* were used as shock troops to deal with emergencies. Şefik soon found himself in disagreement with his German and Austro-Hungarian superiors, accusing them of treating his soldiers as 'cannon fodder' rather than allies with equal standing. Intense German pressure saw Şefik recalled on 7 October 1916.

Initially appointed head of the İzmir provincial recruitment centre, Şefik was later transferred to command various weak reserve divisions conducting coastal defence and home guard duties in the Aegean region. He ended the war as Commanding Officer of the *57th Division*. Under the provisions of the Mudros Armistice Agreement, most of the army units including the *57th Division* were to be disarmed and disbanded. Şefik largely ignored the provisions, managing to keep his weak division intact, conducting a successful fighting withdrawal during the initial phase of the Greek invasion between May and August 1919. He became one of the organisers of local forces in the South Aegean region during the difficult months of 1919 and 1920. However his opposition to the radical transformation of the Western front saw him transferred to rear duties. Although he was cleared of charges of brutality against civilians and financial misconduct, he was never again assigned to positions of influence.

Şefik retired from the army in 1931, dedicating his remaining years to clearing his reputation by publishing his personal accounts. He enjoyed some attention during the last years of his life but never received full credit for his achievements at Gallipoli and in the Independence War. He died a broken man in 1964.

Şefik was a hard-working, talented and courageous officer. He was a rare figure —volunteering for active service whenever possible and proving an excellent combat commander. He fought in all the wars of the Ottoman Empire between 1897 and 1922. He possessed the remarkable ability to concentrate almost obsessively on a single issue — such as the landings at Arıburnu — and mobilise all his resources to meet it. However he was a very difficult subordinate who was always ready to question orders and never hesitated to voice his criticism. He also had little time for false modesty — he knew he was an excellent officer and was eager to be recognised for his achievements. While this explosive combination ultimately ruined his military career, it was instrumental in the Ottoman success at Anzac. If ever an Ottoman officer was the right man in the right place at the right time, it was Mehmed Şefik Aker on 25 April 1915.

Under the new arrangement, Şefik assumed command of the right zone and lent his *3rd Battalion* to the *26th Regiment* in the south, receiving the *Bursa Gendarmerie Battalion* in its stead. He was tasked to defend the coastline between Ece Bay and Kabatepe. He positioned all his battalions on the coast, keeping just two gendarmerie companies as regimental reserves. From north to south, one gendarmerie company was sited at Ece Bay, the *1st Battalion* covering the coastline between Büyükkemikli (Suvla Point) and Ağıldere, while the *2nd Battalion* covered the area between Ağıldere and Kabatepe. Following a detailed reconnaissance he identified the Arıburnu (Anzac) region as critical terrain. He regarded this feature as the potential first step for a landing force since it provided the shortest approach to the Kocaçimen Bloc (Saribair Range) and was also replete with valuable firing positions to cover both north and south coastal defence lines. Crucially, he decided to emplace his artillery behind this position. Şefik knew from previous experience that, while naval artillery fire had little effect on entrenched infantry, it was devastating against units caught in the open.

Ottoman soldiers in a basic trench. At the beginning of the campaign most trenches resembled this one — an earthen entrenchment without barbed wire, sandbags or other additional means of fortification. Ottoman soldiers were accustomed to dig protection pits and trenches when they came under fire (image courtesy of ATASE).

Şefik needed good roads to move his units quickly and receive essential logistic support, but he had no engineers and had received no construction or entrenching material. He simply had to use what resources he possessed and gave priority to the digging and fortification of trenches. The platoons dug the main platoon positions first and then constructed the support trenches to the rear. Having finished these, the men began digging alternative positions and connecting trenches. Şefik was keen to retain the machine-gun company in reserve but ordered the preparation of machine-gun positions with good potential for enfilading and crossfire. Documents reveal that several machine-gun positions had been prepared on Arıburnu Knoll, 400 Plateau, Ağıldere (near the Fisherman's Hut) and Kabatepe. Unavoidably, road-building remained at the bottom of the priority list. While his men completed these back-breaking entrenching tasks, Şefik did not neglect their training. All units rehearsed defensive movements in accordance with the current coastal defence doctrine which Şefik had adapted to suit local conditions.

Under Şefik's defensive plan, his platoons on the coast would wait and watch from secure and well-covered support trenches behind the main positions. Two observation posts would cover both sides up to a distance of between 400 and 600 metres while battalion reserves would be ready to launch counter-attacks or occupy blocking positions within 30 minutes. His platoons would man the main position from communication trenches until the boats of an attacking force reached the effective range of the infantry weapons. Once the invasion force was sighted, the men from the observation posts would join the platoon in the main position. Şefik frequently practised his unit in quick targeted fire, ordering second line ammunition stocks to be distributed to the platoons. Every soldier would carry 150 rounds and receive 60 rounds from the platoon stock positioned nearby when needed. With almost 18,000 rounds per platoon in the hands of highly trained and experienced soldiers, the platoons were capable of surprisingly deadly firepower.

Ottoman soldiers demonstrating various positions in a well-constructed trench during the summer of 1915 (image courtesy of ATASE).

Another important defensive principle espoused by Şefik was his total refusal to allow his forward units to retreat. These men were to defend their positions and die there if necessary so as to gain time for the reserve to move forward. Şefik never tried to disguise the grim reality of war. He often repeated to his subordinates the analogy of a 'nail well stuck'. He was convinced that the enemy was at his most vulnerable during the final approach to the beach.

Enemy soldiers trapped in boats would have little opportunity to return fire and would present ideal targets for rapid platoon fire. On the other hand, if enemy soldiers secured a beachhead, it could prove very difficult to dislodge them. Şefik had little faith in the ability of reserves in faraway central locations to react in time.

An Ottoman field camp. One bell tent was allocated to each nine-man squad.

Every passing day and every rehearsal reinforced Şefik's belief that the Allies would launch an amphibious operation and that one of the main landing sites would be somewhere close to the Anzac region. By the end of the year his belief verged on obsession. He constantly repeated his certainty that the enemy would invade and reiterated the importance of the Anzac region in his verbal and written orders. A number of chance incidents reinforced this belief. For example, on 19 February 1915, a day after Şefik had moved his command post to Kabatepe, a battleship fired several shells into the fort that dominated the position. To him this display of force and the renewal of the Allied naval attack against the Straits defences represented the final proof.

27th INFANTRY REGIMENT
1915

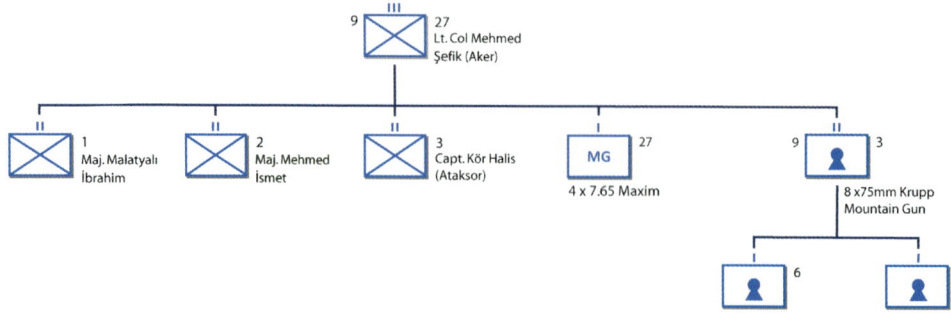

While Şefik waited impatiently for the landing to materialise, his soldiers began to tire of heavy work and suffered from exposure to the severe winter conditions in their open trenches. With the return of the *3rd Battalion* and the *8/3rd Mountain Artillery Battery*, he moved two battalions back to Kocadere for some relief and kept just two battalions (including the gendarmerie) on the coast. Şefik issued a new set of orders to the reserve battalions articulating the response to an enemy landing, directing them to immediately race to Topçular Sırtı (Gun or Third Ridge) at the sound of gunfire and wait for orders to reinforce the coastal positions. He identified Third Ridge as a possible target for any landing in this region, convinced of the importance of occupying the ridge well before the enemy.

With the arrival of the *19th Division* on 26 February, command responsibilities on the peninsula were amended and the *27th Regiment* was placed under command of the *19th Division*. The *9th Division* headquarters moved to the Asiatic shore to take responsibility from the *Menderes Detachment*. Şefik soon established a good relationship with his new commander, Mustafa Kemal, who was very impressed with the *27th Regiment*'s defensive system and preparations. The arrival of the *19th Division* would prove a welcome development with enemy naval bombardments against Kabatepe soon to become a daily affair. These bombardments proved time and again the veracity of Şefik's belief that naval artillery had limited effect on entrenched infantry, but also demonstrated its lack of accuracy. The frequently targeted Kabatepe did not receive one direct hit. Instead of frightening the Ottoman soldiers, these early limited naval bombardments heartened them and bolstered their belief in the security of their positions.

A 75mm Krupp *feldkanone* L/30 M1903 field gun in firing position. Note the pre-registered firing list on the back of the protective shield (image courtesy of ATASE).

On 2 March, Şefik issued a highly prescient order. He reiterated his belief in importance of Arıburnu (Anzac) and warned his battalions to defend it at all costs. Both reserve battalions were tasked to send one company each immediately to reinforce Anzac in case of a landing. In similar fashion he positioned the *7/3rd Mountain Artillery Battery* (four 75mm Krupp L/14 M1904 guns) at Yeşiltarla (the Cup) and tasked it with the provision of fire support to Anzac and Kabatepe. A week later the 15cm short howitzer battery (six guns most probably Krupp *schwere Feldhaubitze* M1902) was placed under tactical command of the *27th Regiment*. Şefik positioned four guns behind Palamutluk (the Olive Grove) and two guns at Çamtepe on 10 March. He specifically ordered the battery at the Olive Grove to prepare fire plans to support the Anzac region in case of a landing.

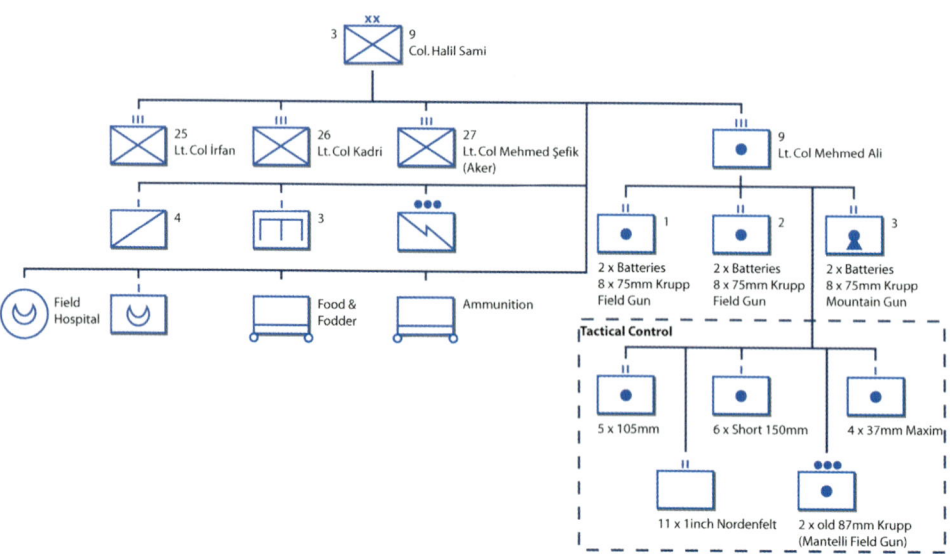

The *9th Division* returned to the peninsula on 25 March, having handed responsibility to the *11th Division*. The defensive command system and responsibilities were changed yet again, with the *19th Division* moving to become the corps reserve and the *27th Regiment* returning to under command of the *9th Division*. With these new arrangements, Kabatepe and Anzac were handed off to the *25th Regiment* and the *27th Regiment* was ordered to cover the coastline between Ağıldere and Koyun Limanı. Şefik was unhappy with this new arrangement. He was reluctant to leave protection of the vital ground to other units having invested so much in his defensive plan. He lobbied to remain and was greeted with success: on 31 March the Anzac region was returned to him. The *27th Regiment* would remain in its original and preferred position.

Mustafa Kemal (Atatürk) Pasha

Mustafa Kemal poses for popular war jounal *Harb Mecmuası* in front of the Kireçtepe Monument. Mustafa Kemal received little public attention until the end of the war because of the Ottoman government's policy of attributing victories to the army in general and ignoring individual contributions.

Mustafa Kemal was born in Salonica (Selanik) in 1881. He graduated from the Imperial Military Academy in İstanbul in 1902 and the General Staff College in 1905. He was a bright student, although never at the top of his class. His interest in politics began early and he was exiled to Syria after being identified as the leader of a small secret organisation. The realities of life in the Ottoman Army came as a shock, prompting him to found another secret organisation. He was particularly disturbed by the Ottoman military's heavy handed policy towards the people. The intervention of friends in high places saw him assigned to Salonica, the capital of opposition to Sultan Abdülhamid II, in 1907. However he was too late to play any meaningful part in the conspiracy formulated by a group of General Staff officers under the leadership of Enver, Cemal and Talat. A year later, Abdülhamid was forced to reinstate the constitution after a series of armed rebellions and mass public disorder.

Having served in several staff positions, Mustafa Kemal volunteered to go to Libya to fight the Italian invasion. He was appointed commander of the Derne region where he served with distinction before seeking to return to İstanbul with the declaration of war by the Balkan states. He arrived just in time for the last phase of the war and served as the Operations Chief of the *Composite Corps* in Gallipoli. He gained valuable experience on the defence of the Gallipoli Peninsula during this period, although his vocal criticism of the government saw him exiled as the Military Attaché to Sofia in 1913. His bitterness increased substantially when the Ministry of Defence declined his application to transfer to a combat unit following the declaration of mobilisation on 2 August 1914.

However the manpower crisis eventually saw him appointed Commanding Officer of the *19th Division*. Mustafa Kemal achieved remarkable success in raising his division in record time. He arrived on the Gallipoli Peninsula on 25 February and spent a month as the commander in charge of the southern coastal defence. He was instrumental in the early success of the Ottoman defence, committing the *57th Regiment* to the fight against the Anzac landing without authorisation, placing his career on the line on 25 April. Despite his obvious success against the invasion forces, he did not stop the Anzacs single-handedly as generally portrayed. He became the operational commander responsible for the counter-attacks against the Anzacs between 27 April and 19 May. Enver Pasha blamed him for the failure of these attacks and held him responsible for the massive casualty toll. Only Liman von Sanders' timely intervention saved Mustafa Kemal from dismissal.

The August offensives provided an opportunity for him to redeem himself. Von Sanders appointed Mustafa Kemal commander of the Anafarta region (Sari Bair and Suvla) when Colonel Ahmed Feyzi disobeyed the order to attack British units in Suvla on 8 August 1915. Mustafa Kemal committed all available forces against the enemy and waves of massive infantry attacks destroyed the Allied troops' chances of success. It is not often in wartime that a single battlefield commander can make a decisive difference. Despite this he did not receive the credit he sought and his relationship with Enver Pasha remained strained. He became more unsettled when the stalemate settled on the peninsula and his suggestions for the conduct of an active defence were ignored. He fell seriously ill for a period of time and took leave for treatment on 10 December.

Mustafa Kemal assumed command of *XVI Corps* in Edirne on 27 January 1916 and was promoted brigadier general on 1 April 1916 after considerable delay. He opposed plans for a deployment to Galicia-Poland, and *XVI Corps* was instead transferred as a part of the *Second Army* to the Eastern Front which had collapsed under an unexpected Russian offensive. Mustafa Kemal was highly successful during the first offensive operation against the Russians on 2 August. Within three days the cities of Muş and Bitlis were recaptured. However the

Second Army units could not achieve their objectives and the stalemate returned. After participating in a series of desultory operations, Mustafa Kemal Pasha was first appointed commanding general of the *Second Army* on 7 March 1917 and, a few months later, assumed command of the recently activated *Seventh Army* in Syria.

In the spring of 1917, the German General Staff unveiled a revolutionary plan to establish a German-led army group (the so-called *Heeres Gruppen Kommando F*) in the Middle East. The *Seventh Army* was activated as part of this army group. Originally, the *Yıldırım* (Thunderbolt) Army Group was tasked to reconquer Baghdad in Iraq and Iran, taking the *Sixth* and newly formed *Seventh Army* under its command. However, the situation changed dramatically after the enemy concentrations against Gaza and Beersheba increased in strength. Mustafa Kemal Pasha was very unhappy with this German plan and, when Field Marshal Erich von Falkenhayn took over command, he was unable to establish a harmonious relationship with his new commander. Mustafa Kemal Pasha voiced his frustration with von Falkenhayn and criticised the entire plan in writing. He later resigned and returned to İstanbul. However his fame and widespread support ensured that Enver Pasha could not purge him from the army.

Mustafa Kemal Pasha went to Germany with the Crown Prince and sought medical treatment in Austria. He was appointed to command the *Seventh Army* once again on 7 August 1918. In the meantime Liman von Sanders had replaced von Falkenhayn. While Mustafa Kemal Pasha worked well with his former commander von Sanders, the overall situation deteriorated and they quickly realised that they had no chance of victory against Allenby's forces. On 19 September 1918, Allenby launched his long-awaited assault, which saw highly mobile British colonial infantry easily breach the Ottoman main defensive line, the cavalry tearing through and racing to block the Ottoman lines of retreat. Over the following days Mustafa Kemal Pasha tried to save his units under the relentless British cavalry pursuit and eventually succeeded in collecting the remnants of the *Fourth* and *Seventh armies*. He fought with determination amidst the confusion and disorder to retain as much territory as possible until the Armistice. While Aleppo was lost on 25 October, further advances into the Anatolian plains were halted.

Mustafa Kemal Pasha was destined to play an even greater role during the Turkish Independence War of 1919–22 and the foundation of the Turkish Republic. The Gallipoli Campaign was certainly an important chapter of his military and political career. Although he preferred not to talk about his achievements in Gallipoli, he remained faithful to his former comrades and did his best to support them. His detailed report on the defence against the Anzac landing and following battles remained unpublished until 1968. Mustafa Kemal, now the President of Turkey, died after a long illness on 10 November 1938.

While the disastrous years of the First World War destroyed many military reputations, Mustafa Kemal Pasha's star rose. Contrary to popular legend he made many mistakes but he was wise enough not to repeat them. He gained a reputation as the general whose arrival on the scene invariably turned the situation. His mostly brilliant, driving and uncompromising leadership would turn a battle like no other in the Ottoman Army. At his best he was audacious, unpredictable, a lateral thinker and also attracted his share of good luck.

THE OTTOMAN DEFENCE AGAINST THE ANZAC LANDING: 25 April 1915

MUSTAFA KEMAL AND THE *19TH DIVISION*

Colonel Mustafa Kemal (Atatürk) in an observation post in the summer of 1915. Mustafa Kemal acted like a corps commander during the crisis of 25 April and later during the August offensive.

Major Mustafa Kemal (Atatürk) was the Ottoman Military Attaché at Sofia when war broke out. Although relatively young (just 33 years old) he was already a renowned and highly regarded officer. Mustafa Kemal was one of the early founders of the secret military organisations that eventually dethroned Abdulhamid II and reinstated the constitution. Nevertheless he was overshadowed by Enver, Cemal and Talat (the future CUP triumvirate) following the successful 1908 revolution. Highly disillusioned, Mustafa Kemal became a key figure in the opposition faction within CUP. This faction opposed not only the increasing power of Enver but also the military's continuing involvement in politics. This led to the fracturing of Mustafa Kemal's relationship with Enver and the other CUP leaders. Despite volunteering to fight the Italians in Libya where he served with distinction, although the arduous campaign conditions permanently affected his health, and despite his important part in the last phase of the Balkan Wars, Mustafa Kemal received no credit for his actions, punished instead for insubordination and, in a sense, exiled to Sofia.

With the outbreak of war, Mustafa Kemal lobbied hard to secure a posting to a combat unit. Like most others he was expecting a short war and, as an ambitious officer, was anxious to participate in the fighting before the war should end. However Enver Pasha clearly regarded him as a troublemaker and ensured that he was kept well away from any position of importance. Finally, with the intervention of some of his more influential friends and given the increasing need for talented officers, Enver Pasha, freshly returned from the disastrous Sarıkamış Campaign, relented. Mustafa Kemal was appointed Commanding Officer of the *19th Division* on 20 January 1915.

Mustafa Kemal faced enormous problems in building his division. It took him two months to replace his problematic chief of staff, Lütfi, with a young and highly talented General Staff officer, Major İzzeddin (Çalışlar), who joined the division in Maydos on 22 March. Even finding rifles for his soldiers presented an almost insurmountable difficulty. Confronted with so many challenges, Mustafa Kemal decided to address each issue in a systematic fashion. He began by amassing the resources and men necessary to activate the *57th Regiment*. The regiment's commander, Major Hüseyin Avni, was ten years older than him, but was a loyal, sturdy and hard-working officer, his battalion commanders young, talented captains. Mustafa Kemal then turned his focus to other infantry regiments (*55th* and *56th*) hoping to replicate his success. However his luck had run out. The Ottoman High Command decided to replace the *55th* and *56th regiments* with two from the *Fourth Army*. There were two compelling reasons for this decision. The first was the need to provide the *Fourth Army* with better trained regiments which had finished their mobilisation during the summer of 1914. The second was the need to assign at least one ethnically Turkish regiment per division to the *Fourth Army* in Syria. Mustafa Kemal's objections came to naught and, despite his protests, the decision stood.

THE OTTOMAN DEFENCE AGAINST THE ANZAC LANDING: 25 April 1915

19th INFANTRY DIVISION
1915

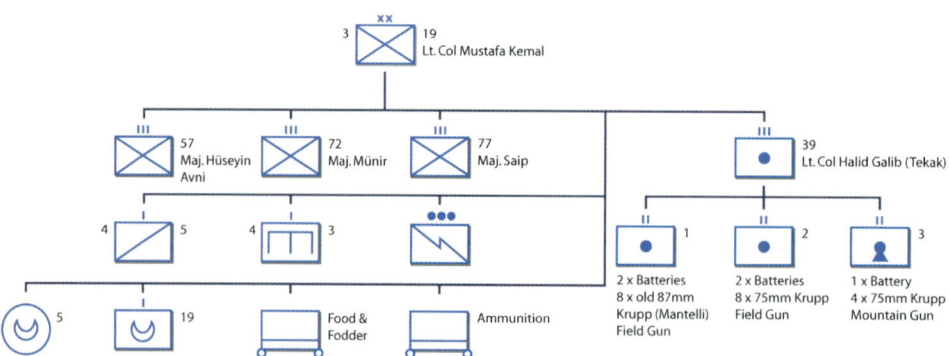

On 21 February Mustafa Kemal received orders to proceed immediately to Maydos. He hurriedly finished his preparations and arrived in Maydos on 25 February, bringing with him just the *57th Regiment* and the *20th Machine-gun Company* (later renamed the *57th*) as the building of his combat support units had proven a more difficult undertaking than he had anticipated. The *39th Field Artillery Regiment* was activated with the arrival of a field artillery battalion (eight 87mm Krupp L/24 M1885 field guns) from the *15th Division* and renamed the *1st Field Artillery Battalion* on 2 April. Unfortunately the artillery battalion had arrived without its draft horses and water buffalos had to be used to tow the guns for some period of time. The *2nd Field Artillery Battalion* (eight 75mm Krupp L/30 M1903 field guns) arrived a little later, fortunately with its draft horses. The *3rd Mountain Artillery Battalion* was raised with four 75mm Krupp L/14 M1904 mountain guns although its remaining four guns would not arrive until very late on 28 April.

An infantry company on a route march. Route marches were an important part of unit training given the lack of transportation and good quality roads (image courtesy of Nejat Çuhadaroğlu).

While the combat support units and other supporting arms were established slowly, Mustafa Kemal began combat training at the earliest opportunity. First he ordered route and cross-country marches to break in soft feet and new boots. He then began a continuous program of rehearsal for reinforcing the coastal defences and for launching counter-attacks. This training proved its worth when small parties of Royal Marines landed at Helles and he ordered the *57th Regiment* to race to Kirte (Krithia). Painstaking rehearsals slowly but surely produced good results, although the overall performance of the *72nd* and *77th regiments* remained poor. In contrast to modern perceptions and some contemporary accusations, the ethnicity of these units was not the reason for their poor performance as only half the men were Arabs. The regiments also contained nomadic Turks, Kurds, Yazidis and Nusayris. Many of these men were unwanted soldiers dumped from their original divisions during the transfer of regiments. A number of them were either old or very young conscripts, while others hailed from social groups with practically no military tradition and limited conscription experience. They needed time to adjust to the new experience of military training.

An infantry company rests during a field exercise (image courtesy of Nejat Çuhadaroğlu).

72nd INFANTRY REGIMENT
1915

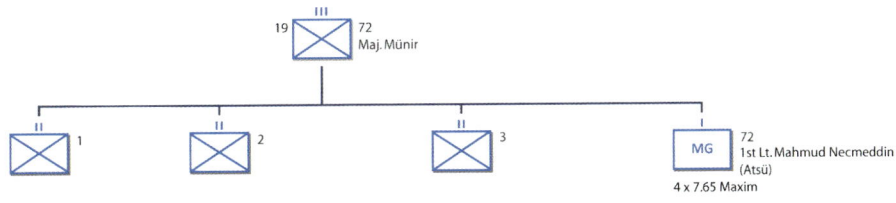

In addition to these time-consuming training and activation tasks, Mustafa Kemal also had a number of defensive duties to perform. He assumed command of the Maydos regional command which was in charge of the coastal defence of southern Gallipoli. His command now comprised the *19th Division, 26th* and *27th regiments*, the *Gallipoli Gendarmerie Battalion* and various artillery units. He was pleased with his new command as, not only did he now command more troops, but he was also arguably in charge of the most vital ground. He had finally received what he had been asking for since the beginning of the war. In this spirit of satisfaction and optimism, he conducted a detailed reconnaissance and inspection. He identified the problems in each unit and attempted to solve these with the assistance of his subordinates. He invited the *Fortified Zone Commander* Cevad Pasha to explain to him the various structural problems and demonstrate the improvements he had made, scheduling an inspection on 18 March. It would never occur, overtaken by the commencement of the main Allied naval attack.

An infantry company leaves its field camp for a training exercise. Note the presence of field kitchens at the rear. The field kitchen, previously regarded as a luxury, became an essential part of the army in the field during the First World War (image courtesy of Nejat Çuhadaroğlu).

The failed naval attack played an important role in convincing Mustafa Kemal, like others, of the certainty of an amphibious operation. From his personal notes it is apparent that he was able to accurately deduce his enemy's intentions and calculate the possible invasion sites. In similar fashion to Şefik, he identified Helles and Kabatepe as the main landing sites. Helles had the singular advantage of allowing naval support from both sides of the peninsula while Kabatepe presented the shortest and easiest way to sever the vital south from the remainder of the peninsula. As far as he was concerned, any landings at Bolayır or on the Asiatic shore would constitute the beginning of a very long campaign.

Unlike Şefik, Mustafa Kemal was a dedicated team player. He was not obsessed with detail, but rather preferred to deal with the larger, more crucial issues, leaving the details to his subordinates. He was a keen judge of character, adept at identifying talented individuals and devolving responsibility to them. Rather than impose his will on his men, he allowed them to reach their own solutions to build their confidence. This also allowed him the luxury of time to deal with more pressing issues. At the same time, however, he could be fierce, ruthless and relentless. Mustafa Kemal impressed his men with the fact that he could be anywhere at any time and was not easily fooled. He was quick to punish anyone who did not fulfil his expectations, pushing his officers to the limit and achieving remarkable results. He quickly recognised that Şefik had accurately assessed the situation and was performing well, so gave him full authority to continue. When he discovered problems in the *26th Regiment*'s area of responsibility, however, he dealt with each one in turn, ironing out difficulties as he went.

77th INFANTRY REGIMENT
1915

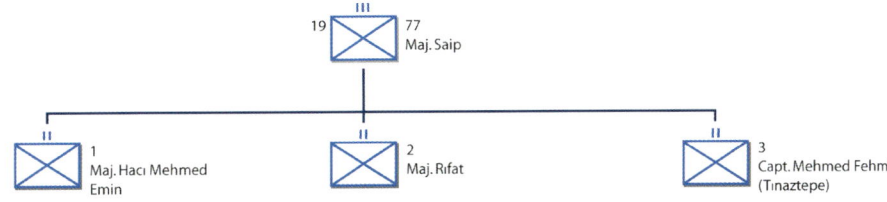

Ottoman soldiers clean their rifles at the rear of the lines. The Ottoman commanders paid close attention to field maintenance given the general lack of spare parts (image courtesy of ATASE).

The happy reign of Mustafa Kemal was cut short with the arrival of the *9th Division* Headquarters and the *25th Regiment* from the Asiatic shore on 23 March. Colonel Halil Sami took over from him and Mustafa Kemal, now corps reserve commander, had time to focus on the problems of his own division. While the *19th Division* had improved significantly in training and organisation, serious flaws remained. For example, the *57th Regiment*'s battalions arrived on the peninsula without their fourth companies. These companies were finally activated at the end of March with the arrival of raw recruits from depots. Improvisation was the order of the day and commanding officers tried various methods to raise the standard of these companies to a level consistent with the remainder of the battalion. The *77th Regiment* came from its home province with a less than ideal weapons inventory. It had no machine-guns and the quantity of rifles was well below the establishment number of 1100. After much discussion and a series of requests, Esad Pasha changed the establishment number of rifles for infantry battalions to 1000 and ordered the combat support and service support units to be armed with old surplus rifles. The 7.65mm Mauser rifles collected from the service units were then issued to the *77th Regiment*. However neither machine-guns nor trained machine-gunners could be found to activate the machine-gun company.

A regiment rests during a field exercise. Note the headbands and Maxim MG 09 machine-guns. *III Corps* was famous for its frequent conduct of field exercises (image courtesy of Nejat Çuhadaroğlu).

On 19 April, after several delays, Mustafa Kemal managed to organise a divisional exercise. The scenario he used and the reaction of the division are important in assessing the alertness of the commanding officers and their men to the impending invasion. The opening situation of the scenario saw the divisional command centre receive information of enemy naval activity and possible landings at Ece Bay and on the coast between Suvla and Kumtepe. Mustafa Kemal ordered the divisional cavalry to send patrols to Turşun (headquarters of the

Gendarmerie Battalion), Ece Bay, Anafartalar, Kabatepe and Kumtepe. The *57th* and *77th regiments* and a mountain battery were ordered to be ready to advance to Bigalı and Maltepe respectively while the *72th Regiment* began the march to Maltepe. The first reports arrived from the cavalry patrols confirming that these were genuine landings (according to the scenario) at Suvla and Kabatepe rather than a series of feints. Mustafa Kemal then ordered a company from each battalion (role-playing as battalions) to advance to the dominant ground. While the units were ordered back after a brief march, the exercise provided valuable lessons. For example, Mustafa Kemal decided as a consequence of the exercise to move his headquarters from Maydos to Bigalı. He also planned to address problems of coordination and information flow between the units during the next exercise which was scheduled for 25 April.

THE DEFENCE AGAINST THE ALLIED NAVAL ATTACKS

As discussed previously, the Ottoman General Staff assessed the most vulnerable areas of the empire as its capital, İstanbul, and the Dardanelles Straits. Previous conflicts and crises had clearly established a pattern in which the enemies of the empire had tried to force the Straits in order to dictate their terms to the Ottoman government. In the face of this threat the General Staff concentrated most of the army corps and divisions around İstanbul, Thrace and western Anatolia. Nevertheless only the *9th Division* (*25th*, *26th* and *27th regiments*) was initially assigned to reinforce the *Dardanelles Fortified Zone Command* against possible landings. Obviously at this stage the General Staff was gambling on the enemy's inertia for some period of time. The General Staff was also expecting a naval attack with limited amphibious landings against established fortifications. Thus the other divisions were to remain as a strategic reserve while the General Staff toyed with various plans including sending two corps to the Romanian border or landing them close to Odessa so as to reduce the burden on Austria-Hungary, currently engaged with the Russians.

Despite enormous expectations, the alliance with Germany did not produce an immediate influx of weapons and military supplies. Serbia's geographic position between the two nations meant that there was no direct railway link between them and the entire line of transportation between Germany and İstanbul was subject to the whims of neutral Bulgaria and Romania. Only a small portion of the military aid promised could reach İstanbul and it took time to arrive. However, when Enver Pasha asked for a new mission of specialists to reorganise and reinforce the defence of the Straits on 16 August his request was immediately approved. Additional naval personnel who had filled the technical and administrative vacancies created by the departure of the British Naval Advisory Mission under Admiral Limpus were also included. This new group, officially designated the *Sonderkommando Kaiserliche Marine Türkei*, was despatched under the command of Admiral Guido von Usedom, the 'hero of China'. The mission's 26 officers and 520 soldiers left Germany for İstanbul travelling in disguise, the men reaching their posts by the end of August. Von Usedom was appointed Inspector-General of both İstanbul and the Dardanelles fortifications and assumed responsibility for other naval defensive measures. His deputy, Vice-Admiral Johannes Merten, was given the task of supervising and mentoring the Dardanelles defences.

THE OTTOMAN DEFENCE AGAINST THE ANZAC LANDING: 25 April 1915

Kaiser Wilhelm II is briefed on the defence of the Strait against the Allied fleet's 18 March attack. The Dardanelles became a frequent tourist stop for VIPs following the end of the campaign. Enver Pasha is on the left of the Kaiser, Esad (Bülkat) Pasha is in between, with Admirals Johannes Merten and Guido von Usedom on the right (image courtesy of Nejat Çuhadaroğlu).

The British-French limited naval bombardment of the outer fortifications by four battleships on 3 November 1914 was instrumental in heightening awareness of a possible invasion and on 12 November *III Corps* was ordered to assume responsibility for the Dardanelles. Its commander, Esad Pasha, was already well aware of the situation. The *9th Division* was originally his organic division, while his other unit, the *7th Division*, was covering the northern isthmus of the peninsula. His third division, the *19th Division*, had been recently activated and was in desperate need of further training and equipment. He decided not to meddle with the Straits naval defences, instead focusing on the defence against major amphibious operations.

Esad (Bülkat) Pasha posing for a staged photo behind a 75mm Krupp *gebirgskanone* L/14 M1904 gun, most probably on Third Ridge (image courtesy of ATASE).

Colonel Cevad deployed his *2nd Fortress Artillery Brigade* (*3rd, 4th* and *5th Fortress Artillery regiments*), *8th Heavy Howitzer Regiment* and miscellaneous combat and combat support units into 14 permanent fortifications and around 40 mobile batteries. A bewildering variety of mostly antiquated artillery pieces of all calibres and types now covered the Straits. In addition, eight contact mine belts (the number of mine belts would eventually reach 11) were laid and two fixed torpedo launchers were deployed. Von Usedom and his team provided crucial help to the Ottoman defenders in planning and training. However, despite continued promises, Germany did not provide much-needed new guns, ammunition and equipment.

Artillery battery personnel pose in front of a generator and a limber during the summer of 1915. The Ministry of War sent not only its best units but also its best weapons and the most modern equipment it possessed (image courtesy of ATASE).

The Allied fleet began its bombardment of the outer forts methodically on 19 February and completed it on 25 February. Small demolition teams of Royal Marines landed at Helles and Kumkale and destroyed the remaining guns between 27 February and 3 March facing little resistance. These easy successes had a profound effect on the attackers. First, they reinforced the widely held belief in the poor fighting qualities of the Ottoman Army. Second, serious concerns over opposed landings were all but dissipated as the confidence of the Allied forces mounted. Interestingly, only a few Allied staff officers paid attention to the failed Marine landings on 4 March. The Marine teams met unexpected resistance and had to be extricated under heavy naval bombardment.

Royal Marines take cover behind the ruins at Seddülbahir during one of their landings between 27 February and 3 March 1915. Their success in destroying Ottoman fortress guns with few casualties was instrumental in reinforcing the misconception that the Ottoman forces would disintegrate in the face of serious landings.

The *Fortified Zone Command* took these early failures seriously. While the toll of casualties numbered less than 50, the *5th Fortress Regiment* was disbanded and its personnel reassigned to other units. Infantry companies from the *9th Division* were assigned to provide perimeter security for the fortresses and more mobile reserves were established nearby. Two days later, the fleet began its bombardment of the intermediate fortifications. But this time it came under sustained fire and the damage inflicted was far greater. The Ottomans took any opportunity provided by pauses in the action to repair damage and improve fortifications. It quickly became apparent to the attacking force that there was no way to silence the guns let alone destroy them. In similar fashion, firepower effectively curbed the operation of the minesweepers and most mine belts remained more or less intact.

Battery commander Captain Mehmed Hilmi (Sanlıtop) and Lieutenant Fahri in front of a 240mm Krupp L/35 fortress gun at Rumeli Mecidiye Fort. This gun was to become famous as the gun that sank French battleship *Bouvet*. In fact artillery fire damaged *Bouvet* and she sank after hitting a mine (image courtesy of ATASE).

Under these adverse conditions and amidst a crisis of confidence, the new fleet commander, Admiral John de Robeck, gambled on forcing the Straits using all the naval power at his disposal. The armada, organised in four battle lines, entered the Straits. The powerful modern battleships fired salvo after salvo from a distance in an attempt to dominate the forts. Under cover of their fire, a second line of battleships joined them, using short-range bombardments to reduce the forts. By now the Ottoman defenders were well aware of the Allied routine and their capacity to sustain damage. They held their fire and waited patiently in their redoubts for the ships to reach effective fire range. One by one the Allied ships were devastated by the accurate, relentless fire. The mobile howitzers wreaked havoc on the wooden decks of the ships with their plunging fire. But by far the most damage was inflicted by the mines. First, the French battleship *Bouvet* struck a mine and sank quickly. Then *HMS Inflexible*, *HMS Irresistible* and *HMS Ocean* also stuck mines one after the other. *HMS Inflexible* managed to limp away from the battle zone, but the other ships were evacuated and left to their fate. De Robeck had no alternative but to halt the operation and withdraw.

Following this disaster de Robeck dared not mount another attempt to force the Straits. He consulted newly appointed Mediterranean Expeditionary Force Commander General Ian Hamilton and both agreed on the need for a combined operation to break the Straits defences. With increased confidence the Ottoman defenders waited for another naval attack as the weeks passed. They had suffered fewer than 100 casualties and lost only four guns destroyed. Other than this the defensive system remained intact with sufficient ammunition for future battles and eight undamaged mine belts.

A German propaganda postcard commemorating the 18 March naval victory.

LIMAN VON SANDERS AND A NEW DEFENSIVE CONCEPT

The *Fortified Zone Command* had successfully defended the Straits against the British-French armada with the help of its German advisors. With the tell-tale signs of an amphibious operation increasing with each passing day, the Ottoman High Command decided to deploy more divisions to the area. Experiences from the Ottoman-Italian War clearly pointed to the importance of command and control, both of an increased number of divisions and of the Fortified Zone. This experience told the Ottomans that a field army and two army corps headquarters were required to command the increasing number of units and to coordinate the overall defence effort. Again, in similar fashion to the Ottoman-Italian War, instead of tasking the available *First Army* Headquarters, a completely new army, the *Fifth Army*, was activated with Liman von Sanders appointed commanding general on 24 March 1915.

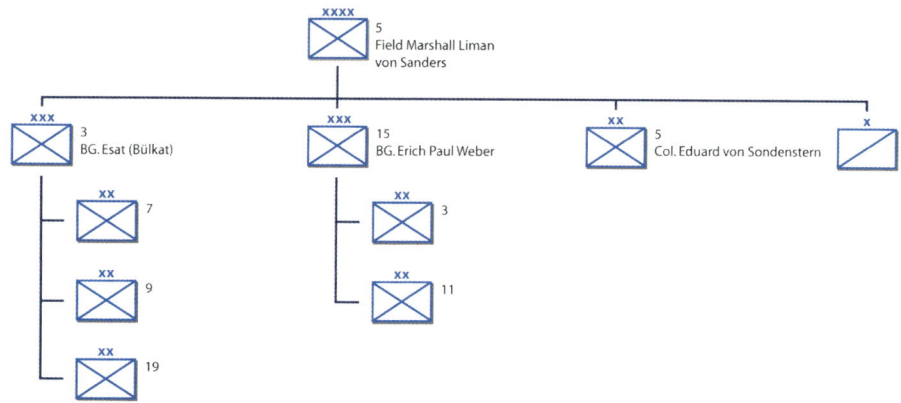

Lieutenant Colonel Kazım (İnanç) poses in one of the three cars available at that time at Gallipoli. Kazım was the Chief of Staff of the *Fifth Army*. He established a very good relationship with von Sanders and remained his Chief of Staff throughout the war. Kazım played an important role in forging good relations between von Sanders and the Ottoman officers in the latter stages of the war, but regrettably not at the outset (image courtesy of ATASE).

THE ORIGINAL OTTOMAN COASTAL DEFENCE CONCEPT

Von Sanders and his small staff arrived and took command of the whole Dardanelles defence system on 26 March. He was briefed by Esad Pasha and then decided to see the situation on the ground for himself instead of relying on maps and overlays. Von Sanders and a group of officers inspected the *9th Division* defensive positions on 31 March, detecting a number of problems with the defensive layout. His brief inspection over, von Sanders dismissed the previous defensive plans and existing deployments as flawed and refused to listen to advice from the *Fortified Zone Area Command*. He radically overhauled the entire defensive system and reorganised the command and control structure, categorically rejecting the Ottoman defensive concept and its assumptions as unsuitable for defence against a modern amphibious attack. He was convinced that it was a mistake to deploy units in strength along the entire length of the coast. He also assessed the naval firepower as a significant threat, asserting that forward defence of the coastline under direct naval fire was far from the optimum defensive strategy. Instead he placed thinly manned observation and screening posts in overwatch above the beaches while maintaining the main bodies as mobile reserves. Von Sanders also moved most of the artillery batteries and machine-guns from the coastline to covered reserve positions.

VON SANDERS' DEFENCE CONCEPT

Von Sanders' concept of defence in depth was based on early identification of the enemy's intent and the main landings by his screening force and rushing the mobile reserves to crush the enemy forces and deny them a foothold on land. Surprisingly he did not consider capitalising on the inhospitable terrain and taking advantage of the vulnerability of the enemy infantry in boats during the final approach to the coast. He appeared unaware of the poor road network and ignored the fact that the peninsula did not provide the depth required for mobile defence or that the Ottoman infantry and artillery units had limited mobility. The logistic trains were even less mobile and units were forced to stockpile at least second line ammunition, food and fodder to maintain them during the initial phase of any attack. Moving the units away from the coastline also saw the piling up of stocks away from decisive points.

Von Sanders also paid no attention to the fact that the widely dispersed observation posts and platoons did not have the necessary means of communication to alert the command centres and reserves to an invasion. Phone lines were connected only to fortified places, battalion headquarters and some company command posts. Most company commanders had no visual contact with their platoons and had only runners for communication. Even if they managed to inform the command centres, poorly manned posts in lightly entrenched positions without effective fire support would be unable to fix and canalise enemy forces until the arrival of the reserves.

In addition to thoroughly overhauling the defensive concept and system, von Sanders identified the Bolayır-Saros region and Beşika Bay as the probable main landing sites in direct contrast to previous appraisals. Cevad Pasha and his staff argued compellingly that, while the capture of Bolayır would certainly put the defence in difficult position, it would not lead to total collapse. On the other hand, if the enemy managed to capture the dominant grounds of the Kilitbahir Plateau and Kocaçimen (Saribair) bloc there would be no alternative but to evacuate the fortifications on the European shore.

Chapter 2

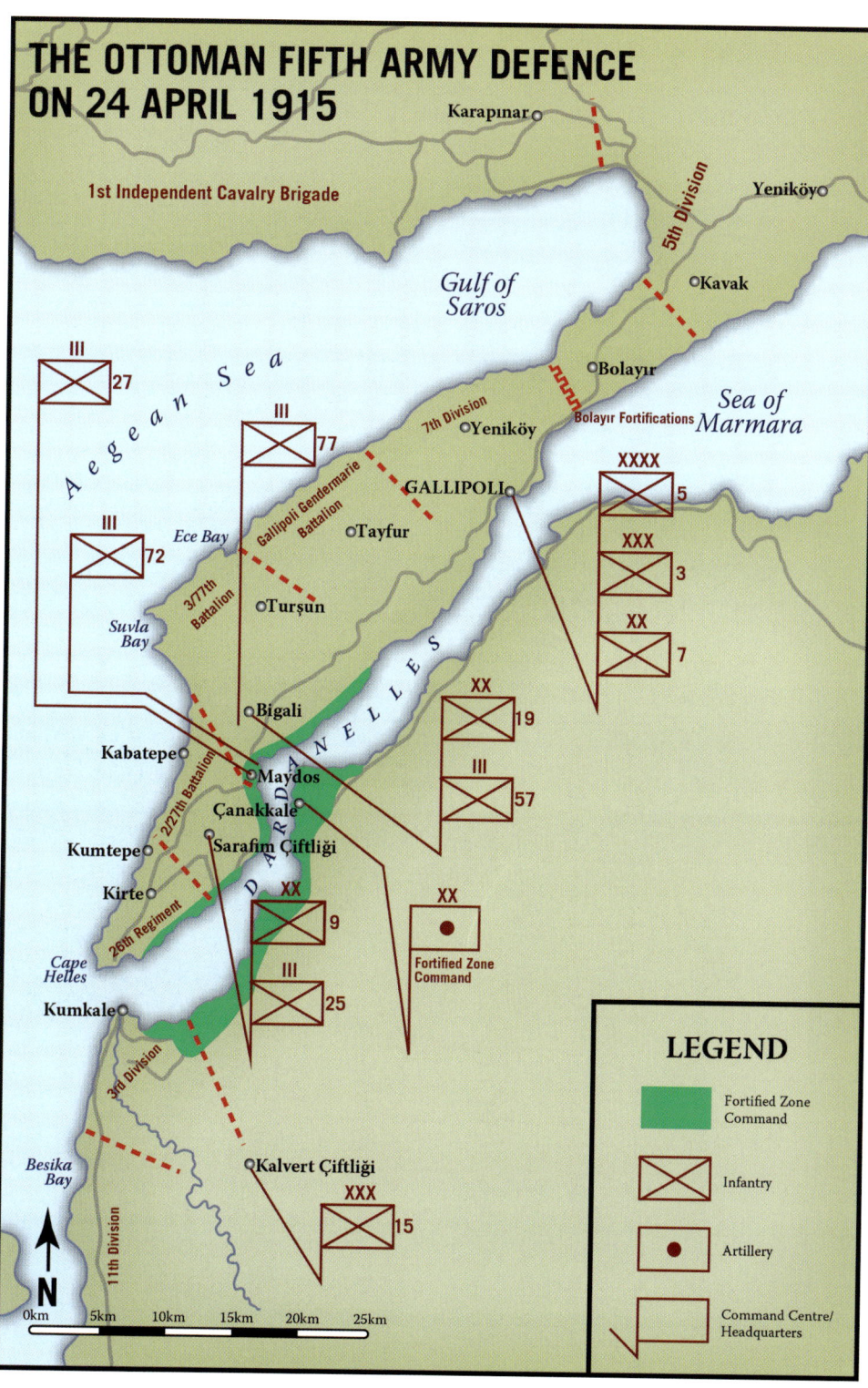

The Ottoman Fifth Army Defence on 24 April 1915

THE OTTOMAN DEFENCE AGAINST THE ANZAC LANDING: 25 April 1915

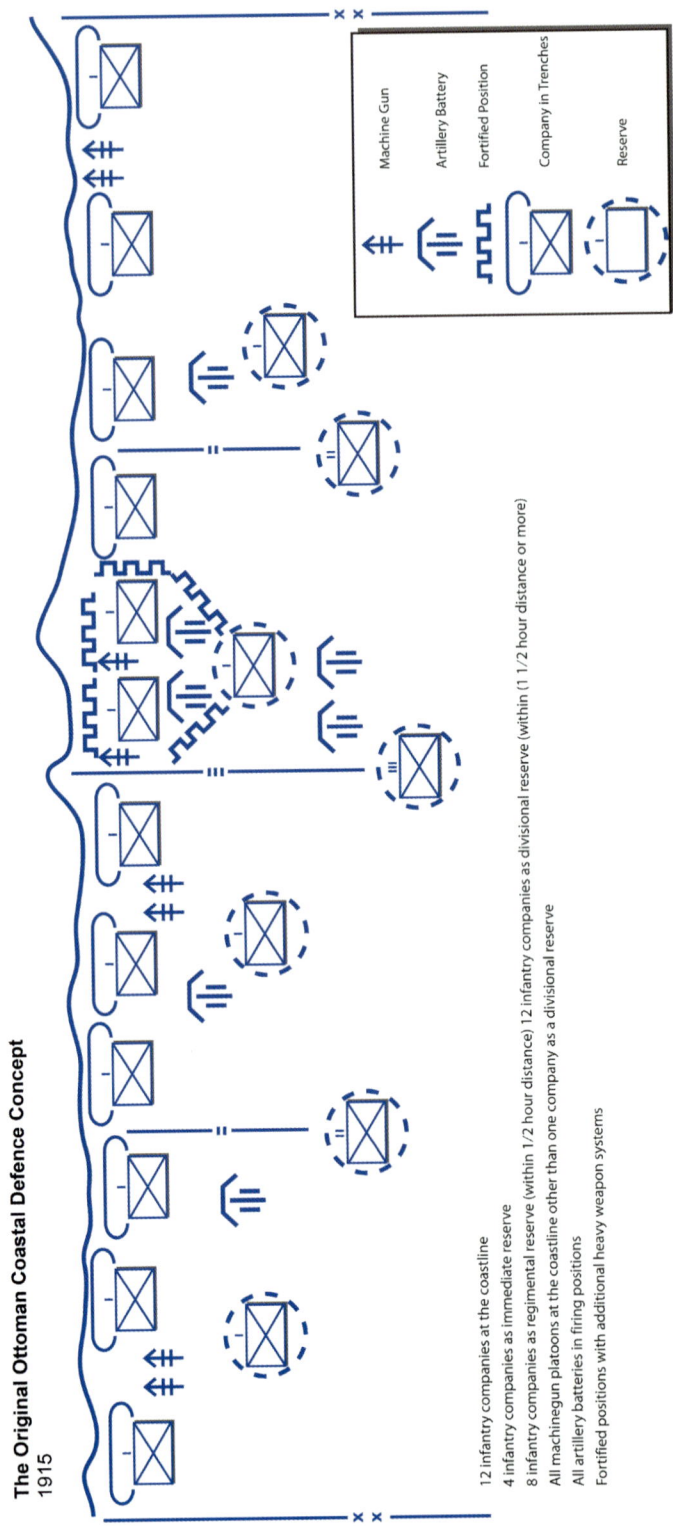

The Original Ottoman Coastal Defence Concept 1915

12 infantry companies at the coastline
4 infantry companies as immediate reserve
8 infantry companies as regimental reserve (within 1/2 hour distance) 12 infantry companies as divisional reserve (within (1 1/2 hour distance or more)
All machinegun platoons at the coastline other than one company as a divisional reserve
All artillery batteries in firing positions
Fortified positions with additional heavy weapon systems

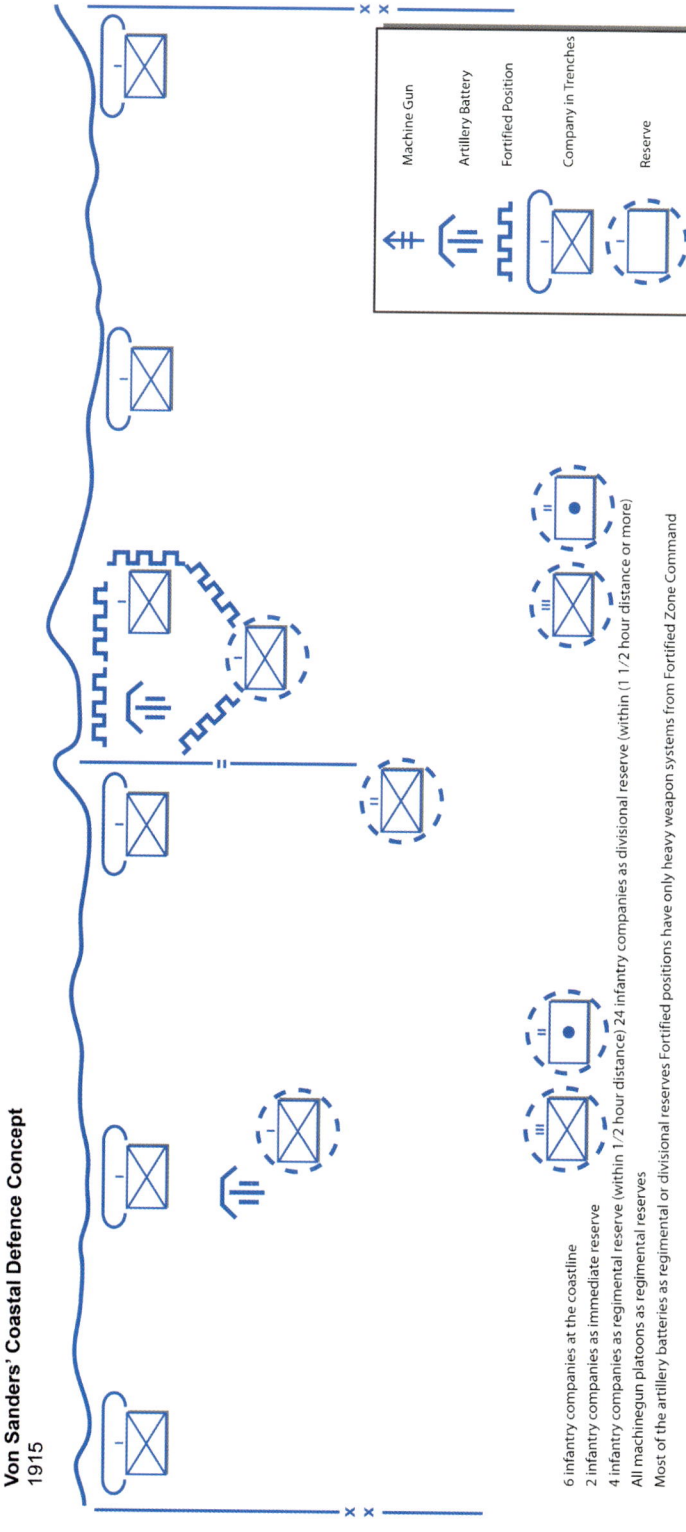

Von Sanders' Coastal Defence Concept
1915

6 infantry companies at the coastline
2 infantry companies as immediate reserve
4 infantry companies as regimental reserve (within 1/2 hour distance) 24 infantry companies as divisional reserve (within (1 1/2 hour distance or more)
All machinegun platoons as regimental reserves
Most of the artillery batteries as regimental or divisional reserves Fortified positions have only heavy weapon systems from Fortified Zone Command

While von Sanders stubbornly clung to his evaluation, he was alarmed by the consequences of massing all his available forces around these sites in case the enemy landed at a number of other sites simultaneously. Accordingly, he divided his units into three groups: Saros (*5th* and *7th divisions*), Gallipoli (*9th* and *19th divisions*) and Asia (*3rd* and *11th divisions*), thereby effectively dissipating combat power throughout the area of responsibility. He ordered the divisions to maintain reserves at all levels and commit small squads of troops to fixed defensive positions in order to achieve economy of force. The *5th* and *19th divisions* he retained as an army reserve directly under his personal command. The dispositions of the divisions were contrary to all the principles of defence. There was no centre of gravity, a very weak screening force without fire support and effective communication to the command centres, and cumbersome groups of reserves some distance away. The result of this defensive concept was that only one battalion (*2/27th Battalion*) was allocated to the Kabatepe region, a reinforced battalion (*3/26th Infantry*) to Cape Helles and another (*2/26th Battalion*) to the left and right flanks, and a company to Kumkale (*6th Company* of the *3/31st Battalion*).

The Arif Fountain, constructed by the *5th Division*, was one of many fountains built by front-line units to provide reliable and continuous water supply particularly during summer (image courtesy of Nejat Çuhadaroğlu).

While von Sanders held the Turkish soldier in high regard, he had a very low opinion of the Ottoman officer corps in general, regarding them as poor performers in the field of applied military sciences and generally unreliable. He did not believe in the viability of the German mission command (*auftragstaktik*) system within the Ottoman Army. The mission command system advocated that commanders merely point out objectives, aims and intentions, assign general tasks and allocate resources and then allow their subordinates to perform the required tasks using their initiative. Von Sanders did the opposite. He centralised the decision-making process as much as he could. He began to issue detailed orders and regulations and conducted frequent inspections to check whether his orders had been carried out exactly as prescribed. One of the dangerous outcomes of this restrictive command style was von Sanders' general distrust of his Turkish subordinates with the exception of some isolated individual cases. He also refused to change his orders even under compelling circumstances. In most cases, he preferred to see the situation for himself before making any changes to his orders. This also meant that, by dealing with all aspects of military life in detail, von Sanders simply did not have the time to concentrate on serious issues.

Moreover, while von Sanders had great respect for Esat Pasha, he regarded the corps as a simple 'post box' — basically an unnecessary and duplicating link between him and the divisions. He did not allow corps and divisional commanders to use their initiative. His operational orders contained strict clauses which severely restricted action without his personal authorisation. His tough attitude towards his subordinates was not confined to his Ottoman allies and he treated Erich Paul Weber, German commanding general of *XV Corps*, harshly, sacking him later in the campaign. While coercion and fear were essential elements of the command culture at the time, Ottoman officers disliked the brutal application of discipline and coercion by a foreign general. Von Sanders lacked the tact to keep this implicit, often bullying his subordinates almost arbitrarily. In short, his command style and the drastic changes he initiated were instrumental not only in creating confusion but also in promoting widespread hostility against him.

A cavalry patrol resting somewhere near Saros. The northern region was covered by the *1st Independent Cavalry Brigade* for an extensive period of time (image courtesy of Nejat Çuhadaroğlu).

In contrast to the belief of many modern commentators, von Sanders' interference did not improve the coastal defences and may even have weakened them. His new defensive concept was instrumental in promoting confusion, aroused serious opposition and impeded preparations to repel a possible invasion. Just a month prior to the 25 April landings, relations between the Ottoman commanders and their German advisor reached an all-time low, creating an incendiary atmosphere that damaged the decision-making process and belief in the wisdom of the defensive concept that was to protect them from invasion.

Three officers from the *72nd Regiment* pose in front of a ruined mill at Maydos after the British aerial bombing on 23 April. The bombing destroyed a portion of the town and caused military and civilian casualties. Mustafa Kemal decided to move the *72nd Regiment* out of the town to a more secure and central position (image courtesy of ATASE).

CHAPTER 3
THE INITIAL DEFENCE ON THE COAST

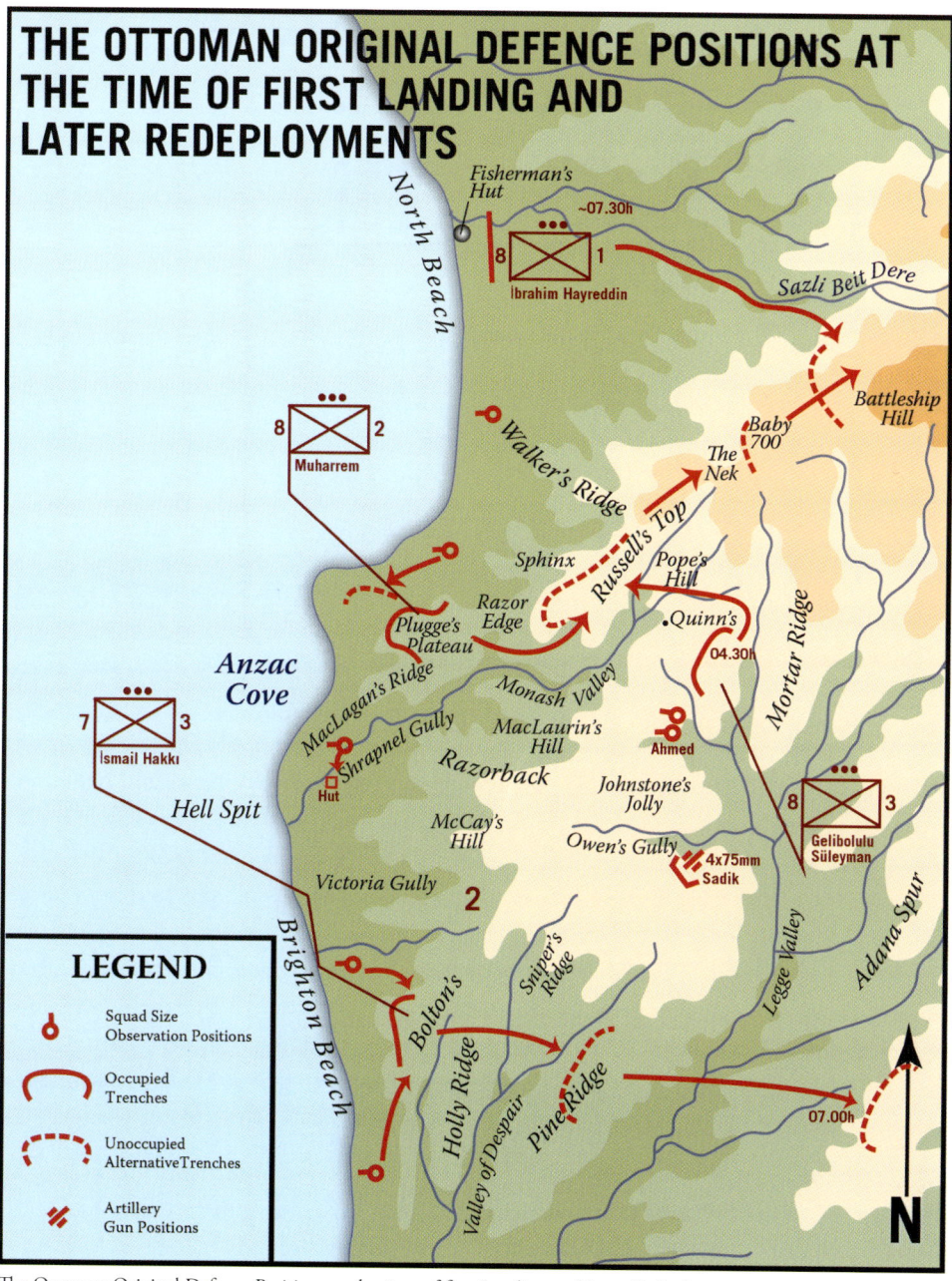

The Ottoman Original Defence Positions at the time of first Landing and Later Redeployments

The riddle of the machine-guns

German 7.65mm Maxim MG09 machine-gun on its original tripod. This was the standard weapon of the Ottoman *Machine-gun Corps*.

One of the most enduring riddles of the Anzac landing is without doubt the question of the Ottoman machine-guns. According to a number of Australian documents and eyewitness accounts, at least four and possibly six machine-guns fired on the first wave as it landed and still more machine-guns appeared later on. Official historian Charles Bean speculates that one or two must have been in Kabatepe, one on Arıburnu Knoll, one beyond Walker's Ridge and certainly one at the Fisherman's Hut during the initial landing. In fact, in Bean's first volume, the Ottoman machine-guns pop up in almost every account of a serious clash. Most of the eyewitness accounts appear to support Bean and some even contain anecdotes of the capture of machine-guns or at least parts of these weapons. Thus it is important to ascertain precisely how many Ottoman machine-guns were present at the landing and how many arrived later during the day.

First, it is instructive to examine Ottoman organisation and doctrine. According to the Ottoman table of organisation and equipment, machine-guns were provided to infantry regiments in a four-gun company. Various systems of employing machine-guns had been tried and, in the end, given the Balkan Wars experience and current German doctrine, machine-guns were allocated under the control of regimental commanders. Clearly the shortage of machine-guns significantly affected this decision. The German Maxim machine-gun was accepted as the standard weapon and the Ottoman government purchased some 200 7.65mm Maxim MG 09 machine-guns (the export version of the German Army's standard 7.9mm MG 08). A large number of these were lost during retreats or surrenders and the government managed to purchase only a few more due to financial constraints. The German alliance did not assist with the provision of armaments such as machine-guns. Thus a number of regiments entered the war without machine-gun companies or with obsolete machine-guns such as the Hotchkiss M1900 and the Maxim MG99. The *26th Regiment* (*9th Division*) which faced the initial landings at Helles and the *77th Regiment* (*19th Division*) did not have machine-gun companies on 25 April 1915. Ottoman doctrine, like its German equivalent, stipulated the use of a machine-gun company as a whole and permitted only the separation of platoons. The use of machine-guns in isolation was strongly discouraged.

Second, I have examined all the war diaries of the units that took part in the battle and read numerous reports and returns. I have also read all the available personal war narratives and checked all the military maps, overlays and sketches. Neither in the Ottoman documents nor in personal war narratives is there any mention of machine-guns at Arıburnu and Kabatepe during the landings. In fact, there are many entries clearly stating that the machine-guns were deliberately kept in reserve. Şefik, the Commanding Officer of the *27th Regiment*, ordered the preparation of machine-gun positions on the coastline when he took over the command of the regiment on 10 November 1914. Contemporary documents state that several machine-gun positions had been prepared on Arıburnu Knoll, 400 Plateau, Ağıldere (near the Fisherman's Hut) and Kabatepe. However, even before the change in defence doctrine, Şefik kept the machine-gun company in reserve, albeit with a reaction time of half an hour.

Third, Ottoman documents and personal accounts provide a detailed narrative of the events of 25 April. How, when and where the machine-gun companies were employed is clearly recorded. According to these documents, the first machine-guns (the *27th Machine-gun Company*) arrived with Şefik at around 7.40 am. Şefik positioned the machine-gun platoons on both sides of Scrubby Knoll. While he changed their positions from time to time, they remained on Third Ridge until the evening of 25 April when one platoon was repositioned on Johnston's Jolly. The *57th Machine-gun Company* arrived after Mustafa Kemal at Chunuk Bair at around 10.00 am. The company was positioned on the western slopes of Chunuk Bair and generally remained there. The last to arrive was the *72nd Machine-gun Company* which was sited in firing positions between Chunuk Bair and Scrubby Knoll at around 3.30 pm. Other than these three companies (12 machine-guns), no other machine-gun units were available on 25 April.

This begs the question of whether there were other weapons that could have been mistaken for machine-guns. The order of battle for the *9th Division* includes eleven 1-inch Nordenfelt multi-barrel (mostly three or four barrel) rapid fire guns (organised in one company) and four 37mm Maxim guns ('pom-pom' or 1-pounder guns, organised in one platoon) under the tactical control of the *9th Field Artillery Regiment*. These guns and their personnel were positioned by the *Fortified Zone Command* between February and March. The *Fortified Zone Command* did not retain these guns when it handed responsibility for the defence to the *Fifth Army*.

How many of these obsolete guns were used against the Anzac landing? There were only two Nordenfelt guns organised as a platoon at Kabatepe on 25 April. Previously there had been six, but some were damaged beyond repair and others had been moved to Helles. There were six Nordenfelt guns at Kumtepe, the remainder sited at Helles. Clearly these obsolete guns (mostly dismantled from ships) could not be classified as machine-guns but rather as rapid fire guns. Contrary to expectations, the two-gun platoon at Kabatepe did not provide any meaningful fire support. It opened fire at around 4.50 am and one gun broke down just before noon while the other exhausted its ammunition in the afternoon. The other Nordenfelts and 37mm Maxims were similarly useless beyond boosting the morale of the defenders. Most of them either broke down or were captured and the remaining guns were all discarded during May.

Chapter 3

The night of 24/25 April 1915 was clear and lit by bright moonlight. In the brilliant clarity of the light two privates from *3rd Platoon (2nd Battalion, 8th Company)*, Bigalı İdris and Gelibolulu Cemil, sharing the night watch on German Officer's Spur (Merkez Tepe), spotted the approaching armada at around 2.00 am. They alerted the nearby company command post at Boyun Mevkii, waking Captain Faik who climbed to the observation post. Faik wrote later that he was surprised to see the silhouettes of so many ships on the horizon. At first he could not discern whether these vessels were approaching or stationary. The Ottoman units on the peninsula had been accustomed to frequent enemy naval activity for almost two weeks, but this sight struck him as unusual. Faik ran back to his command post and telephoned the battalion command post at Kabatepe (Gaba Tepe). The battalion commander, Major Mehmed İsmet, tried to calm Faik and ascertain the particulars of the sighting. As far as İsmet was concerned, this enemy naval activity followed the same pattern as the previous fortnight and he saw no need to alarm the division and neighbouring units. İsmet reasoned that, even if Faik's suspicions were correct and enemy forces were actually planning to attack, they would almost certainly be heading towards Kabatepe. İsmet advised Faik to calm down and continue observing the enemy movements.

2/27 INFANTRY BATTALION
1915

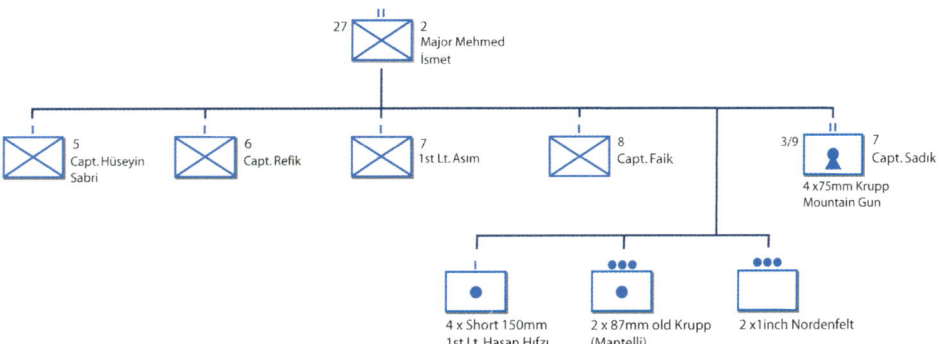

Faik, however, did not share İsmet's lack of concern and was unhappy with his commander's advice. He returned to the observation post, immediately noticing the increased number of ships which by now were moving very obviously towards the coastline. He decided to bypass his battalion commander to warn the *9th Division* Headquarters. It was now around 2.30 am and duty officer Deputy Officer Nuri transferred the message to the Divisional Chief of Staff, Major Mehmed Hulusi (Conk). Hulusi, like İsmet, did not regard the sighting as cause for concern and did not even bother replying to Faik's report. The indifference of his chain of command left Faik no alternative but to wait for events to unfold. Possibly dispirited by his commanders' responses, Faik committed the serious error of failing to warn his two platoons on the coast to be ready just in case. While there were no telephone lines to the other platoons, he had runners he could despatch with messages. Despite having this option Faik alerted only his reserve, the *3rd Platoon*, and waited anxiously for sunrise.

8/2 INFANTRY COMPANY
1915

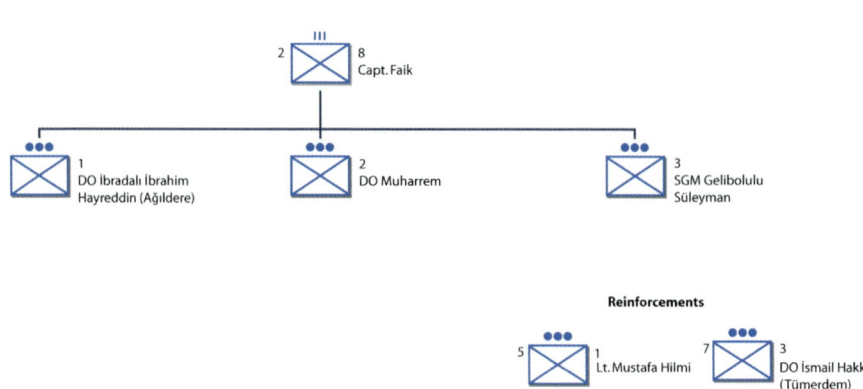

It is unclear precisely when the *2nd Platoon* at Plugge's Plateau (Hain Tepe) became aware of the boats heading directly toward its position. Witness accounts from veterans some 70 years after the war have generally proven unreliable and serve only to raise more questions regarding the specifics of the initial reactions than they answer. According to its commander, Deputy Officer Muharrem, the *2nd Platoon* was slow to read the intentions of the amphibious landing force. The sudden realisation that there were boats approaching the coast left Muharrem in a command paralysis and, instead of ordering his platoon to man the main trenches at Arıburnu Knoll via the communication trench (as they had so often practised), he remained in the support trenches with his men. His troops opened fire from their positions, approaching the edge of the steep slopes as closely as they dared, just minutes before the invading force landed. Because of their precarious and exposed position, this was not an organised and coordinated defensive fire and certainly not a fierce fusillade as commonly described in modern literature. Moreover a broad stretch of dead ground provided the attackers effective cover immediately beyond the thin strip of beach. The Anzacs in the front boats reached the beach safely with few casualties and immediately began climbing the slopes. The squad at the northern outpost retreated to the trenches at Arıburnu Knoll ahead of the enemy landing party and joined the firefight, but panicked when they realised that the main body of the *2nd Platoon* was not coming to assist from the support trenches. Some members of the squad escaped along the communication trench while others remained in their positions and were killed by the invaders. It is unclear what happened to the squad at the southern outpost, although it is likely that they joined the firefight from their original location. This southern squad appeared to retreat towards Shrapnel Gully (Büyükdere) after exhausting most of their ammunition. Understanding their ultimate fate through Ottoman records is problematic, although Australian accounts suggest that the defenders on this southern sector took refuge in a hut where they were captured and killed rather than retreating inland.

Chapter 3

Arıburnu Knoll from Plugge's Plateau. Note the dead ground the knoll creates. The *2/8th Platoon* was supposed to occupy the main trenches when the boats of the invading force entered the effective range of their rifles. Deputy Officer Muharrem experienced command paralysis and the platoon remained in the support trenches at Plugge's. It was left to the men from the observation post to the north to occupy these trenches before they were overrun by the quickly advancing Anzacs (AWM G00906).

Almost half of the Ottoman soldiers at Plugge's Plateau were wounded or killed during the initial exchanges of fire, largely due to the fact that their upper bodies were exposed as they took aim at the approaching enemy. Silhouetted on the horizon, they presented excellent targets to the invading forces. Unsurprisingly, Muharrem was quickly wounded in both shoulders and evacuated. Those of his remaining soldiers who were unwounded escaped towards the western part of the Russell's Top (Yüksek Sırt) trenches where they joined the *3rd Platoon*. The Anzacs who reached these Ottoman support trenches glimpsed the retreating forms of the *2nd Platoon* men as they disappeared up the slopes.

Faik reacted to developments as soon as the first shots were fired. He left two squads under Sergeant Ahmet on the seaward slopes of German Officer's Spur and rapidly moved the remaining seven squads to the Russell's Top trenches, reaching the position at around 4.40 am. They occupied the support trenches just in time and opened fire with their rifles, initially targeting incoming boats. Faik sent Private Gelibolulu Cemil to the *7th Mountain Artillery Battery*'s position behind Yeşiltarla (near the Cup) to request the battery to open fire against the enemy and, if possible, persuade the gunners to move position to a point somewhere near Hill 971 (Kocaçimen Tepe). He actually meant Chunuk Bair (Conkbayırı) but, unaware of the name of the feature, used Hill 971 instead. Battery commander Captain Sadık, however, refused the request to move on the basis that he had been given clear orders only to support the Kabatepe region. He sent Cemil back with a proposal to discuss the situation prior to any further action. Faik had no time to discuss the battery's position with its obdurate commander and returned to the fight without artillery support.

With the end of resistance on Plugge's Plateau, the trenches on Russell's Top became untenable. Once the main body of the Anzac forward elements (A Company, 12th Battalion under the command of Lieutenant Colonel Lancelot F. Clarke) discovered the exact location of the trenches, thanks to lines of dry brown bushes supposed to camouflage the trench line, they subjected them to withering fire, while small groups of advancing enemy began to infiltrate from Shrapnel Gully. Faik tasked Sergeant Lapsekili Muharrem and two soldiers to halt the enemy's progress with hand grenades. While the grenades provided some initial respite, they were harassed by Anzacs sniping at them from several directions and approaching steadily. Casualties among the Ottoman defenders in these advanced positions increased by the minute. Platoon leader Sergeant Major Gelibolulu Süleyman had his left foot blown to pieces before Faik himself was wounded in the groin. He ordered his soldiers to stand their ground until the reserves could arrive.

A 75mm Krupp *gebirgskanone* L/14 M1904 gun in its firing position. The 75mm Krupp mountain guns provided the main fire support on 25 April. Their accurate shrapnel fire was the main cause of Anzac casualties (image courtesy of ATASE).

In the meantime Major İsmet remained unaware of the danger and failed to appreciate the accuracy of Faik's warnings even when the *7th Company* at Kabatepe visually spotted enemy boats. Against orders, soldiers began opening fire in the direction of the boats. While Company Commander 1st Lieutenant Asım tried to enforce fire discipline, İsmet reported this sighting to the *9th Division* command post without waiting to clarify the enemy's intentions. He wasted almost an hour during which he could have reacted to the unfolding situation. Finally, at around 5.20 am, he sent an urgent message to the division explaining the seriousness of the situation and asking for reinforcements.

Chapter 3

THE ARTILLERY RIDDLE

Artillery was the deadliest weapon of the First World War by a significant margin. Unsurprisingly, artillery — particularly shrapnel fire — caused more casualties among the attacking Anzac troops than any other weapon (including machine-guns) on 25 April 1915. It is important to assess not only the number and types of artillery used but also when these joined the battle.

At the time of the landing there were three Ottoman artillery units in the region. The first was the heavy howitzer battery consisting of six short 150mm howitzers, probably Krupp *schwere feldhaubitze* M1902, with an effective range of 7450 metres. These guns may also have been the older version Krupp M1893 with the same calibre but with a shorter range of approximately 5000 metres from *III Corps* artillery and under the command of 1st Lieutenant Hasan Hıfzı. The battery was deployed in two halves: four howitzers were positioned at Palamutluk Sırtı (the Olive Grove) and two guns at Çamtepe. Only the howitzers at the Olive Grove were within range of Anzac Cove and these began firing on naval vessels and coastal positions at around 6.00 am. According to Ottoman records, the siting of their firing positions and the lack of effective forward observation prevented them firing on positions further inland.

The second artillery unit was the artillery platoon fielding two 87mm field guns of the Krupp *feldkanone* L/24 M1885 type at Kabatepe. These guns were described in the Ottoman sources as Mantelli guns after the steel cladding on the barrel. They had an effective range of 6800 metres for high explosive shell and 5200 metres for shrapnel. The platoon was drawn from the *Fortified Zone Command*. As a weapon system, the M1885 was an outdated gun and difficult to maintain in working condition due to worn barrels and faulty parts. One of the two guns was broken during a firing exercise a few days prior to 25 April, leaving only one gun operational against the landing. The single gun began firing at 4.45 am and fired a total of 114 shrapnel and 37 high explosive shells throughout the day. Although the slow-firing system hampered its effectiveness and HMS *Bacchante* bombarded its position from 7.00 am, it effectively harassed the second and following wave landings and considerably damaged enemy morale. It also fired inland on visible groups of soldiers as the opportunity presented, but in these instances its effect was largely psychological.

The third and potentially the most important artillery unit was the *7th Mountain Artillery Battery* consisting of four 75mm mountain guns of the Krupp *gebirgskanone* L/14 M1904 type. With an effective range of 4800 metres, these guns belonged to the *9th Field Artillery Regiment, 3rd Mountain Artillery Battalion* under the command of Captain Sadık at Yeşiltarla (near the Cup). The battery was specifically positioned to provide support to defenders opposing the landing at Kabatepe. Under specific orders to maintain that position, Sadık refused to countenance any move in order to provide fire support to the *8th Company* as requested early in the morning. He stubbornly waited for orders from his commander to change his position but notification came too late. Lieutenant G. Thomas's platoon from the 9th Battalion and Lieutenant E.W. Talbot-Smith's platoon from the 10th Battalion overran the *7th Mountain Artillery Battery*'s position while the gunners were frantically trying to pack the guns and ammunition at around 7.00 am. Sadık managed to escape with one gun and most of the ammunition but left behind three guns and most of the equipment.

Şefik, Commanding Officer of the *27th Regiment*, and his battalions began to reach Third Ridge at 7.40 am. He commenced the march without waiting for his artillery battery (*8th Mountain Artillery, 3/9th Battalion* armed with four 75mm Krupp mountain guns) which was at Çamburnu at the time. Sadık arrived at Third Ridge half an hour later with his lone 75mm Krupp mountain gun column and Şefik positioned the gun close to Scrubby Knoll from where it began firing at 8.30 am. The *8th Mountain Artillery Battery* finally arrived at 10.30 am. Şefik placed the *3/9th Mountain Artillery Battalion* commander, Major Manastırlı Nazif, in charge of this battery and Sadık's single gun. Nazif organised the artillery and sited them in positions around Scrubby Knoll. The five-gun battery began to fire as a unit at 11.00 am. At midday Şefik moved two guns to Anderson Knoll in order to provide better fire support to his counter-attack.

Mustafa Kemal and his *57th Regiment* began to arrive at Chunuk Bair–Hill 971 at around 9.30 am. He positioned the *6th Mountain Artillery Battery* (*39th Field Artillery Regiment, 3rd Mountain Artillery Battalion* armed with four 75mm Krupp mountain guns) at Suyatağı (literally 'creek') Mevkii south of Chunuk Bair. The battery began firing at approximately 10.30 am. Due to a mistaken report of fresh landings around Kumtepe, Mustafa Kemal ordered his two regiments and remaining artillery to head south to meet this reported threat. The *2nd Field Artillery Battalion* (*39th Field Artillery Regiment* consisting of two 75mm Krupp rapid fire batteries each with four field guns) did not arrive at Third Ridge until around 4.00 pm due to the confusion of marching back and forth. Mustafa Kemal positioned the batteries north of Scrubby Knoll (between Sancaktepe and Üçüncü Tepe). The 75mm Krupp *feldkanone* L/30 M1903 was a highly efficient modern field gun with an effective range of 5900 metres for high explosive shell and 5400 metres for shrapnel.

Mustafa Kemal's command also included the *1st Field Artillery Battalion* (*39th Field Artillery Regiment* consisting of two 87mm old Krupp field batteries each with four field guns). This battalion had limited mobility due to the lack of draft horses and water buffalos were used to tow the guns instead. The battalion arrived just before sunset at Kocadere village, so Mustafa Kemal held it there until the next day. Its eight 87mm field guns did not fire on 25 April.

As a final note, all the artillery batteries carried their first and second line ammunition stocks with them. Regulations stipulated that each battalion (except heavy artillery) was allocated 2200 shrapnel and 1000 high explosive shells. While the exact number of shells for each battery on 25 April 1915 is unclear, it is evident that the *1/39th Field Artillery Battalion* (eight 87mmm old Krupp field guns) had 2157 shrapnel shells while the *3/39th Mountain Artillery Battalion* (four 75mm Krupp mountain guns) had 2282 shrapnel and 759 shells. The *3rd Battalion* had received the ammunition stocks for the *6th Battery* but not the guns to fire them. Those guns arrived on 28 April.

Chapter 3

The 87mm Krupp *feldkanone* L/24 M 1885 was an obsolete field gun but commonly used by the Ottoman Army throughout the war. Originally designed for black powder, its barrel was not strong enough for modern charges so an additional steel cladding was added. The cladding resembled a mantle, hence the Turkish nickname 'Mantelli' (image courtesy of Nejat Çuhadaroğlu).

At 4.45 am, with improved visibility, the two-gun 87mm (Krupp *feldkanone* L/24 M 1885) *Field Artillery* (Mantelli) *Platoon* was ordered to open fire on the boats and the landing parties. But only one gun was operational, the other having broken down a few days earlier, and the slow-firing system laid only a meagre barrage on the landing enemy. Similarly, the two-gun 1-inch multi-barrel Nordenfelt platoon, which had already joined the firefight, was also plagued by technical problems. By midday one gun had broken down and the other had exhausted its ammunition. Both the Mantelli and Nordenfelt platoons were increasingly targeted by British naval gunfire after 8.00 am which seriously limited their effectiveness. Amid these difficulties the single 87mm Krupp gun still managed to fire 114 shrapnel and 37 high explosive shells throughout the day, providing artillery support to the beleaguered front-line defenders. The four-gun 150mm (Krupp *schwere feldhaubitze* M1902) howitzer battery in Palamutluk Sırtı (literally 'Oak Grove' but later named the Olive Grove by the Australians) opened fire on the ships and landing boats at around 6.00 am. Given the limitations of their firing positions and lack of effective fire observation teams with direct connection to the battery, these slow-firing guns were less effective against land targets but provided useful fire against ships and points on the edge of the coast. Their value lay in their ability to impede the landings following the second wave and force the escorting warships to move away from the coast. In reality, the Ottoman defenders did not receive satisfactory artillery fire support until the arrival of the mountain and field artillery batteries with the reserves at around 11.00 am.

A gun crew manning a 150mm Krupp *schwere feldhaubitze* M1902 demonstrating for a press visit, most likely somewhere behind Palamutluk Sırtı (the Olive Grove). Note the presence of a German officer close to the gun and a foreign journalist at the rear. A four-gun 150mm howitzer battery fired on naval vessels and the coastline on 25 April (image courtesy of ATASE).

İsmet had Captain Hüseyin Sabri's *5th Company* as a reserve but was reluctant to send the entire company to reinforce the *8th Company* which was bearing the brunt of the Anzac landing. He was adamant that the enemy's main landing would be at Kabatepe and had only two platoons from the *7th Company* manning the fortifications there. So he sent the *1st Platoon* of the *5th* under Lieutenant Mustafa Hilmi to reinforce the *8th Company*. Hilmi set off just after 6.00 am taking his 68-strong platoon towards Sancak Tepesi (north of Scrubby Knoll) following the Legge Valley (Karayürek Deresi) path. He soon came across elements of Sadık's battery hurriedly retreating in a very disorganised manner behind Lone Pine (Kanlısırt) and was spotted by the forward elements of the Anzac advance (probably Lieutenant Noel M. Loutit's party from the 10th Battalion and Lieutenant James Haig's unit from the 9th Battalion). Somehow he managed to slip past without taking casualties and began to collect the remnants of the *8th Company* who had either taken refuge in the creek bed or were fleeing through the scrub. He also met soldiers evacuating the wounded Faik to Kocadere village. Hilmi learnt the seriousness of the situation from Faik and decided to establish a defensive position on the slopes of Sancak Tepesi. He found a few more soldiers there and organised a defensive line overlooking German Officer's Spur and Lone Pine. He managed to consolidate the position just prior to 8.00 am with almost 90 soldiers and from there the bright morning light allowed the defenders to see the size of the amphibious landing that had assembled off the coast.

Deputy Officer İsmail Hakkı (Tümerdem) was on duty on Bolton's Ridge (Keltepe) with his 80-strong *3rd Platoon* (*2nd Battalion*, *7th Company*) and noted the unusual ship silhouettes at around 2.45 am. He had no means of direct communication with his company commander at Kabatepe so sent a runner to Muharrem's southern observation post. The post commander was unable to provide additional information. Hakkı spotted approaching boats a few minutes before the landing and ordered his men to open fire immediately, having heard the first shots from Plugge's Plateau. He pulled his observation posts back to the main trenches while continuing to fire on the Anzacs (soldiers of the 9th and 10th battalions) appearing near Shrapnel Gully. Detecting enemy movement close to Plugge's Plateau and the Cup, Hakkı decided to send reconnaissance patrols to investigate. At the same time he sent runners to Kabatepe for reinforcements and extra ammunition. An hour later a single wounded soldier from the reconnaissance patrols returned, reporting the loss of Plugge's Plateau and the absence of friendly troops nearby. The runners from Kabatepe returned with orders from Lieutenant Asım to defend their area of responsibility at all costs.

As the morning wore on, the platoon was increasingly targeted by enemy infantry fire from the north and the north-east. To make matters worse, more landings from the enemy's second wave had occurred close to Hakkı's position. Had he remained any longer he knew that he and his men would have been overrun by the enemy's advance. The platoon skilfully withdrew first to Pine Ridge (Albayrak Sırtı) and then to the seaward slopes of Anderson Knoll (Kavak Tepe) without taking casualties. In both places they dug new defensive positions and opened fire on any target that appeared within range. Hakkı was fortunate that the Anzacs did not attack his new positions and he remained ensconced and able to fire from a safe distance. The patrols that had been sent to establish contact with friendly forces eventually met regimental commander Şefik (Aker) at around 7.20 am. Şefik ordered them to continue the defence in their present position and wait for reinforcements.

The *1st Platoon* (*2nd Battalion*, *8th Company*) was in the vicinity of the Fisherman's Hut (Balıkçı Damları) and was the northernmost platoon of the company defensive line. It was more or less isolated from the other units, apart from occasional contact with Muharrem's northern observation post. The platoon leader, Deputy Officer İbradalı İbrahim Hayreddin (Ağıldere), initially occupied support trenches further north of the position. The platoon's southern observation post informed him of unusual sounds and lights coming from the sea at around 4.00 am. He decided to move to the main trenches behind the Fisherman's Hut and called the northern observation post from there. Realising the imminent threat, the platoon opened a well-coordinated fire against the enemy boats and pinnaces at the limits of their rifles' range. Helpless to intervene, they watched the Anzacs overrun the *2nd Platoon* positions on Plugge's Plateau. İbrahim wisely rationed the ammunition to be used against the distant targets. By 5.00 am a group of boats had begun to move towards their position, easily discernible in the post-dawn light. By this time, at points to the south of İbrahim's position along Anzac Cove, an estimated 4000 enemy troops had already landed. The boats heading towards his position provided İbrahim the opportunity to inflict serious losses on the attacking force. He ordered his soldiers to wait for the boats to enter the deadly range of the rifles, some 200 metres out. The soldiers of B Company, 7th Australian Infantry Battalion, had little chance against these well-prepared and ably led defenders. The firefight essentially turned into target practice. More than half of the assaulting soldiers were hit before reaching the shore, causing terrible casualties in the landing boats. The troops represented bobbing targets unable to take cover from the accurate and sustained rifle fire of İbrahim's *1st Platoon*. The remaining Australian troops scrambled to shelter behind a sand bank. While his men peppered the landing Australians from his northern sector, his southern outpost was busy keeping two Australian platoons (Lieutenant Rupert A. Rafferty's platoon from the 12th Battalion and Lieutenant Frederick P.D. Strickland's platoon from the 11th Battalion) at bay as they attempted to advance north along the beach. İbrahim left a squad to pin the survivors behind the sand bank with occasional fire and moved the remaining soldiers to the southern trenches to face the relief force. He also sent a small team armed with hand grenades to deal with the enemy soldiers trying to outflank them from a dry creek.

Deputy Officer İbradalı İbrahim Hayreddin (Ağıldere) was the commander of the *1/8th Platoon* at the Fisherman's Hut. Although he was a reserve officer, he achieved remarkable success in his initial defence of the Fisherman's Hut and gaining valuable time at Battleship Hill before the arrival of the *57th Regiment*. He was wounded later in the day and was evacuated. He returned to his unit and survived the war (image courtesy of Yetkin İşcen).

İbrahim was pleased with the initial defence, but was aware that the enemy was advancing inland towards the high ground and his soldiers had almost exhausted their ammunition. He withdrew the majority of his troops before they could be cut off by the large numbers of Anzac troops who had landed to the south. He left one squad in its trenches and moved the others from Sazli Beit (Sazlı Dere) to the next high ground, Rhododendron Ridge (Şahin Sırtı). The rearguard then joined the main body. Following the northern slopes of the hills to avoid enemy fire, they eventually reached Chunuk Bair. Several soldiers from the *2nd* and *3rd platoons* joined İbrahim where he watched the advance of the *27th Regiment* from Third Ridge (Topçular Sırtı or Gun Ridge) to join the defence. Their presence halted the enemy's advance and, from their hastily prepared positions, they began to fire at targets appearing around Battleship Hill (Düztepe) and Baby 700 (Kılıç Bayırı).

The most controversial incident of the day for the Ottoman defenders was undoubtedly the capture of the three 75mm Krupp mountain guns behind the Cup. A mountain artillery battery had been sited in this location during the reorganisation of the land defence at the beginning of March. The battery was to support the Kabatepe fortification against a landing from a position that promised good cover from enemy naval gunfire. While this was the ideal location, it seriously limited the mountain guns' ability to support other units such as the *8th Company* platoons on the coastline, without moving further north. The *7th Mountain Battery* (*3rd Battalion*, *9th Field Artillery Regiment*) under the command of Captain Sadık had assumed responsibility for the guns in the middle of April. Sadik was a perfect example of a narrow-minded technician who lacked initiative and had little capacity to understand the rapidly changing nature of combat. His battery had serious problems such as the lack of phone connection to Kabatepe and the divisional command centre, no liaison and coordination with the *8th Company* and a limited number of pack animals to move the battery in a single lift. He did not try to improve the situation and was apparently unconcerned by his isolation from other units.

The *2nd Battalion*'s commander, Major İsmet, did not send direct orders to Sadık to support the *8th Company* during the initial landings. He simply ordered Captain Faik to make use of the mountain battery's fire support when needed, unaware that Sadık would refuse to change position on the basis that he had been ordered to support Kabatepe only. Sadık was reluctant to take responsibility — possibly the reason he had asked Faik to come to his location to discuss the issue. Documentary evidence suggests that he also did not try to contact Kabatepe to ask for an assessment of the situation and seek clarification. He stubbornly held his position until he saw that Plugge's Plateau had been captured. Even then there was still time to manhandle the guns and open fire on the Anzacs who were rapidly moving towards the interior. Instead, he ordered his men to dismantle the guns, pack up the ammunition and move to Third Ridge. He sent an ammunition party first and personally led a group carrying a gun and optical equipment. But it was too late for the remainder of the battery. Several small Australian parties (Lieutenant G. Thomas's platoon from the 9th Battalion and Lieutenant E.W. Talbot-Smith's platoon from the 10th Battalion) discovered the location of the battery while the Ottoman gunners were desperately trying to dismantle the remaining three guns and pack the ammunition. They had no chance to spike the guns or offer any serious resistance. Most of them were killed in their position, although a few managed to save themselves by scattering in different directions. Sadık and his party later joined the incoming *27th Regiment*. He was eventually court-martialled for his conduct and expelled from the military.

THE OTTOMAN DEFENCE AGAINST THE ANZAC LANDING: 25 April 1915

COMMAND CRISIS AT THE TOP

Between 4.30 and 5.50 am on 25 April the first warnings of an impending landing operation arrived at all the Ottoman command centres on Gallipoli from various channels. Halil Sami, Commanding Officer of the *9th Division*, and his staff initially assessed the sightings as simply a naval demonstration and did not react. However when reports of physical landings began to materialise, messages from the front-line units quickly began to choke the lines of communication. The initial inaction and misreading of the situation saw four platoons of the *2/27th Battalion* at Anzac and the *3/26th Battalion* at Helles face the first two waves of the landing alone. Moreover Halil Sami did not inform the chain of command through the correct hierarchy. His staff officers sent their first reports directly to Lieutenant Colonel Kazım (İnanç), Chief of Staff of the *Fifth Army*, while his corps commander, Esad Pasha, received his information from the *19th Division* commander, Mustafa Kemal, at 5.50 am — almost half an hour after *Fifth Army* Headquarters had been alerted, despite the fact that both of them were sited within walking distance of each other.

Merkez Fort (better known as Fort Sultan) on the Bolayır line. Note the old heavy mortar on the right and the 150mm Krupp fortress howitzers on the left. The Bolayır line was originally constructed during the Crimean War to protect the Gallipoli Peninsula from a possible Russian attack. It showed its worth during the Balkan Wars against the Bulgarians. Convinced that a landing would occur at Bolayır-Saros, von Sanders waited for three days on a hill near to this fort.

Esad Pasha immediately called Liman von Sanders but learnt to his dismay that von Sanders had left for the Bolayır fortifications. Although there were almost no first-hand reports of the actual landings at *Fifth Army* Headquarters, von Sanders, who was fixated with the idea that the landings would occur at Bolayır and Saros, rushed to the Bolayır fortifications, leaving most of his staff behind. Esad Pasha, a much cooler head, took his time and evaluated the increasingly urgent reports in order to ascertain the genuine landing sites and respond accordingly. He discussed the situation with his divisional commanders and staff for an hour. In the end he came to the conclusion that his worst fears had been realised and the enemy's main effort must be either at Anzac or Helles. Esad Pasha's task was not an easy one. He had to manage von Sanders' mistrust of Ottoman officers and of his own independently minded Ottoman subordinates while, at the same time, ensuring that the Ottoman and German officers avoided infighting during the gravest crisis of the war thus far. Instead of giving clear orders to Halil Sami and Mustafa Kemal, the *9th* and *19th Division* commanders respectively, on how to respond to the invasion, Esad Pasha decided to go to Bolayır. This was his first big mistake of the day.

Chapter 3

Ottoman soldiers depart İstanbul in a small sailing vessel (from a sketch by a German journalist). Maritime transport remained the primary means of transportation given the Allied submarine threat. The Ottoman Army used a wide variety of ships, ranging from small sailboats to steam-powered liners (image courtesy of Nejat Çuhadaroğlu).

Esad Pasha was unable to find von Sanders at the Bolayır fortifications, locating him instead on a nearby hill watching the ships at Saros Bay, seated behind bushes and accompanied only by his aide-de-camp, Captain Erich R. Prigge. When Esad Pasha moved to approach him, von Sanders angrily told him to lie down and crawl to his position to avoid detection. Esad Pasha obediently lay down and crawled. His position, subordinate to von Sanders, required that he provide sound and timely advice if he felt his commanding officer was not reacting to the realities on the ground, but his loyalty and obedience to von Sanders meant there was no possibility of confrontation between the pair. Accounts of this meeting note that Esad Pasha merely expressed his opinion that the enemy's principal landings were at Helles and Anzac and then asked for the release of the *19th Division* and heavy artillery to bolster the Ottoman defences. However von Sanders was not receptive to polite advice at this stage of the battle. Dangerously overconfident in his belief in the superiority of his own defensive plan, von Sanders resolutely refused to comprehend the gravity of the situation and the reality of the landing points as the main enemy effort. He continued to wait for a main landing at Bolayır for another two days, well after the Allied aims and plans were evident for all to see, and ignored all the other landings, regarding them as evidence of an elaborate ruse. Esad Pasha managed only to gain permission to move his tactical command post from Gallipoli to Maltepe by sea. When he arrived at his new command post at around 12.00 noon, having lost almost half a day, he discovered that his subordinates had already committed themselves. From the Ottoman perspective, it was just as well they did.

THE OTTOMAN DEFENCE AGAINST THE ANZAC LANDING: 25 April 1915

ŞEFIK AND THE ARRIVAL OF THE *27TH REGIMENT*

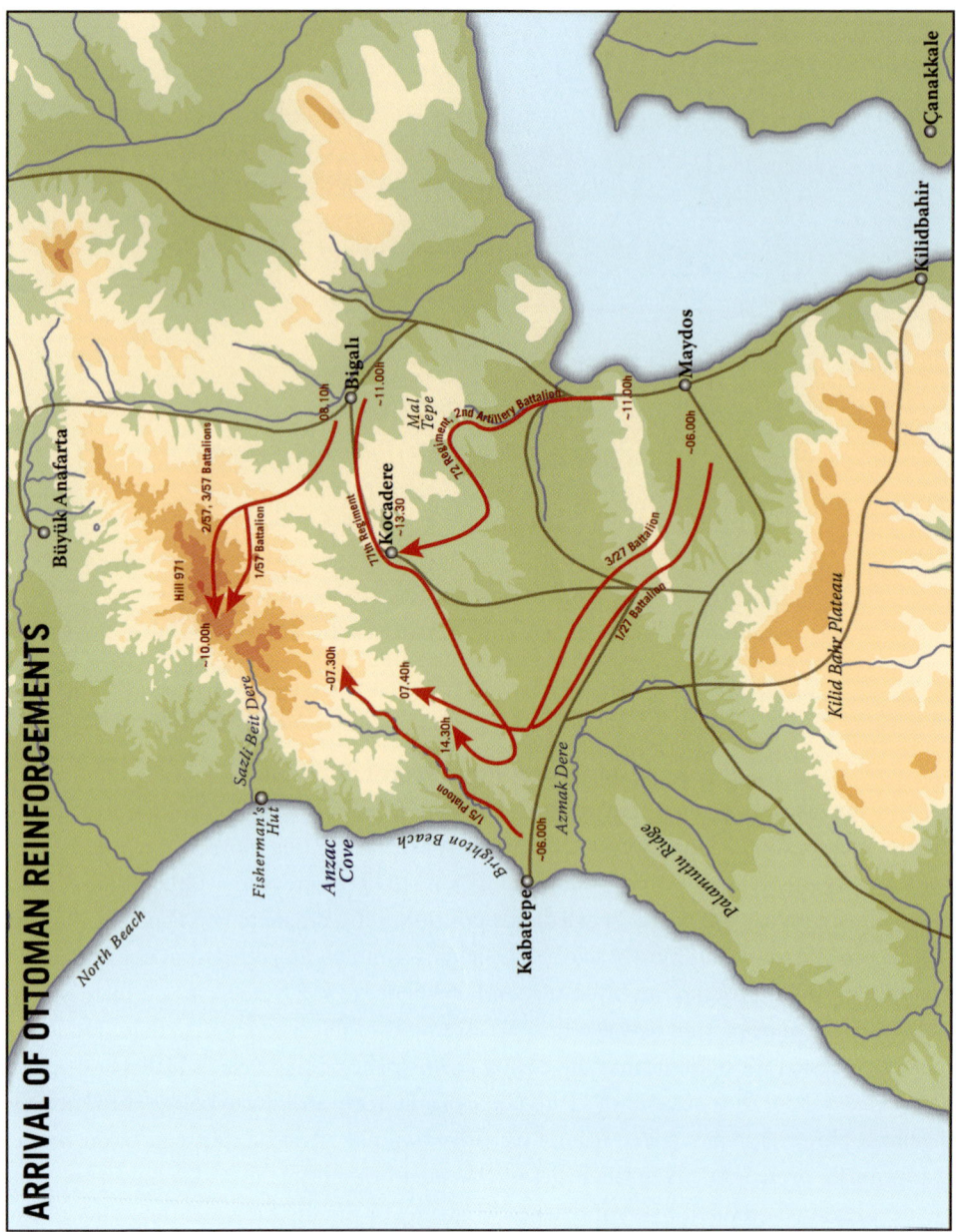

The Arıburnu region — including North Beach and Brighton Beach — formed the mainstay of Lieutenant Colonel Şefik's defensive obsession. He was convinced that an Allied main landing would occur in this location and, on his arrival there in early March, began construction of a comprehensive defensive system in anticipation. This construction activity was halted suddenly with the introduction of von Sanders' new defensive concept. Under von Sanders' organisation, only one battalion was left to defend the region while the remaining battalions of the *27th Regiment* were tasked as the northern reserve of the division. Moreover the battalion on the coast was placed under direct command of the division. Şefik was unhappy with the new defence system as it essentially designated Arıburnu as a secondary defensive area in support of the Kabatepe fortified point.

A cavalry troop mounts in readiness to move out. The Ottoman cavalry played an important — albeit mostly forgotten — role at the beginning of the campaign by conducting reconnaissance, covering secondary landing sites and supplying dispatch riders (image courtesy of Nejat Çuhadaroğlu).

On the night of 24/25 April, Şefik put his two battalions through a combination of a field exercise and forced march. The tired regiment returned to its encampment at around 2.00 am. Şefik woke to artillery fire coming from the west a few hours later. To him the situation was clear. The long-anticipated landing had begun. He called Kabatepe to be told that no attack had been made against the fortified point; rather the landing had been made at Arıburnu as he had long forecast. He alerted his regiment and ordered the distribution of iron rations. While his soldiers were busy with their preparations, Şefik called the divisional command centre to request permission to march to oppose the landing. The Chief of Staff, Major Hulusi, shared neither Şefik's enthusiasm nor his logic. To Hulusi it was still less than apparent whether the landing was real or a feint. He cautioned against making rushed and possibly incorrect decisions, suggesting the need to wait. This apparently reasonable proposition did not satisfy an increasingly agitated Şefik. He called the division repeatedly until the divisional commander, Colonel Halil Sami, relented and, at 5.45 am, granted him permission to advance against the landing at Anzac. In addition to the release of his two battalions and a machine-gun company, the *8th Mountain Artillery Battery* (*9th Field Artillery Regiment, 3rd Mountain Artillery Battalion*, armed with four 75mm Krupp *gebirgskanone* L/14 M1904 guns) at Çamburnu was also placed under Şefik's tactical command. He decided not to wait for the battery, which would require at least half an hour's march to join him. Şefik left a company with orders to escort and protect the battery while sending several cavalry patrols to reconnoitre forward. His initial aim was to reach the key terrain of Third Ridge before the enemy.

The regiment was divided into two marching groups: Şefik and the *1st Battalion* followed the new southern path while the *3rd Battalion* and machine-gun company followed the northern route. Both groups stayed away from the Maydos-Kabatepe main road to avoid being spotted by enemy balloons and planes. This proved to be a wise decision as, not only was HMS *Manica*'s balloon in the air, enemy planes continually flew over, forcing them to take cover. The battalions were reunited near Kavak Deresi behind Third Ridge as Şefik had planned. They met a wounded soldier from the *8th Company* who gave them a concise account of the company's defence and warned them that enemy forward elements had already reached Anderson Knoll. While Şefik writes in his account that this information concerning the enemy's forward elements turned out to be false and he only saw enemy movement at Legge Valley and Lone Pine, the advance guard actually came under fire and, after a brief firefight, drove the enemy (probably Lieutenant Noel M. Loutit's party) off the western slopes of the ridge. Similarly Şefik's account does not mention meeting İsmail Hakkı's soldiers near the hill. According to contemporary reports, however, he ordered them to stay and provide flank security. Şefik suggested launching a counter-attack from Anderson Knoll to take advantage of the enemy's apparent vulnerability there, but gave up when he realised that the enemy advance further north was posing a greater danger to the continued defence of that part of the coast.

HMS *Ark Royal*, as the first aircraft carrier, played an important role in providing daily air observation reports on the Ottoman defence (image courtesy of Nejat Çuhadaroğlu).

Şefik's account also records that the vanguard reached Hill 165 [later renamed Kemalyeri (Scrubby Knoll) after Mustafa Kemal's tactical command post] at precisely 7.40 am. He was evidently unhappy with statements that appeared in various Turkish and foreign books after the war which claimed that Mustafa Kemal and the *57th Regiment* had reached Third Ridge well before anyone else. In order to correct the record, he places significance emphasis in his own account on the fact that his units managed to cover the distance in less than two hours. In Şefik's support, observers at Maltepe corroborated his timings by claiming that they saw a large group of Ottoman soldiers advancing on the eastern slopes of the ridge at around 7.30 am. Whatever the true arrival time, it took a relatively long period for the whole column to reach its destination. Moreover, Şefik had to allow his units some time for rest and reorganisation before committing them to the battle.

Şefik was quick to appreciate the severity of the situation. The enemy was advancing in two main directions — one group was heading towards Hill 971 while the other larger group was pressing directly against the ridge where his regiment was currently positioned. In reaching Third Ridge before the Anzacs, Şefik achieved his primary aim by occupying a position of considerable natural strength. Nevertheless, simply occupying and defending Third Ridge was not a viable option for him. He preferred to drive the enemy off the key terrain on Second Ridge, but his two-battalion regiment was not strong enough to do so without effective fire support. For that reason he decided, in his words, 'to hug the enemy' by establishing a close physical presence thereby halting their advance and pinning them down until reinforcements could arrive. He also hoped to recapture the three lost mountain guns.

Soldiers in a forward trench. Note that all the soldiers were wearing pre-1912 khaki fezzes instead of *kabalak* (*Enveriyye*) (image courtesy of ATASE).

THE OTTOMAN DEFENCE AGAINST THE ANZAC LANDING: 25 April 1915

Ottoman reinforcements march towards the front line. Reinforcements were late moving to the peninsula due to von Sanders' expectation that the landing would occur in the Bolayır-Saros region (image courtesy of Nejat Çuhadaroğlu).

While he labelled this action as the first counter-attack of the day it was, in military terms, more an 'advance to contact' operation. Şefik deliberately paid limited attention to the enemy's northern group since he could not cover both directions, and preferred to pit his strength against the southern threat. He sent a report to the division via Kabatepe informing the headquarters of his decision to launch a counter-attack from his current location and asking the *19th Division* to proceed to Hill 971 as soon as possible. He needed artillery for a successful counter-attack but the battery he had summoned prior to the march was nowhere to be seen. The company that had been left behind to escort and safeguard the battery arrived behind Third Ridge alone. The divisional commander, unaware of Şefik's reason for leaving the company in position, sent the men on their way shortly after the departure of the regiment. As a result, the battery lost its way and did not reach Scrubby Knoll until around 10.30 am, too late to take part in the first operation.

Fortunately, Captain Sadık and his one-gun column with its ample supply of ammunition appeared from the direction of Kocadere village. Despite Sadık's depressing news of the capture of the three guns, his arrival was nonetheless a welcome development. Şefik placed the gun near Scrubby Knoll facing Lone Pine and ordered it to fire on the Australian soldiers around the captured mountain guns at around 8.30 am. He then clarified his operational order. He assigned the *3rd Battalion* to the north against German Officer's Spur and the northern part of Johnston's Jolly (Kırmızı Sırt) and the *1st Battalion* to the south against Lone Pine and its southern extension. Each battalion was ordered to leave one company as a reserve while the third platoons of each company were to establish a second line. He placed machine-gun platoons (each with two guns) on both sides of Scrubby Knoll (Deputy Officer Saadet to the north and Lieutenant Halil to the south) to provide covering fire. It was a difficult decision to commit battalions without effective artillery fire support, but circumstances demanded immediate action to blunt the Anzac advance as each passing minute saw the enemy land more troops and occupy more key terrain.

According to Şefik's account, the battalions left their positions at around 8.30 am, although the real start of the operation is more likely to have occurred at around 9.00 am. While they easily drove the isolated Australian forward elements from the western slopes of Third Ridge, both battalions encountered serious difficulties from the outset. The dense scrub and vegetation in and around Legge Valley, while providing good camouflage, effectively split the Ottoman attack formations and disrupted coordination between the units. The *3rd Battalion* came under intense fire from the north and Captain Kör Halis (Ataksor) had to allocate two platoons to subdue this threat — one from the *10th Company* and Mustafa Hilmi's *1st Platoon*. The *3rd Battalion* further fragmented as the advance progressed. The *10th* (less one platoon) and the *12th companies* — the latter had been released from reserve — were assigned to the northern part of Mortar Ridge (Edirne Sırtı) while the *9th* and *11th companies* were allotted to the southern part. The single mountain gun and two machine-guns began to encounter difficulties supporting the battalion, particularly the northernmost platoons, due to the distance and terrain. Compounding these difficulties, Halis was wounded in the arm. Although he refused to be evacuated and remained in command, he was forcefully carried away a few hours later. It was unsurprising therefore that three companies of the battalion were stuck at Hill 180 between Baby 700 and Mule Valley (Kesikdere) while the fourth company further south could not even establish contact with the enemy.

A recently formed machine-gun company (later named the *26th Machine-gun Company*) armed with captured British Vickers machine-guns provides a demonstration for Liman von Sanders in Bigalı on 30 August 1915. From left to right: Fahreddin (Altay), von Sanders, Esad Pasha and Kazım (İnanç) (image courtesy of ATASE).

An İstanbul city ferry loaded with sick and wounded. Several passenger ships and ferries were converted to hospital ships to carry the ever-increasing causalities from the Dardanelles (image courtesy of ATASE).

Major Malatyalı İbrahim's *1st Battalion* was more fortunate during the initial advance but also encountered difficulties when it reached the edge of Johnston's Jolly and Lone Pine. The topography at Johnston's Jolly presented unique problems for both sides. The plateau was flat and devoid of any vegetation other than sporadic trees and bushes and could be swept with deadly fire from at least two directions. Lone Pine also had areas bare of natural cover (particularly the Daisy Patch) but there was sufficient vegetation to camouflage the advance. The Anzacs took advantage of this and maintained a strong position there. As a consequence, the *1st Battalion* was stuck on the eastern edge of Lone Pine and its southern extension, Pine Ridge, pinned down by determined Australian fire.

Şefik was unsettled by the slowly developing advance and increasing enemy fire and infiltration. However, at 10.30 am, in the midst of his despair, the 'lost' mountain artillery battery appeared. Fortunately, the *3rd Mountain Artillery Battalion* commander, Major Manastırlı Nazif, also arrived shortly after. Nazif quickly positioned the mountain guns close to the single gun and this five-gun battery began to fire in unison at around 11.00 am. In the meantime his cavalry and foot patrols to the north established contact with the forward elements of the incoming *57th Regiment*. Instead of the two battalions Şefik was hoping for, an entire regiment and a mountain artillery battery came to his aid. He immediately sent a written report explaining the situation and asking for a coordinated two-pronged counter-attack against the enemy to be launched at 11.30 am.

Chapter 3

Stretcher-bearers carry wounded and sick from a city ferry. The *Fifth Army* evacuated serious cases and convalescents to İstanbul and other cities to reduce the burden on the field hospitalities (image courtesy of ATASE).

A group of soldiers rests in Bigalı Village. Note the wide variety of uniforms and headgear. Bigalı was the command centre of the *19th Division* while the *57th Regiment* was camped nearby on the night of 24/25 April (image courtesy of ATASE).

119

MUSTAFA KEMAL AND THE ARRIVAL OF THE 57TH REGIMENT

When the first news of the landing at Anzac Cove arrived, Mustafa Kemal's *19th Division* Headquarters and divisional units were in the Yeldeğirmeni Plains near Bigalı (Boghali) village while his regiments had encamped further south around Maltepe and Mersintepe. On the coast his *3/77th Battalion* reported an amphibious landing north of Kabatepe and naval gunfire at 5.20 am. Mustafa Kemal had already been woken by the sounds of gunfire. Having confirmed the reliability of the reports, he alerted his regiments and informed Esad Pasha, his corps commander. He also sent cavalry patrols in the direction of Turşun village, Anafarta and Kabatepe to establish his own observation and reconnaissance system, just as his men had practised a few days before. As the former commander of the defence of southern Gallipoli during March, he knew that the initial reports must be taken seriously and units despatched immediately. However the *19th Division* was reserve for the *Fifth Army* and he had to wait for von Sanders' orders before he could react. By this time von Sanders had departed for Bolayır without leaving any orders. He discussed the impasse with Esad Pasha, but Esad Pasha hesitated and was reluctant to use his initiative without first consulting von Sanders.

Mustafa Kemal was in a most invidious position. He knew that a rapid reaction was required before it was too late but, at the same time, von Sanders' defensive concept seriously limited his initiative. The Ottoman officers were trained in and operated under the German mission command (*auftragstaktik*) system. An important principle of this system was never to hesitate in a command void. Ottoman officers were not accustomed to receiving detailed and restrictive operational orders, and thus Mustafa Kemal and Halil Sami decided to take the initiative. However each adopted a different approach to the task at hand. Halil Sami was the commander in charge of the regiments that had been fighting off the enemy landings at Helles (Seddülbahir) and Anzac. The patchy intelligence and contact reports made it difficult to read the enemy's intentions and thus determine where best to send his men to mount the most effective defence. The confusion generated by conflicting reports of landings and enemy sightings left him all but operationally blind, hampering Ottoman efforts to repel the attackers before they gained a foothold. Halil Sami was happy to delegate power to his subordinates and allowed them plenty of discretion to fight their own battles. This was evident in his response to *27th Regiment* commander Şefik who pressured him for authorisation to move against the landing at Anzac. The same occurred at Helles where the *26th Regiment*'s commander, Lieutenant Colonel Kadri, became the de facto commander. However, delegations of power did not work well with the *25th Regiment* commander, Lieutenant Colonel İrfan. He actively shied from responsibility, delegation and the use of initiative. Like Halil Sami, he was happy to allow his battalion commanders to react to developments.

Esad Pasha poses with a group of officers, probably during the autumn of 1915. Note the German officers who flank him on both sides. Esad Pasha preferred to let Mustafa Kemal and Halil Sami exercise tactical command and remain in charge of the front and rear command posts (image courtesy of Nejat Çuhadaroğlu).

Major Hüseyin Avni, commander of the *57th Regiment*. A loyal and trusted subordinate, he was Mustafa Kemal's right-hand man on 25 April. He was killed in action on 13 August 1915 (image courtesy of ATASE).

The *19th Division* cavalry patrols began to send reports from around 7.30 am. According to the first reports of Deputy Officer Hasan Raşid (from Kabatepe) and 2nd Lieutenant Mehmed Salih (from Kocadere), the enemy landing at Anzac was serious and there were already fierce clashes around Hill 971. Mustafa Kemal ordered the *57th Regiment* commander, Major Hüseyin Avni, to prepare to march to the ridge west of Kocadere (Third Ridge). Fortunately for the Ottomans, Halil Sami had already requested Mustafa Kemal to send a battalion to support the *27th Regiment* at 7.30 am. This request was the pretext that Mustafa Kemal had been seeking. Like Şefik, he had also identified the landing at Anzac Cove as the most dangerous to Ottoman prospects of holding the peninsula. At this stage he was unaware of the serious situation at Helles given the stream of contradictory orders and reports coming from the *9th Division* command centre. Instead of sending a battalion as had been requested, Mustafa Kemal decided to move with his entire regiment — the *57th Regiment*, the *57th Machine-gun Company* and the *5/3rd Mountain Artillery Battery* in support. He gave preliminary orders to his two other regiments and rushed towards Anzac Cove without authorisation from his chain of command other than sending a report to the corps headquarters at 8.00 am informing them that he was advancing towards Anzac.

57th INFANTRY REGIMENT
1915

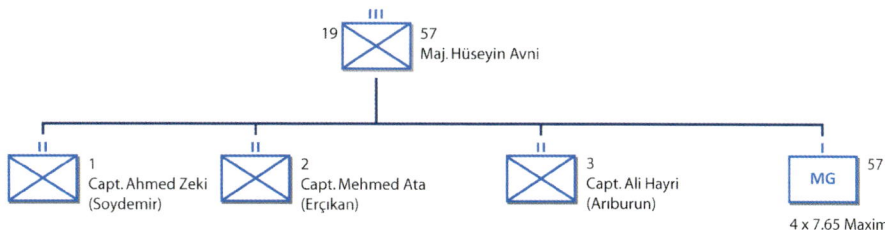

Mustafa Kemal began the march at 8.10 am at the head of the *57th Regiment* with a small group of staff officers accompanying him. His aim was to reach Chunuk Bair or at least Hill 971 before the enemy. There were no roads or suitable paths on which to travel so they were forced to cut a track through the dense scrub and low vegetation. Accounts suggest that they moved north of Kocadere village and were probably divided into two groups. The *2nd and 3rd battalions* with the mountain artillery battery moved in a northerly direction while the *1st Battalion* went south, although its exact route remains unclear. It is not certain when the forward elements reached the battlefield proper, but Mustafa Kemal's report claimed that the *57th Regiment* launched its counter-attack at 10.00 am. The distance to be covered was six kilometres as the crow flies and would take at least one and a half hours with probably only the fittest soldiers completing the march. While Mustafa Kemal's account appears reasonable, contemporary sources also record that Hüseyin Avni informed the division that the main marching group was passing Abdal Geçidi (mountain pass) at 10.00 am and that the *1st Battalion* had lost its way with several officers sent to find and escort it. The battalion arrived at the ridge half an hour late. The timing in Mustafa Kemal's report may well have referred to the time of the initial clashes of the forward elements of the *57th Regiment* with the Anzacs well before the start of the counter-attack.

Mustafa Kemal reached Chunuk Bair some time before the marching infantry. From this ideal observation point he spotted the enemy's advance along the high ground and noticed a group of Ottoman soldiers in a disorderly retreat. These soldiers almost certainly belonged to İbrahim Hayreddin's mixed platoon which had been fighting there for more than three hours. Mustafa Kemal concluded that the current situation required drastic action. He halted the fleeing soldiers and ordered them to fix bayonets and stand their ground.

As the soldiers established a makeshift defensive perimeter, Mustafa Kemal realised that he could not wait for the rest of his regiment to arrive. He ordered the *2nd Battalion*'s commander, Captain Mehmed Ata (Erçıkan), who had just arrived, to launch an immediate attack in the direction of Battleship Hill. He then placed the mountain battery in a fire position in a small creek on the eastern side of Chunuk Bair, later renamed Suyatağı Mevkii. He looked for the *1st Battalion*, which was coming from the south, but could see no sign of it. He angrily sent orders to its commander, Captain Ahmed Zeki (Soydemir), to join the attack immediately from the south. The hasty piecemeal attack achieved its aim and drove the forward elements of the Australians (a composite company under Captain Eric W. Tulloch) off Battleship Hill, but the attack lost its momentum under increasing enemy fire from Baby 700.

Captain Ahmed Zeki (Soydemir) was the Commanding Officer of the *1/57th Battalion*. His battalion lost its way during the march and he was late joining the attack. Zeki was wounded in action and evacuated at around 4.00 pm. He returned to his unit a few months later and survived the war (AWM ART02868).

It is important to identify the timings of this first action against Battleship Hill since both Mustafa Kemal and Şefik later claimed that their respective units were responsible for the earliest counter-attacks. Mustafa Kemal reported to Corps Headquarters at 10.24 am that he had launched an attack. Six minutes later he sent a message informing headquarters that the *27th Regiment* had arrived. However Hüseyin Avni reported to Mustafa Kemal at 11.30 am that the *2nd Battalion* had launched a counter-attack with two companies with the *1st Battalion* following from the south. It is also clear that Şefik sent a request for the battalions to launch a combined counter-attack at 11.20 am. As far as can be gleaned from other documents — including regimental war diary entries — the first companies commenced the attack at around 11.30 am and were joined by the others after 12.00 noon which fits perfectly with the recorded flow of events.

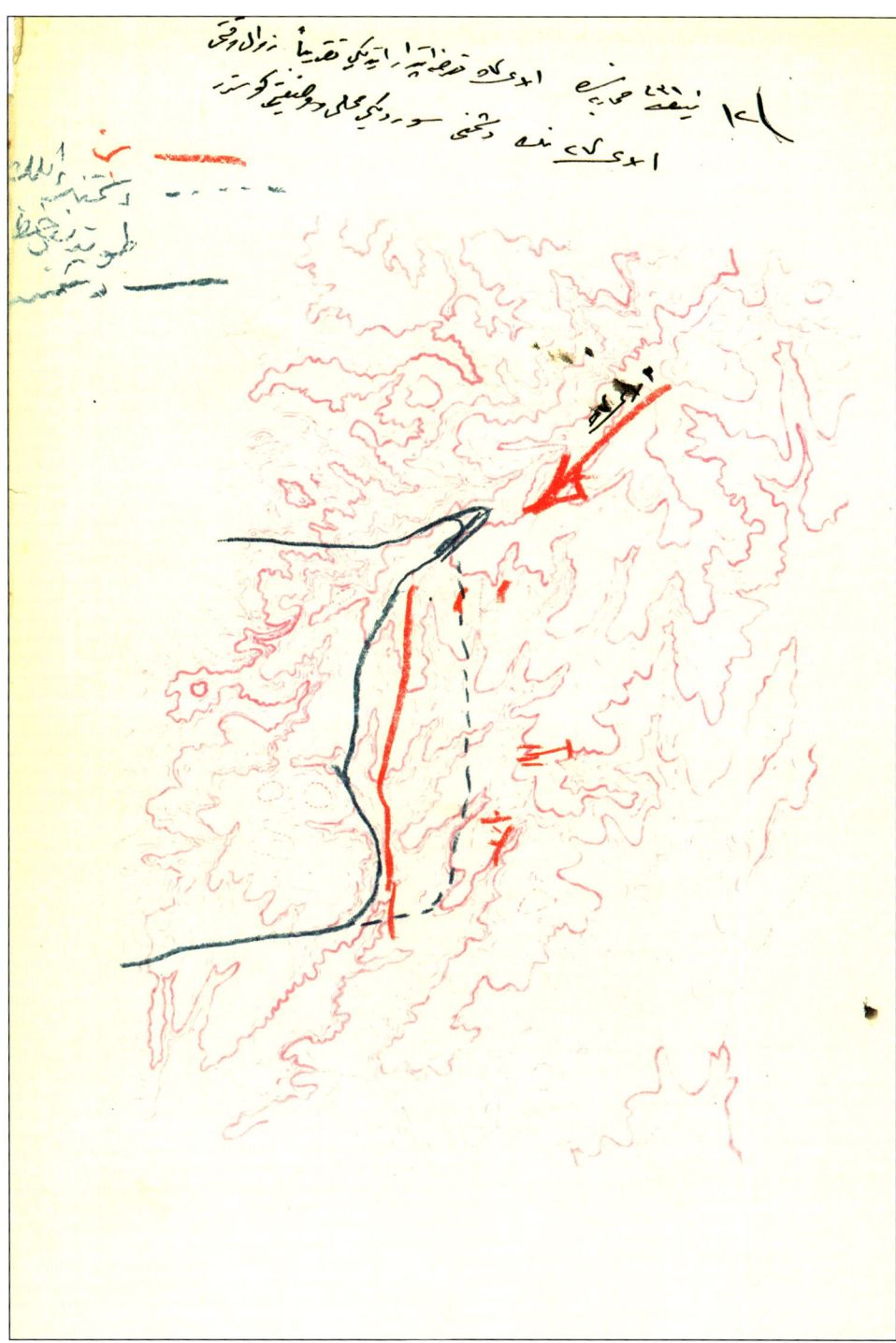

The situation at the beginning of the counter-attack by the *57th Regiment* at noon. The composite company under Captain E. W. Tulloch is shown on the eastern slopes of Battleship Hill. Mustafa Hilmi's *1/5th Platoon* and a platoon from the *10th Company* are shown as two short, disconnected red lines to the north. The two reserve companies are marked to the south of the artillery position (map courtesy of Serdar Ataksor).

THE OTTOMAN DEFENCE AGAINST THE ANZAC LANDING: 25 April 1915

By 11.30 am Mustafa Kemal believed the time had come to launch a major coordinated counter-attack. He began by rallying as many troops and stockpiling as many weapons as he could find. He established contact with Şefik and took him under his command while his two battalions attempted to push the Australians back over Second Ridge. He divided the landing area into two sectors and gave responsibility for the southern sector to Şefik. He sent a message to Şefik explaining his plan and his requirements for the *27th Regiment*, and then ordered him to attack the enemy's flank, concentrating on Lone Pine. This was a classic example of a mission-oriented order which consisted of just a few sentences. With their previous military education, well-established military doctrine and common experiences, both Mustafa Kemal and Şefik understood the situation in almost identical terms and knew what to do. There was no need to issue long and complex orders to enforce command and coordination. Mustafa Kemal sent orders to his units in the rear to march forward at 10.40 am. The *72nd Regiment, 1st Field Artillery Battalion* (two old 87mm Krupp *feldkanone* L/24 M 1885 field batteries) and *2nd Field Artillery Battalion* (two 75mm Krupp *feldkanone* L/30 M1903 rapid fire field batteries) were ordered to march to Maltepe while the *77th Regiment* and medical company were ordered to Kocadere village. Having issued these orders Mustafa Kemal sent a short message to *III Corps* providing a concise situation report.

A field artillery battery (armed with 75mm Krupp *feldkanone* L/30 M1903) during a firing exercise. Note the medical evacuation training conducted simultaneously with the firing (image courtesy of Nejat Çuhadaroğlu).

Mustafa Kemal was clearly disobeying orders by committing his entire division without authorisation from Esad Pasha and von Sanders. Although the Ottoman military doctrine encouraged commanders to exercise their initiative, Mustafa Kemal certainly exceeded his authority to fill what he saw as a command void jointly created by von Sanders and Esad Pasha. On so many occasions, great captains of war have gambled in chancing their arm against the enemy and Mustafa Kemal was certainly gambling in planning his counter-attack against the landing. In doing so he was risking not only his career but the entire operation.

Esad (Bülkat) Pasha was one of the most decorated and prestigious officers of the Ottoman Army at the beginning of the war. He could not fill the command void on 25 April because of his loyalty and obedience to von Sanders (image courtesy of Yetkin İşcen).

At this critical stage a dispatch rider from the *9th Division* arrived with alarming news of fresh landings at Kumtepe. Kumtepe had been identified as critical terrain due to its proximity to the Kilidbahir plateau and Maltepe and had been the subject of considerable concern to Ottoman commanders for some time. Mustafa Kemal immediately left the command of current operations to the *57th Regiment* commander Major Hüseyin Avni and issued an order to the *77th Regiment* commander, Major Saip, to march to Palamutluk (Olive Grove). He himself rushed to Maltepe to meet the *72nd Regiment*. On the way he met Saip and verbally reiterated his order. Mustafa Kemal reached Maltepe at around 12.40 pm. Fortunately, Esad Pasha met Mustafa Kemal before he was able to lead the *72nd Regiment* to Kumtepe. Mustafa Kemal described the military situation to him, outlining his response. Esad Pasha, as a highly experienced combat commander, compared the information from Mustafa Kemal with the message of the landings at Kumtepe and realised that the report from Kumtepe was mistaken.

Two dispatch riders. Divisional and corps cavalry were divided into small teams of dispatch riders to perform the vital task of communication, particularly during a crisis (image courtesy of ATASE).

Esad Pasha had been in Maltepe for almost half an hour when he discovered that his subordinates had already committed themselves to offensive action against the landing. Esad Pasha was an ardent proponent of mission command and believed that his divisional and regimental commanders possessed a better knowledge and understanding of the tactical situations in their areas. Instead of reprimanding Mustafa Kemal for using his initiative and making executive decisions without guidance from his chain of command, he encouraged him to continue his operations against the Anzacs. However, Esad Pasha did clarify the command relationship and began to monitor his subordinates closely, intervening when necessary by establishing an effective command over them. Esad Pasha informed von Sanders of developments and persuaded him of the necessity to continue the defensive arrangements while asking for more reinforcements. Von Sanders, who was still preoccupied with the possibility of a landing against Bolayır or Saros did not object to Esad Pasha's decision.

The timely arrival of Esad Pasha was a fortunate break for the Ottoman defenders facing the northern front against the Anzac landings, but this was not the case for those fighting the British landing at Helles. Esad Pasha made his second big mistake by underestimating the danger posed by these landings. Mustafa Kemal's decision to commit his division at Anzac and the continuous reports coming from this region overshadowed the magnitude of the threat at Helles. In contrast to the reasonably swift reaction at Anzac Cove, Halil Sami, Commanding Officer of the *9th Division*, went into a state of command paralysis over the landings and lost touch with developments as they were reported by his subordinate commanders. In most cases he simply allowed them to proceed without interfering. In the rare cases he actually issued a command it was invariably the wrong decision such as his infamous order to withdraw from Krithia (Kirte) on 27 April. Fortunately for the Ottomans, Halil Sami's subordinates decided to ignore most of his orders and held their ground. Most damagingly, Halil Sami made only limited attempts to keep his superiors and neighbouring units updated with the progress of operations in the Helles area. The relatively few reports that he did send were contradictory. As a result, Esad Pasha and the other field commanders gained a false impression of the situation at Helles.

Having gained Esad Pasha's approval to maintain his course of action, Mustafa Kemal ordered the *72nd Regiment* and two artillery battalions to Kocadere and sent new orders to the *77th Regiment* to return and support the attacks of the *27th Regiment* from the south. As fate would have it, Major Saip confused the exact location of the Olive Grove, which was southeast of Kabatepe, believing it to be an extension of Anderson Knoll. Instead of marching further south in the direction of Kumtepe, he simply ordered his regiment to march to the junction of Kabatepe road and Kavak Deresi. The dispatch rider and later Mustafa Kemal eventually found him and pointed him and his regiment towards Anderson Knoll.

Water carriers loading their barrels at Esad Pasha Fountain. Esad Pasha took over responsibility for building roads and logistics infrastructure using labour battalions (image courtesy of ATASE).

THE OTTOMAN DEFENCE AGAINST THE ANZAC LANDING: 25 April 1915

THE COORDINATED COUNTER-ATTACKS OF THE *27TH* AND *57TH* REGIMENTS

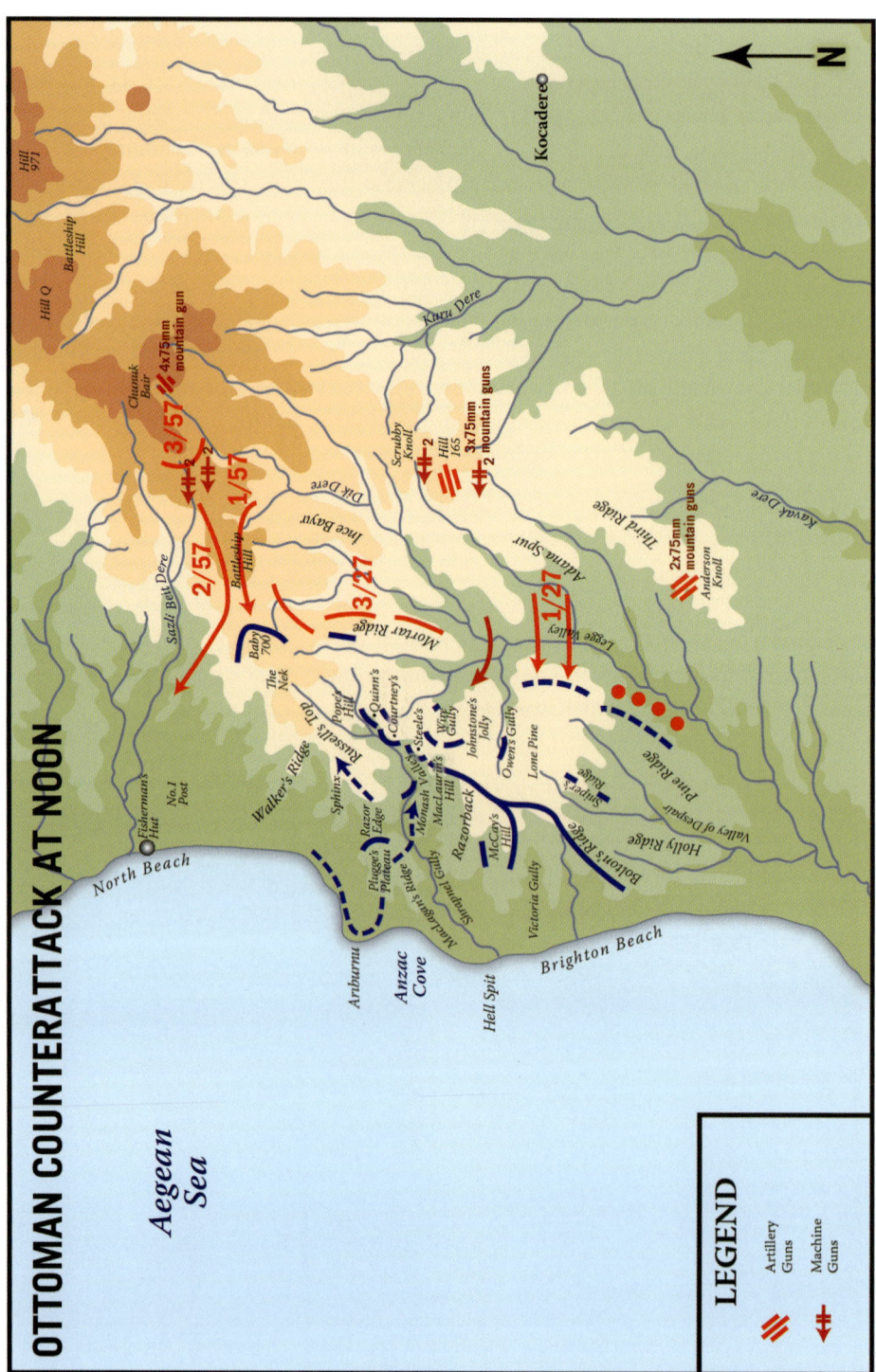

Major Hüseyin Avni took over command from Mustafa Kemal at 12.00 noon and personally led the counter-attack in the northern sector of the Anzac landings. Zeki's *1st Battalion* was pinned down in front of Baby 700 by a large group of Australians (while the actual numbers are unclear, it appears to have been approximately a company-size composite unit from the 9th, 11th and 12th battalions, a company from the 1st and two companies from the 2nd Battalion. The New Zealanders from the Auckland Battalion arrived at around 2.30 pm). Ata's *2nd Battalion* wheeled north following the northern slopes of Baby 700 (Kabak Sırtı) and Walker's Ridge (Sırça Tepe), intending to drive the weak enemy outposts off those features. Ata's northernmost company reached the Fisherman's Hut at around 2.00 pm and began to establish a defensive line to close off any attempts by the Anzac troops to break out north. Hüseyin Avni ordered the *3rd Battalion* to reinforce the *1st Battalion* and fill the void created by the movement of the *2nd Battalion*. While the mountain battery and machine-gun company had been providing effective fire support, both battalions were unable to bring their combined weight to bear on the enemy due to the narrowness of the ridge and the difficulty of the terrain. Occasional naval gunfire was also instrumental in creating havoc along the densely manned front line.

The 75mm Krupp *feldkanone* L/30 M1903 was the main artillery weapon of the Ottoman divisions during the war. However it a played relatively minor role on 25 April. The eight-gun *2/39th Artillery Battalion* entered the battle late in the afternoon at around 4.00 pm (image courtesy of Nejat Çuhadaroğlu).

Şefik was tasked to attack Lone Pine, but Halis's three companies (*9th*, *10th* and *12th*) were already bogged down in precarious positions between Battleship Hill and German Officer's Spur. It was impossible to either attack or break contact without providing the enemy the opportunity to advance and consolidate their gains. So he left these companies in their original positions and ordered Major İbrahim to take the *3rd Battalion*'s only available company (the *11th Company*) under his command and launch an attack against Lone Pine with four companies (the *1st*, *2nd*, *4th* and *11th companies*). Deputy Officer İsmail Hakkı was ordered to take his platoon and recapture his former position at Pine Ridge. Şefik kept the *3rd Company* in reserve for the time being. In order to subject Lone Pine to effective crossfire he decided to reposition two mountain guns on Anderson Knoll.

THE OTTOMAN DEFENCE AGAINST THE ANZAC LANDING: 25 April 1915

The situation in the southern sector after Şefik moved two 75mm mountain guns to Anderson Knoll at around 12.00 noon. This contemporary map provides us some very important information. The blue dotted line shows the furthest point reached by the Anzacs according to the Ottoman staff of the *27th*. Interestingly, the site of the initial clashes with Lieutenant Noel M. Loutit's party on the ridgeline is not marked. The southern end of Adana Spur appears to show the furthest position reached by the Anzacs on this map. Similarly, the location of one of the machine-gun platoons is also unmarked and should have been slightly to the north of the northern artillery position. The artillery line of fire (red arrows) and the area that they covered (blue shaded) clearly shows why Şefik decided to move the mountain guns to Anderson Knoll. The crossfire was particularly effective on Lone Pine, the site of the lost Ottoman guns (map courtesy of Serdar Ataksor).

Chapter 3

Captain Kör Halis (Ataksor) was the Commanding Officer of the *3/27th Battalion*. He was a highly talented and brave infantry officer but he was wounded during the first counter-attack and was forcefully evacuated a few hours later. He returned to his unit and took over the command of the regiment from Şefik in August 1915. He survived the war (image courtesy of Serdar Ataksor).

The *1/27th Battalion* launched its attack half an hour after the *57th Regiment* at around 12.30 pm. With the availability of better fire support the attack progressed slowly but eventually succeeded. The 26th Indian Mountain Artillery Battery moved into a fire position just before the Ottomans, but immediately came under withering counter-battery fire which capitalised on the Ottoman gunners' superior positions and better registration. In less than an hour the Indian battery's position had become untenable, particularly with the approach of the advancing Ottoman infantry. At 2.30 pm the Indian battery was withdrawn to the coast having failed to provide any meaningful artillery assistance to the invading force. By this time the landing had developed into an infantry soldier's battle. Officers and NCOs from both sides who dared stand and issue orders to their units were immediately shot. Two companies of the *3/27th Battalion* facing north lost all their officers at around 2.00 pm and the battalion scribe (essentially a member of the administrative branch with quasi-officer status), Mehmed Vehbi, took command until the following morning. Soldiers in small groups — most independent of one another — moved towards the enemy, instinctively using whatever cover they could find in very difficult terrain. Some troops attacked the enemy wherever they came across them, a scenario equally true for Anzac and Ottoman. Others tried to infiltrate behind the enemy and fire on opportunistic targets. Small counter-strokes were frequently launched to eliminate enemy strongpoints. With combat experience from the Balkan Wars, intensive training and better knowledge of the terrain, the *27th Regiment* enjoyed a distinct advantage. Despite their dire equipment shortages, at least one-third of the Ottoman soldiers were carrying hand grenades while the Anzacs lacked anything similar with which to counter their attacks.

THE OTTOMAN DEFENCE AGAINST THE ANZAC LANDING: 25 April 1915

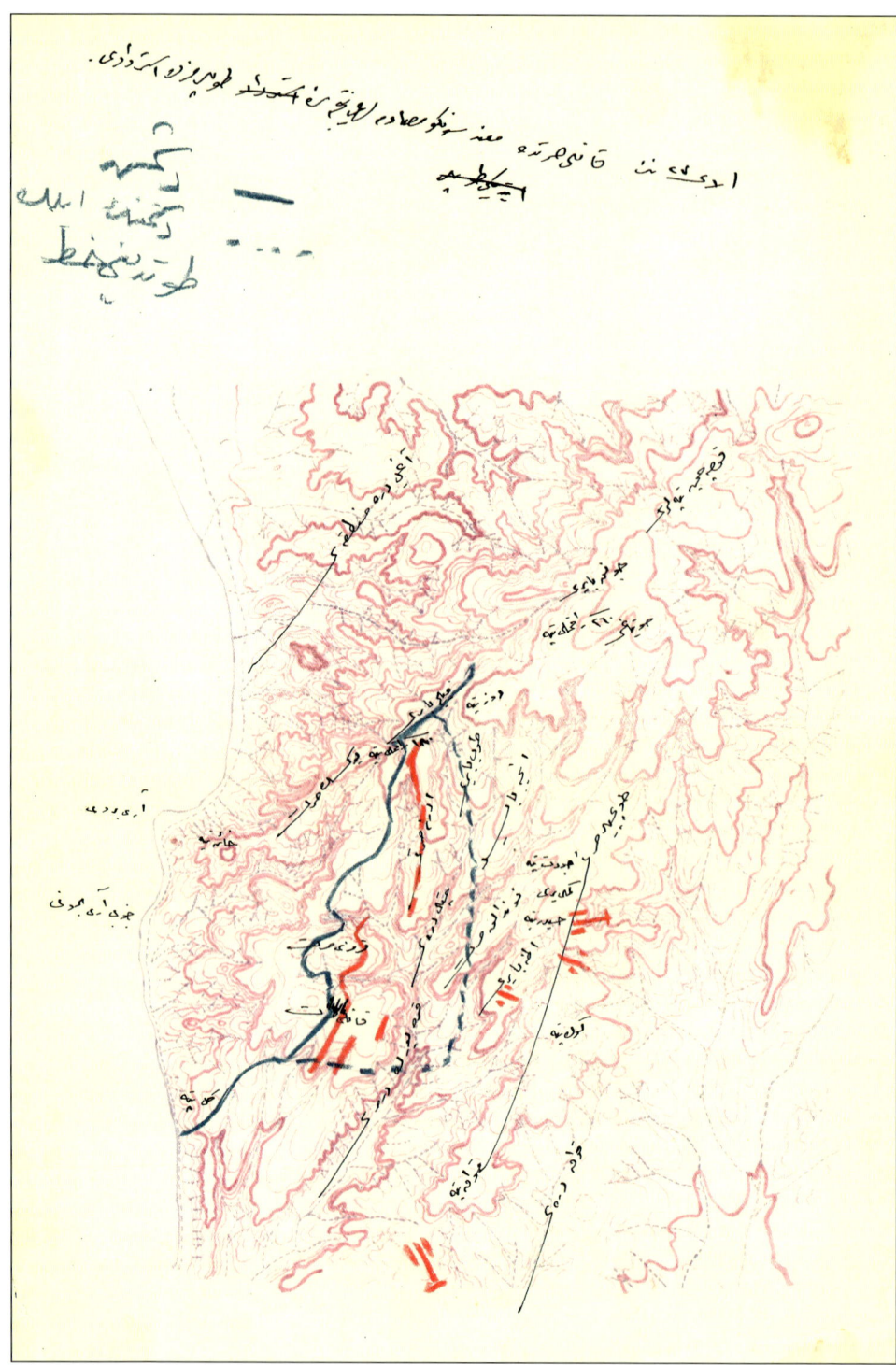

The recapture of the lost guns by the *1/27th Battalion* at around 4.30 pm. The third platoons manning the second line are marked as two short disconnected red lines behind. Deputy Officer Saadet's machine-gun is shown on Adana Spur. (map courtesy of Serdar Ataksor).

Chapter 3

Ottoman infantry in a trench. Note the non-standard ammunition pouches (image courtesy of ATASE).

Şefik skilfully directed the attack from his observation point on Scrubby Knoll. He repositioned the machine-gun platoons as required to provide immediate relief to platoons pinned down by strong enemy positions. He sent the *3rd Company* to reinforce the attack and recapture the lost guns at around 2.00 pm. The arrival of the *3rd Company* changed the balance at the Cup and the lost guns were finally recaptured at around 4.30 pm. The guns were secured and carried back behind the Ottoman lines after sunset. Surprisingly, they were more or less intact and, with some emergency repairs and maintenance during the night, they returned to the battle the next day. The *1st Battalion*'s slow advance came to an abrupt halt once it had reached the western edge of Lone Pine and its southern slopes. The battalion had now outranged both the artillery and machine-guns. Moreover, it had been reduced to approximately half of its established combat strength even with the inclusion of the *11th Company*, such was the ferocity and desperation of the defence. Moreover, half the officers and NCOs had been either killed or wounded during the day-long engagements. Only one original company commander remained at the head of his company. There were also a number of lightly wounded soldiers still manning the lines who needed to be sent back for treatment. The command and control problems encountered in the fog of war during that day would only increase during the night.

THE OTTOMAN DEFENCE AGAINST THE ANZAC LANDING: 25 April 1915

Red Crescent Society postcard emphasising the importance of medical evacuation. The divisional medical companies were in charge of medical evacuation and operated casualty clearance stations with four doctors and 255 stretcher-bearers and medics.

When Mustafa Kemal returned to Chunuk Bair at 3.00 pm, he found a difficult situation. Şefik was still trying to recapture the lost guns while Hüseyin Avni had been unable to move onto the ridge and was instead moving down slopes and through creeks in an attempt to outflank the enemy positions. Mustafa Kemal directed the *2nd Field Artillery Battalion* to occupy fire positions to the north of Scrubby Knoll. He also rushed the *3rd Battalion* of the *72nd Regiment* to reinforce the *57th Regiment* while keeping the remaining two battalions in reserve. The introduction of a fresh battalion and eight 75mm Krupp rapid fire field guns

The Arab soldiers

Prior to the war, some British political and military leaders considered the ethnic and religious diversity of the Ottoman Empire a weakness that could be exploited, prompting British intelligence to focus on this element of the Ottoman military. The disintegration of the Empire under the pressure of war confirmed this view in the eyes of some observers. Some Turkish commentators have also been influenced by what has been termed 'the betrayal of the non-Turkish nations'. British views were dominated by prejudice; they regarded the Arabs as poor soldiers who were unable to withstand harsh combat conditions. The poor performance and disintegration of the *77th Regiment* on 25 April 1915 has been cited as evidence of the poor quality of Arab soldiers. However it is worth examining the view that Arabs were poor and reluctant soldiers, ready to desert or flee at any opportunity, against the evidence of their performance in the Gallipoli campaign.

The recruitment district for the *77th Regiment* was the province of Halep (Aleppo) in what is now Syria. For this reason, it was widely known as an 'Arab' regiment. However the demographics of Aleppo province tell another story. There were many ethnic Turks living around Aleppo, although these were mostly nomads. There were also some religious minorities, such as the Yazidis and Nusayris. Consequently, the regiment did not comprise Sunni Arabs alone, but was an ethnic and cultural mix. Unit commanders specifically complained about the non-military bearing of the Yazidis and Nusayris, minority groups which were previously exempted from military service. These groups simply did not have a martial culture and a military tradition of any description. Enforced conscription was regarded as a breach of a centuries-old custom and was actively resisted. It was therefore unsurprising that conscripts from these groups gave their officers a great deal of trouble.

During the night counter-attack of 25/26 April 1915, the *77th Regiment* became disorganised and fled in disarray. Ottoman military authorities initially blamed these soldiers and some two dozen deserters from the *77th Regiment* were summarily executed as an example to other units. Following a detailed examination, the *19th Division*'s commander, Mustafa Kemal (Atatürk), identified the real culprit as the Commanding Officer of the regiment, Major Saip. According to Mustafa Kemal's report and other contemporary accounts, the men of the *77th* fought well, demonstrating a tenacity that surprised their officers. However they were completely dependent on the leadership of their officers and, when they were killed in battle, the regiment simply disintegrated. In the eyes of Mustafa Kemal and the two battalion commanders of the *77th*, these soldiers bore little responsibility for the rout.

The other so-called 'Arab regiment', the *72nd Regiment*, was not committed to battle on 25 April, but joined the fight two days later. It was not an elite formation and its overall combat performance was mediocre and little different to that of other line regiments. Nevertheless both regiments gained a bad reputation which was reinforced in personal war narratives, Turkish and foreign official histories and modern works. Most Turkish histories were written to reflect the nationalist understanding of the war and, accordingly, the portrait of Arab soldiers in the literature of the Gallipoli Campaign is traditionally that of poor and cowardly fighters. In reality they performed no better or worse than the majority of soldiers in the Ottoman military.

dramatically changed the dynamics of the battle as the attackers were comprehensively out-gunned. Mustafa Kemal ordered another counter-attack at 3.30 pm, assigning the *1st, 2nd* and *3rd battalions* of the *57th Regiment* to the first wave, leaving the *3/72nd Battalion* in firing positions behind. Given the rugged nature of the terrain, the Ottoman infantry was forced to launch a frontal attack in heavily packed waves in a manner that has now come to represent the waste of life that characterised the campaign. The first waves literally ran towards certain death while successive waves overran the Anzac defences and finally captured Baby 700. The small groups of soldiers which had infiltrated from both flanks played an important role, moving forward with the frontal attacks. The remnants of the defending forces had no choice but to withdraw or be overrun and killed.

Following the capture of Baby 700, The Nek was the next objective. The Ottoman soldiers who passed the crest of Baby 700 came under intense fire from New Zealand machine-guns (from the Auckland Battalion) and rifle fire from a composite company nearby. But Mustafa Kemal had noted the existence of a choke point. He prepared the *3/72nd Battalion* to reinforce the counter-attack, although it was forced to traverse a broad open space under enemy fire before reaching the attack line. Mustafa Kemal planned to launch a coordinated night attack and needed fresh units to do this. Instead of using the *3/72nd Battalion*, he moved the fourth companies of the *57th Regiment* to the flanks while ordering the artillery to concentrate its fire on The Nek and Mortar Ridge. However the recently activated fourth companies were not ready to perform this hazardous task. The raw conscripts lacked not only the training and experience but also the endurance and stamina of their fellow soldiers in the first three companies. They wilted under the intense fire and took cover. Officers and NCOs managed to move some of them forward, but not all. Hüseyin Avni had no choice but to push his forward units further. The Ottoman soldiers slowly but surely prevailed against the defence which had been weakened by the heavy bombardment. The soldiers of the 1st Australian Battalion under Captain Harold Jacobs abandoned their positions on Mortar Ridge and took refuge in Monash Valley while the last defenders at The Nek withdrew behind the New Zealand machine-guns. At this point the *57th Regiment*'s counter-attack petered out and the Ottoman artillery and machine-guns were unable to fire accurately on the enemy positions. There was no option but to draw breath and wait for night to fall.

Mustafa Kemal halted his major assaults at 6.00 pm, having realising that further progress in both northern and southern sectors during the late afternoon was unlikely. He now paused for the night and to plan his next move. The *77th Regiment* was considered to have failed to pit its full combat weight against the enemy in the southern sector during the afternoon's counter-attack, so Mustafa Kemal issued orders to the *27th* and *77th regiments* to launch a coordinated night counter-attack just prior to 1.00 am to make full use of the bright moonlight. If the southern night attack achieved its aim to drive the enemy off Second Ridge, he hoped to use the entire *72nd Regiment* from the northern sector to press the advantage and squeeze the Anzac forces back to the narrow strip of beach along which they had landed. By contrast he gave a far more limited role to the *57th Regiment*. Hüseyin Avni was tasked to pin down the enemy and, if possible, find weak spots for a breakthrough.

Chapter 3

SAIP AND THE DISINTEGRATION OF THE *77TH REGIMENT*

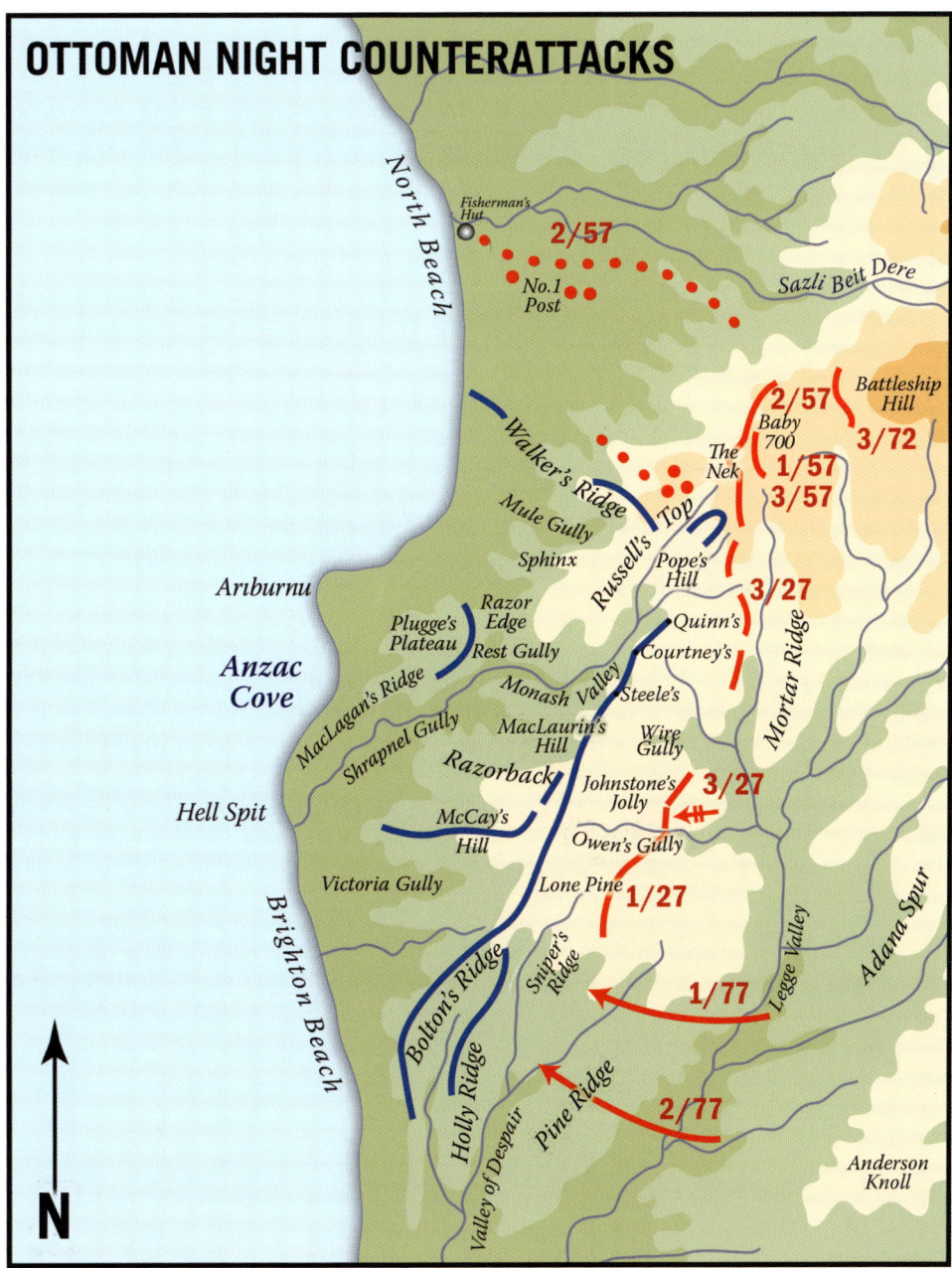

In the meantime Şefik remained optimistic about his chances of pushing the enemy back into the sea despite the problems confronting his battalions. He was also aware of more recent landings later that afternoon. All he needed was a fresh regiment as reinforcement. With high hopes and a considerable degree of expectation he met the *77th Regiment*'s commander, Major Saip, who had come to coordinate his regiment's counter-attack at around 5.00 pm. He reported that his two battalions were already in Legge Valley and he was planning to advance and establish contact with the enemy. Clearly the counter-attack could only be launched in the early hours of the night. Although the chances of a successful attack appeared greater now with the coordination of the *27th* and *77th regiments*, the tactical situation facing the *77th Regiment's* battalions was very difficult and their morale was low. The *1st Battalion*, under the command of Major Hacı Mehmed Emin, was in the northern sector of the regiment's position while the *2nd Battalion*, under the command of Major Rıfat, was in the south. Both the battalions were exhausted and the officers were having difficulty maintaining command and control in the largely unfamiliar terrain. Saip, who was already very confused, did not issue clear orders other than pointing his battalion commanders in the general direction of the attack. As subsequently became clear, there was a crisis of trust within the regiment and the battalion commanders and other regimental officers harboured serious concerns over Saip's capacity to command and lead them in battle.

Hacı Emin tried in vain to establish contact and coordination with the neighbouring units of the *27th Regiment*. He pushed forward blindly, passing south of Lone Pine under sporadic enemy fire. His soldiers were buoyed by the sight of large numbers of enemy dead strewn across the battlefield, but not Hacı Emin himself who anxiously questioned the soldiers of the *27th Regiment* he encountered to glean whatever information he could on the enemy's intentions and positions. His apprehension deepened when he realised that he had lost contact with the *2/77th Battalion* on his left during the advance. His advance platoons finally established contact with the enemy at the western extremity of Lone Pine at around 7.00 pm. He decided to launch a probing attack without waiting. It was a disorganised and isolated attack but the battalion managed to clear the enemy forward posts.

While Hacı Emin was establishing both a solid defensive line and continuing to launch probing attacks thereby building the confidence and morale of his men, the *2/77th Battalion* was in a far better position on Pine Ridge and its southern extension. After suffering disorientation, disorder and confusion during the initial phase of the advance, Major Rıfat met İsmail Hakkı's *3/7th Platoon* on the way and İsmail Hakkı guided him forward. Such had been the success of the main afternoon counter-attack and the disorganisation of the Anzac forces, that there were only small platoon-sized enemy outposts (most of these from scattered Australian units of the 6th Battalion) in front of him, all of which he deduced were comparatively weak. Rıfat's companies moved further south to make use of the cover provided by the creeks and small ridges that extended like fingers from Pine Ridge. They then wheeled north and began to eliminate enemy positions. It was a slow and bloody process but by midnight the *2/77th Battalion* had destroyed or scattered all the enemy units on Pine and Sniper's ridges. Rıfat decided to wheel his forces to the north leaving a covering force facing the outpost on Bolton Ridge. At that point he received an order from Saip to attack enemy forces wherever he found them.

Saip realised that he had lost the confidence of Mustafa Kemal and his subordinates. He was under immense pressure to attack the main body of Anzac troops to the south of the *27th Regiment* but he had serious concerns over the ability of his regiment to carry out

In a staged photo, an infantry platoon prepares for an assault. The Ottoman officers gained valuable lessons from disastrous frontal attacks and developed new tactics and techniques that were to prove far less costly (image courtesy of ATASE).

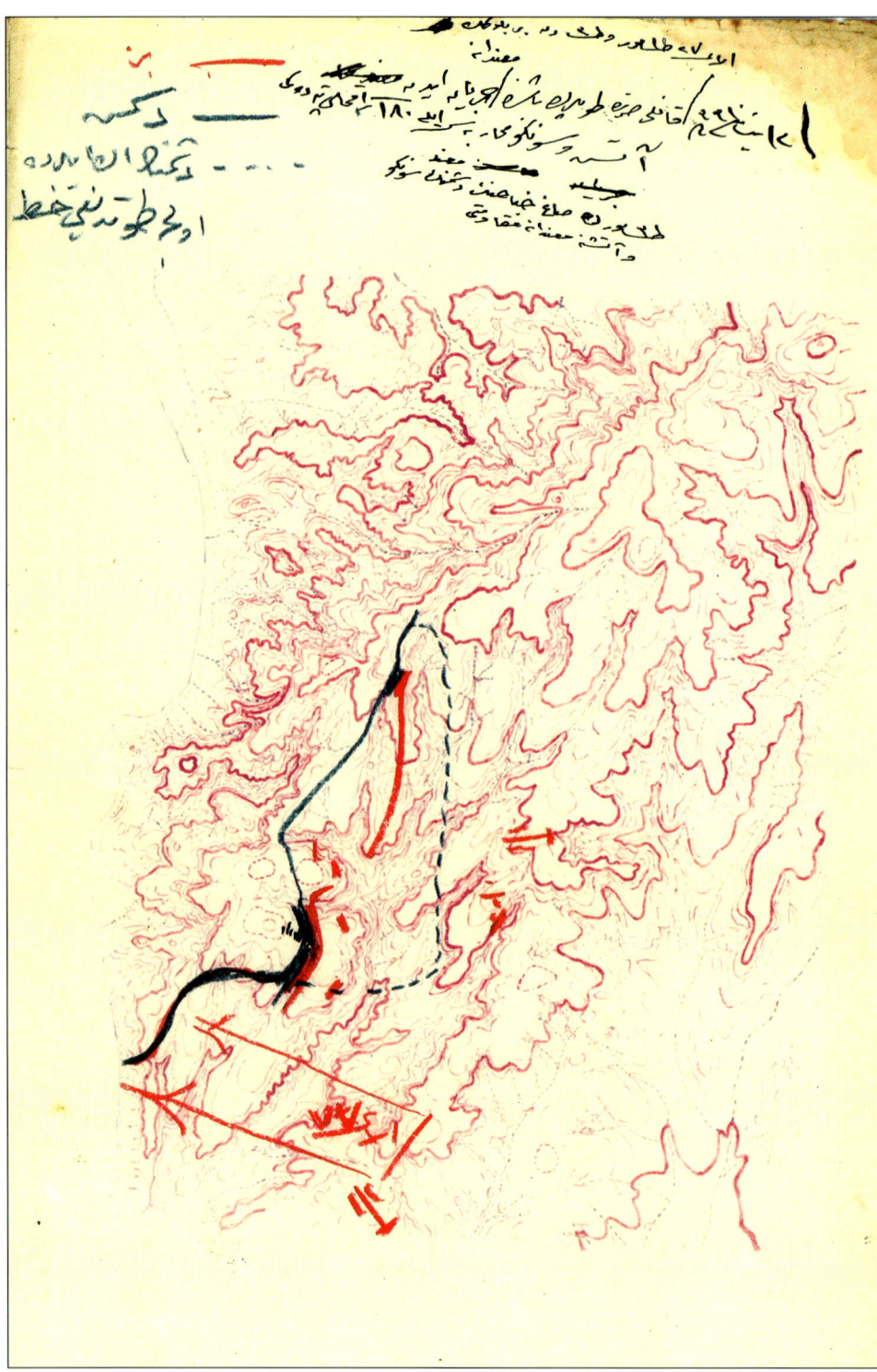

The night counter-attack of the *77th Regiment*. The *1/77th Battalion* actually advanced further north than shown. The *2/77th Battalion* wheeled north after overrunning the Anzacs on Pine Ridge. (map courtesy of Serdar Ataksor).

the order. In contrast to the *27th* and *57th regiments*, his soldiers were not only ill-trained conscripts without combat experience but were also unaccustomed to the Gallipoli terrain. He needed to act and to do so quickly, but wasted valuable time in indecision, watching the advance of his regiment from a distance. In the middle of the night amid frequent orders and requests from Mustafa Kemal and Şefik, Saip called his battalion commanders together. He only managed to find Hacı Emin who complained about various problems and pointed out serious difficulties, most of which became evident in the following attacks. Saip ordered him to immediately attack with the *2nd Battalion*. The runners managed to transmit this order to Rıfat, although it came very late.

Hacı Emin reluctantly launched a small company-sized attack which did not escape Saip's notice. He was called back and reprimanded severely. At around 1.30 am the *1st Battalion* attacked without the support of the *2nd Battalion* — a recipe for disaster. The companies became hopelessly intermingled while charging forward and a sizable percentage of officers and NCOs were shot, while leaderless soldiers scattered across the battlefield. Hacı Emin returned to Saip's command post and tried to persuade him to call off the attack. At 3.00 am, after much hesitation, Saip ordered the withdrawal of the *77th Regiment* to its starting position. Officers rushed back to their companies and halted the attack. The *2nd Company* commander, 1st Lieutenant Vasıf, refused to retreat and moved his soldiers into defensive positions close to the *27th Regiment* under the pretext that any withdrawal would be disastrous.

The *1/27th Battalion* commander, Major İbrahim, was horrified to see the withdrawal of the *77th Regiment* from his southern flank and rushed to find out who had given this order. İbrahim found Saip and explained to him that the withdrawal of the *77th Regiment* had placed the *1/27th Battalion* in a very dangerous situation. He argued that the enemy was sure to use the opportunity to flank his position from the soon-to-be-vacant south. Saip ignored İbrahim's pleas, asserting his seniority of rank and insisting that his orders be followed. After reprimanding İbrahim, Saip ordered him to retreat alongside the *77th Regiment*. İbrahim reluctantly obeyed the order.

At this critical stage, while the *1/77th* and *1/27th battalions* were attempting to break contact and regroup their soldiers for a withdrawal, they heard reports of the *2/77th Battalion*'s counter-attack. Rıfat's battalion simply disintegrated under enfilading fire from the flanks and his soldiers began to flee. Confusion turned to chaos. Soldiers from the *1/77th Battalion* joined their comrades and either ran back or sought cover. İbrahim skilfully controlled his battalion, preventing the spread of confusion and conducting an orderly withdrawal. In similar fashion, İsmail Hakkı controlled his platoon (*3/7th Platoon*) and joined the *27th Regiment* later on. The *77th Regiment* all but ceased to exist as a combat unit with the exception of the *2nd Company* of the *1st Battalion* which chose to remain with the *1/27th*.

The *57th Regiment*'s night counter-attack also encountered serious difficulties from the outset. Captain Ata's *2nd Battalion*, which had borne the brunt of the fighting and taken the most casualties during the day, was in a terrible state and suffering a crisis of morale after losing most of its officers and NCOs. It was unfit for any further offensive operations.

Nevertheless Hüseyin Avni considered that it might prove able to follow the example of the other battalions which were still in relatively good spirits. The advance began at around 11.30 pm with the *2nd Battalion* on the northern flank, the *1st Battalion* on the southern flank and the *3rd* in the centre. The soldiers came under heavy fire immediately after passing the western slopes of Baby 700. The *2nd Battalion* was seriously shaken and broke down under fire. Hüseyin Avni and Ata somehow kept the soldiers under control but it became obvious that a frontal attack was no longer possible. Instead the *1st* and *2nd battalion* commanders began launching minor counter-strokes and sent small parties to infiltrate the enemy lines. While most attempts failed, two small parties discovered a gap between the Australians (a mixed battalion under the command of Lieutenant Colonel G.F. Braund) and New Zealanders (a mixed company-size unit under the command of Captain A.C.B. Critchley-Salmonson) and managed to penetrate as far as Russell's Top. However they lost contact with the rear and hurriedly retreated before the sun rose.

2nd Lieutenant Ata posing in front of a military hospital in İstanbul. Ata was a platoon leader in the *2nd Company, 1/27th Regiment*. He fought at Lone Pine throughout the day and later was evacuated after being seriously wounded. He returned to his regiment a few months later and survived the war (image courtesy of Hakan Akın).

Şefik waited in vain to launch a coordinated counter-attack with the *77th Regiment* on the front line during the night. He heard occasional firefights and a great deal of movement but his efforts to establish contact failed. At last he moved south to try to ascertain the situation. He was horrified to find that the *77th Regiment* had disintegrated in and around Legge Valley where soldiers in small groups had taken refuge. The regiment's heavy equipment and weapons were scattered all around. There was nothing Şefik could do before sunrise except ensure that his own sector maintained discipline and held its ground. He was particularly disturbed by İbrahim's withdrawal which not only wasted the previous afternoon's counter-attacks but also gave the enemy an excellent opportunity to retain Lone Pine. Şefik had to recall the isolated *11th Company*'s platoons from its advance post on Johnston's Jolly to bolster his position, although he left Saadet's machine-guns and a platoon-sized security force in place. Şefik returned to his command post and reported the disintegration of the *77th Regiment* to the divisional command centre. He ensured that arrangements had been made to protect his left flank for possible enemy flanking attacks.

Mustafa Kemal already entertained serious doubts over the ability of Saip and his regiment, and learnt of the catastrophe very late, in an early morning report from Şefik. He immediately went to the south of Kavak Deresi to investigate the situation. It was a sorry sight. Officers and NCOs were desperately trying to collect soldiers and form them into makeshift units. Mustafa Kemal met the *1st Battalion* commander, Major Hacı Emin, whom he had known from the Libyan War of 1911. Hacı Emin briefed him in detail on the entire debacle and accused his regimental commander, Saip, of incapacity and mismanagement. Mustafa Kemal reluctantly cancelled his plans for a major counter-attack from the north on 26 April despite the fact that forward elements of the *57th Regiment* had reported small gains around Hill 180 and The Nek during the night. The next day would bring a fresh plan.

EPILOGUE
THE DAY AFTER

In his notes, Mustafa Kemal labelled 26 April 1915 the most critical day of the landing. The Ottoman resistance to the amphibious assault at Anzac Cove in the first 24 hours after the landing took a massive toll on the defenders. All three regiments (*27th*, *57th* and *77th*) were exhausted and had lost just over half of their combat-effective soldiers. Most damagingly, the toll of officers and NCO casualties was much higher — almost three-quarters had been killed or wounded. Mustafa Kemal knew that the Anzacs were equally exhausted, but that they had a greater likelihood of receiving reinforcements via the Royal Navy, sitting offshore in the Aegean. Apart from von Sanders, who was still waiting for the main enemy landings at Bolayır and Saros, there was a general anticipation of a renewal of enemy attacks at all levels. For the Ottomans the situation looked bleak.

Mustafa Kemal provided an updated situation report to Esad Pasha and asked for immediate reinforcements to continue his harassing attacks throughout the day so as to maintain pressure on the Australians and New Zealanders and prevent them consolidating. Esad Pasha gave him the dismal news that there were no reinforcements other than the *3/7th Mountain Artillery Battalion*. However he promised to send at least two infantry battalions on the evening of 26 April and cautioned him not to launch any major attacks until their arrival.

Throughout the day, the *19th Division*'s line units hurriedly dug new trenches and firing positions while combat service support units attempted to establish logistic and communication lines. Some units that had become bunched up or exposed at first light were moved to more secure locations including the elements of the *11th Company* of the *27th Regiment* in Johnston's Jolly. The machine-gun platoon and infantry platoon providing security came under intense and accurate enemy fire with the arrival of daylight. Machine-gun platoon leader Deputy Officer Saadet was seriously wounded and the position became increasingly untenable. Şefik reluctantly pulled them back. He also reduced the numbers of soldiers on the eastern edges of Johnston's Jolly and Lone Pine and established a second stronger defensive line (overlooking Second Ridge) on the western slopes of Third Ridge.

Simultaneously with Şefik, Hüseyin Avni also established two defensive lines and pulled back all the elements that were caught in exposed or precarious positions. The small groups that had infiltrated the enemy defensive area returned with information on enemy disorganisation and weakness in a number of locations. However Hüseyin Avni had no intention to launch even small attacks in broad daylight. Unlike the previous day, the Royal Navy was now more active. Battleships and destroyers opened fire on any visible target following a short reaction time. The artillery represented its prime target. Şefik described one example of the vigilance of enemy naval guns in his memoir. A 75mm field artillery battery from the *39th Artillery Regiment* had replaced the mixed mountain battery to the north of Scrubby Knoll during the night. The battery commander, Captain Ahmed, decided to register his guns by fire, against the advice of Şefik, early in the morning. HMS *Majestic* easily pinpointed the exact location of the battery, noting the muzzle fire which was clearly visible in the dim light of the morning. Its third shell stuck the middle of the battery destroying one gun and killing half a dozen gunners. Şefik himself barely escaped. He immediately recalled his mountain battery and sent the field guns further north.

A staged photo of a four-gun 87mm Krupp field battery in a firing position. Note the officers on the left side observing the target with binoculars. In contrast to popular belief, light and medium field artillery guns were generally used as direct fire weapons (image courtesy of Nejat Çuhadaroğlu).

The Ottoman reorganisation and regrouping was conducted under the constant threat of imminent enemy attack. Several small-scale probing attacks were launched by both sides during the morning but all failed to achieve any meaningful results. Mustafa Kemal and Şefik were certain that the enemy would try to make use of the apparent weakness of the defence and would probably launch an attack in the afternoon. The 4th Australian Battalion's mistaken advance into Lone Pine from the south at 4.30 pm was regarded as fulfilling this expectation. The Ottoman covering force, artillery and machine-guns opened well-organised and concentrated fire on the hapless soldiers of the 4th Battalion. While many were shot to pieces, some managed to reach Owen's Gully. Şefik read this advance as a probing attack prior to a main assault and requested two companies from the *72nd Regiment* to reinforce his second line. He then spent several tense hours waiting for the Anzac assault. Against all predictions, however, the only activity for the rest of the day comprised a series of isolated individual movements.

THE OTTOMAN DEFENCE AGAINST THE ANZAC LANDING: 25 April 1915

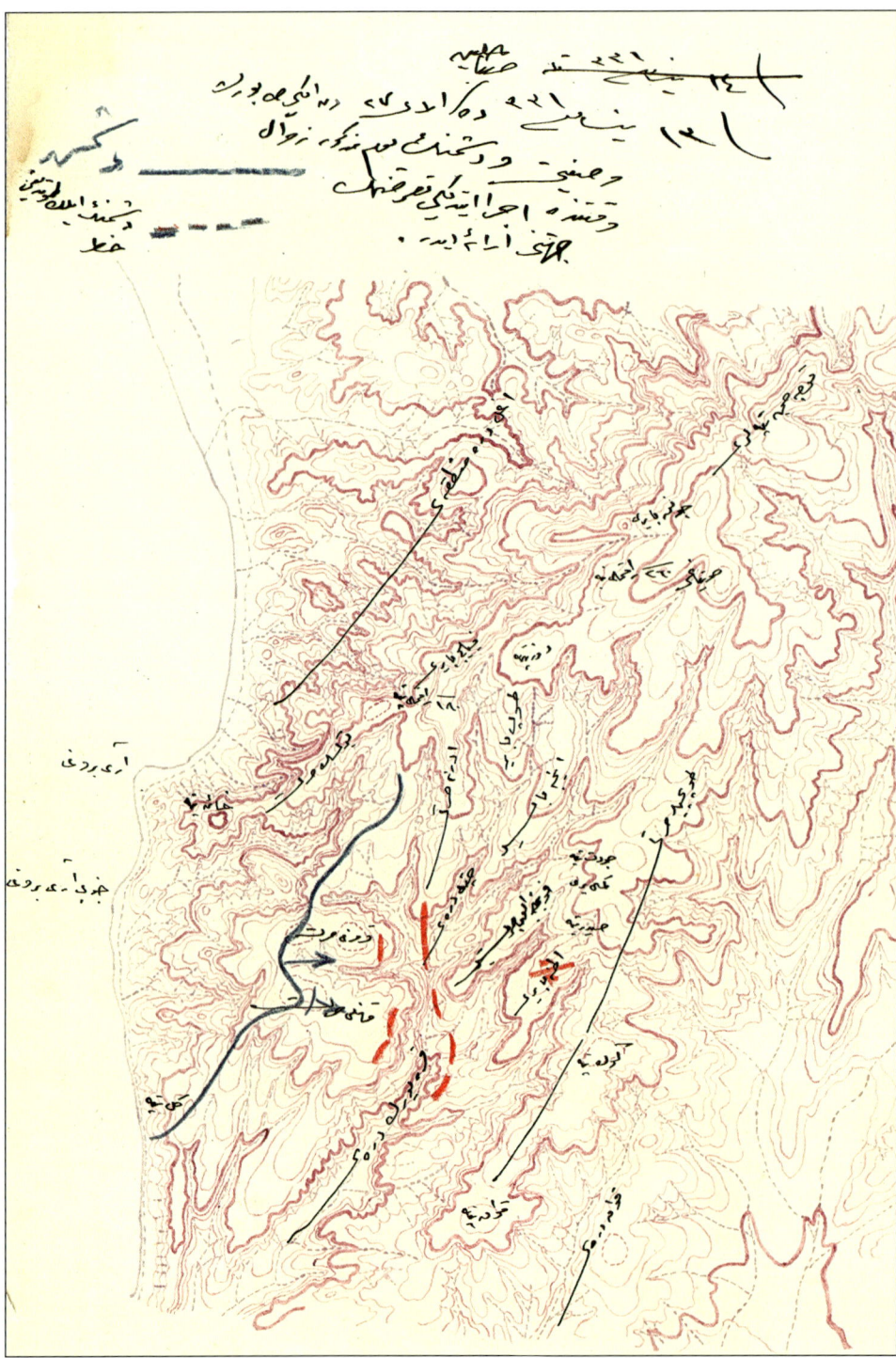

The situation during the 4th Australian Battalion's mistaken advance at around 4.30 pm. Şefik and his officers read the south-north advance as a counter stroke to the covering force. This is an important map which shows the early names of the previously unidentified terrain features (map courtesy of Serdar Ataksor).

An infantry company rests in reserve positions behind the front line. Tented camps were simply too visible to Allied aerial or naval bombings so their use was discouraged after 25 April 1915 (image courtesy of ATASE).

Mustafa Kemal devoted most of the day to reorganising the *77th Regiment*. At 6.00 am he ordered the *72nd Regiment* to move south and reoccupy the positions in Legge Valley that had been evacuated by the *77th Regiment*. The regimental commander, Major Mehmed Münir, had just two battalions (the *3rd Battalion* had been under the tactical command of the *57th Regiment* since the previous afternoon) and also had to leave a company to provide security for Kocadere village and all the artillery, medical and logistics units positioned there. Münir and his seven companies initially moved behind the *27th Regiment*. After completing the necessary coordination and reconnaissance, the regiment began moving to its designated position further south at 8.30 am. Münir kept his main force on the western slopes of Third Ridge and sent a covering force to Legge Valley. He sent two of his companies to stiffen the *27th Regiment*'s defence at 4.40 pm. Consequently, only a reinforced battalion remained to defend the southern flank until the next day.

In the meantime Mustafa Kemal established a security line behind the *77th* using the corps and divisional cavalry to catch any deserters and confused soldiers. Later in the day regimental officers and divisional staff gathered all the remnants of the *77th Regiment*. A composite battalion (400 strong) was created from those soldiers who still possessed a degree of discipline and motivation. This battalion joined the battle two days later under the command of Major Rıfat. Around two dozen soldiers who had constantly resisted attempts to enforce discipline were quickly court-martialled and summarily executed in groups in front of their regiment and other units to set an example. Others were sent back for retraining and reorganisation.

A Red Crescent Society postcard commemorating the land defence of Gallipoli. The successful defence against the initial landings caused much joy and celebration all across the country. The Red Crescent Society and others produced various memorabilia items as a means to attract donations.

GENERAL EVALUATION OF THE OTTOMAN DEFENCE

The Ottoman defence against the Anzac landing was marked by tensions between field army and other command levels, and the command void resulting from these tensions. Liman von Sanders radically overhauled the peninsula's defensive concept and plans, creating widespread opposition and hostility. Of the several serious mistakes von Sanders made in response to the Allied invasion, none was greater than his refusal to abandon his conviction that the invasion would take place at Bolayır and Saros against the reality of the 25 April landings. He not only refused to release reserves and heavy weapons, but also failed to provide any concrete orders. The immense pressure of the developing situation simply exacerbated the command void at the top. Consequently, commanders at field army and corps levels were unable to influence the situation until too late.

Esad Pasha failed to step in and fill the void caused by von Sanders' prevarication and wasted half a day attempting to convince von Sanders of the necessity for action. When the senior Ottoman officer finally arrived at the battle site, it was simply too late to push the Australians and New Zealanders back into the Aegean. In contrast to his obedient and compliant attitude to von Sanders, Esad Pasha was an ardent believer in mission command. He did not expect the same total obedience he showed to von Sanders and instead allowed his divisional commanders to prosecute operations as they saw fit. Esad Pasha attempted to perform efficiently under extremely difficult circumstances, monitoring developments and providing much-needed logistic and administrative support, despite his initial slowness to react. At this stage of the war there was no understanding or doctrine on dividing the responsibilities of the direction of combat into main, tactical and rear headquarters. Esad Pasha became the first Ottoman general to appreciate the importance of separating his staffs into a main and rear headquarters and officially recognising Mustafa Kemal and Halil Sami as the commanders in charge of tactical headquarters on 25 April. Esad Pasha effectively relieved them of logistical responsibilities (of planning for incoming units, the supply of

A memento of victory: high-ranking officers and their staff pose in İstanbul at the end of the Gallipoli Campaign. Left to right front row: Colonel Ahmed Cevad (İstanbul Military Police Chief), Dr Süleyman Numan Pasha (Inspector-General of Medical Corps), Esad Pasha (former commander of *III Corps*), Liman von Sanders (commander of the *Fifth Army*), Vehib Pasha (commander of the *Second Army*), Rauf (Chief of Staff of the Navy). Rear row: Refik Münir, Dr İbrahim Tali, Şükrü, Kazım (Chief of Staff of the *Fifth Army*), Erich R. Prigge (aide-de-camp to von Sanders), Asım, İsmet (Chief of Staff of the *Second Army*) and Abdi (image courtesy of ATASE).

ammunition and food, of furnishing detailed reports and returns and all other crucial but time-consuming administrative staff work), allowing them to focus on immediate operational issues and problems. This flexible attitude, based on trust, was vital for the execution of the successful counter-attacks that stopped the Anzac forces from breaking out of the larger Anzac Cove area, and the eventual success of the campaign.

A logistic train carrying tents, timber and other heavy equipment for establishing a camp in the field. Oxen, water buffalos, camels and mules carried the burden of supplies for the Ottoman expeditionary forces in mostly untracked countryside. Note the age of the officer. Retirees or officers deemed unfit for combat duties usually manned the logistic trains and completed a variety of rear area duties (image courtesy of Nejat Çuhadaroğlu).

High-ranking officers from the *27th Regiment* pose behind the front line at Lone Pine in the summer of 1915. Left to right front row: Major Halis (Ataksor), Lieutenant Colonel Şefik (Aker), Major Cemil. Rear row: Captain Mustafa, Lieutenant Cevdet, Captain Faik, Lieutenant Hamdi (image courtesy of Serdar Ataksor).

The record at divisional and regimental level was better but by no means problem free. Halil Sami reacted to events and sent erratic reports demonstrating that he struggled with the responsibility of commanding a front-line unit under pressure while Mustafa Kemal and Şefik were the outstanding front-line commanders of the day. Instead of seeking to receive clear orders or trying to assess the situation from scraps of delayed and often misleading information which trickled back to the command centres, they rushed forward to the areas of greatest danger. They not only used their initiative well beyond the level of their command, but also acted decisively when confronted with new developments. Both commanders demonstrated outstanding combat leadership by displaying personal courage under fire and inspiring their soldiers to greater deeds as most of them knowingly headed towards certain death in advancing to face the invasion force.

Guards of an Ottoman regimental colour (either the *47th* or *48th Regiment*) proudly posing in Lone Pine after the Anzac evacuation (image courtesy of ATASE).

After the successful landing of the first two waves of enemy it became a race to reach and hold the dominant Third Ridge. The Anzac forward elements reached the ridge first but were unable to retain it due to their numerical weakness and isolation from the main body. With the arrival of Şefik's troops the focus changed to which side could deploy the most troops to the position in the shortest time. Mustafa Kemal reached the ridge in time and the Ottomans won the second stage of the race. However a mistaken message caused much disruption and prevented reserves from being despatched. Mustafa Kemal lost valuable hours by moving back and forth while the *72nd* and *77th regiments* arrived too late to take part in the midday counter-attacks.

Professionalism and improvisation carried the day. The ever-resourceful Şefik kept the Anzacs at bay in the southern sector while Hüseyin Avni not only checked the Anzac forward position at Baby 700 but also flanked the northern Anzac positions from further north. When Mustafa Kemal returned to the front line, he decided to husband the *72nd Regiment* as a fresh unit for exploiting any breakthrough and for continuing counter-attacks on 26 April. However the optimistic Mustafa Kemal made two big mistakes in that first hectic 24 hours: he underestimated the problems that bedevilled the *77th Regiment* and he ordered a disorganised and piecemeal night attack. Although some elements of the *57th Regiment* managed to infiltrate Russell's Top and Pine Ridge was cleared of enemy, the night attack was a failure and the *77th Regiment* disintegrated as a result — a loss that was unnecessary and ultimately placed further stress on Mustafa Kemal and the surviving force elements. To his credit, Şefik realised the futility of counter-attacks against dug-in infantry before anyone else. He understood that, without effective and accurate fire support, coordination, sound planning, preparation and good use of terrain, there was literally no chance of success. As it transpired, it proved impossible to move reserves up in time to exploit the opportunities offered by a counter-attack as the terrain was simply too difficult to traverse quickly. Unfortunately his acquired wisdom was not shared with or developed by others. The erroneous belief that, with determination and the use of cold steel, the enemy could be repulsed from its tiny beachhead was the root cause of the futile and costly mass attacks between 27 April and 19 May in which so many Ottoman soldiers lost their lives for limited gains.

Officers from the *27th Regiment* pose for a group photo on 30 June 1915. Halis (Ataksor) is near the centre of the group wearing a fez (image courtesy of Serdar Ataksor).

Epilogue

The Ottoman junior officers were determined to cleanse the stain of the Balkan defeats from their reputations. They were ready to die rather than face humiliation once again. Furthermore the Ottoman Army had been an officers' army and the current experience of war reinforced this. Soldiers needed their officers to perform well. Yet the prevalent command style and attitude in the army and the nature of the war continuously exposed junior officers to enemy fire. Leading from the front was a leadership ideal that was deeply ingrained in the Ottoman officer corps. The senior military leadership reinforced this ideal with a strict awards system in which mere bravery, however exceptional, was not sufficient to a gain a decoration. Thus officers suffered extraordinarily heavy casualties. In an army in which paternalistic leadership and man-management had been well institutionalised, the loss of company grade officers was a heavy loss indeed.

Two recently commissioned lieutenants (both of them Gallipoli veterans) pose for studio photograph. Notice the presence of bayonets and port epée which, according to regulations, should have been carried by NCOs and officer candidates. As officers these lieutenants should have carried short swords instead of bayonets.

The *27th* and *57th regiments* (except the fourth companies of the *57th*), which were manned by trained and experienced soldiers, performed astonishingly well on the battlefield. Their achievements were clear testimony to the success of the military reforms initiated in the aftermath of the Balkan Wars. Despite the fact that the Ottoman Army was traditionally an 'officers' army' the soldiers of these regiments preserved their élan and continued to fight after losing most of their officers. NCOs or even experienced soldiers simply took command. This was not the case in the *77th Regiment*. Soldiers of this regiment followed their junior officers on most occasions but the death of their officers led to disarray, loss of discipline and disintegration. The so-called 'Arab Regiment' was not alone in making mistakes. Muharrem's failure to occupy the main trenches in Arıburnu Knoll essentially gave free rein to the first wave of the landing and ensured that a foothold was established soon after the first Australian troops came ashore. The recently activated fourth companies of the *57th Regiment* broke under fire and had to be stiffened by other units. Similarly, the *2/57th Battalion*, which had suffered heavy casualties and was pushed too hard at Baby 700 during the evening counter-attacks, simply panicked during the night attack.

A German postcard depicting the Ottoman defence against the landings. The landings on 25 April captured the imagination of many artists, journalists and literary figures. Unfortunately their products bore little resemblance to the reality on the ground. In this example everything seems to be wrong from the date to the uniforms, from the terrain to the tactics (image courtesy of Nejat Çuhadaroğlu).

The Ottoman reaction to the initial landings and the subsequent rapid local mobilisation to counter-attack proved decisively that this war was a young man's war. Esad Pasha was the best example of his generation, but he was dismayed by the horrific casualties wrought by this modern industrialised warfare. His beloved corps was literally smashed to pieces under enemy fire and he felt helpless in the face of such carnage. He simply could not find the will to obey orders that created more casualties for little to no gain. By virtue of his background and his previous military experience, he found himself fundamentally out of touch with the times, living in the wrong era and fighting a war unlike any he had known. In these respects, Esad Pasha faced the same realisation as British veterans of the Boer War when first confronted with the scale of casualties on the Western Front. In direct contrast to Esad Pasha, Mustafa Kemal was almost emotionally immune to the loss of life for this great national cause. He had few illusions regarding the costliness of attack and understood and accepted the need for bloodshed to eject the enemy from the peninsula.

Overall, *III Corps* functioned better than the Allied units thanks to its innovative triangular corps system and bitter experiences of the Balkan Wars. Esad Pasha trained and prepared his corps better than any other. Although he did not deal with the command crisis adequately after the first landings, his subordinate commanders were able to step in and act decisively. The mission command system that had operated poorly during the Balkan Wars worked comparatively well on 25 April. On that day, with those troops and under those conditions, the Ottoman Army's combat effectiveness was superior to that of the British Army, its dominions and its allies.

CONCLUSION

The logic behind the landing was very similar to that of the naval attack that presaged it. The British leadership believed that the Ottomans would 'melt away' when they saw the British flag and the might of its armies and the Royal Navy on the beaches. As far as the Allied leadership was concerned, the Ottoman Army was poorly equipped, badly led, inefficient and demoralised by a succession of defeats. Under this illusion, therefore, it was envisaged that the biggest problem would be one of logistics — moving and landing troops — as, once the landings were effected, resistance would be slight and the advance rapid. As Ian Hamilton later confessed to the Dardanelles Commission, 'I did not know, to tell you the truth that they were nearly as good as they turned out to be.'

The Balkan Wars and the ensuing military intellectual discussions and reforms taught the Ottoman Army many lessons — albeit painful ones — and transformed it from a garrison army of ill-trained and ill-led conscripts into an army of highly motivated experienced veterans. Even the so-called 'Arab regiments' ultimately fought well, suffering horrendous casualties. Moreover, given its history of previous wars, naval and land attacks in the years prior to the First World War, the Dardanelles region was much better prepared. The defence of the peninsula may have been even stronger had von Sanders' defensive concept and plans been abandoned and the Ottoman plans remained in place. Yet von Sanders cannot be blamed for all that went wrong. The Ottomans made their own errors independent of the effect of the German commander's inactivity on the critical first day. Both commanders and troops made mistakes or simply failed.

Esad Pasha poses in a communication trench near Anafarta during his visit to Gallipoli after the Allied evacuation. From left to right: Esad (Bülkat) Pasha, Rüşdü (Sakarya) Pasha, Mehmed Nazım, Ali Rıza (Sedes) Pasha and Fahreddin (Altay) (image courtesy of Nejat Çuhadaroğlu).

Group photo of the *III Corps* key commanding and staff officers in front of a decorative panel of captured enemy weapons at the corps tactical command centre near Scrubby Knoll. From left to right front row (siting): unidentified, Haydar (Alganer), Mehmed Nazım (Chief of Staff, *16th Division*), Hulusi. Second row: Rüştü ([Sakarya], commander of the *16th Division*), Mustafa Kemal (Atatürk), Esad (Bülkat) Pasha. Third row: Wilhelm Willmer (commander of Anafartalar region), unidentified German officer, Hans Kannengiesser (commander of *XV Corps*). Fourth row: Ohrili Kemal (Chief of Operations, *III Corps*), unidentified, Fahreddin (Altay, Chief of Staff, *III Corps*), İzzeddin (Çalışlar), unidentified (image courtesy of ATASE).

THE OTTOMAN DEFENCE AGAINST THE ANZAC LANDING: 25 April 1915

The Ottoman defence against the Anzac landing provides not only a valuable insight into the Ottoman Army's ability to wage war with a contemporary Western force, but also many lessons in terms of countering an amphibious invasion. Regrettably, however, these lessons have been neglected or ignored. The comparative lack of attention paid to the Ottoman defence as a military lesson has much to do with viewing Ottoman military history *sui generis* rather than as an element of global military history that can provide genuine military lessons. To contemporary Western observers the Ottoman Army was not a regular army but a horde. They did not expect it to possess comparative attributes or exhibit similar issues and problems to those faced by Western armies. Modern scholars similarly do not examine the Ottoman military as they examine Western militaries. They do not ask the same questions and certainly do not apply the same analytical approaches. Instead, the focus is on trying to identify anomalies (the presence of some unusual Ottoman commanders — either von Sanders or Mustafa Kemal) in the Ottoman experience to set them apart from the more conventional and thus more easily understood militaries. Military historians in Turkey and Australia should be seeking to undertake comparative research to produce more detailed and genuinely 'joint' operational histories and studies of this battle to combat the prevailing myths and half-truths concerning the Gallipoli Campaign.

Medal ceremony for the *27th Regiment* in İstanbul, attended by Esad Pasha and other key commanders of the Gallipoli Campaign. From left to right: Şefik (Aker), Ali Rıza (Sedes) Pasha, Enver Pasha, a German officer, İsmet (İnönü), Esad (Bülkat) Pasha, Fahreddin (Altay) and Kazım (Orbay) (image courtesy of Nejat Çuhadaroğlu).

Epilogue

Medal ceremony for the *27th Regiment* in İstanbul. Enver Pasha attached two prestigious combat medals to the regimental colours. The regiment, as part of the *9th Division*, was sent to the Eastern front where it was disbanded on 13 September 1916 (image courtesy of ATASE).

PRIVATES

In 1909 a new field service uniform was introduced replacing a century old dark blue uniform. The overall quality of the uniform was poor due to the economic realities of the empire. The shortages of war made it worse after 1916 when units had been forced into a position from which they could not maintain standardization of uniforms and equipment.

Soldier's basic kit included; a soft woolen head gear (officially named as Kabalak but generally known as Enveriyye after Enver Pasha, the coloured piping was introduced during the Summer of 1915), one tunic (with five Bakelite buttons which were later replaced with metal buttons either plain or embossed with crescent and star), a pair of pants, woolen putties, a pair of fatigue shoes or half boots (no easy shoes available for normal use), overcoat (with falling collar which could be turned up to protect neck from the cold and rain), socks, shirts. Most of the soldiers kept their civilian clothes and underclothes for use as replacement behind the lines. Soldiers were usually forced to repair their uniforms, shoes and equipment with whatever material they could find.

Soldier's combat kit included; a leather belt with brass plate belt buckle, leather ammunition pouches (exact copies of the German M 1909 that could hold 45 cartridges in three pockets), knapsack with shoulder straps (simplified version of the German M 1887 with interior framework of wood and no interior divisions), woolen blanket (brown or gray), ration bag (designed to carry three days' rations and some small utensils), canteen (exact copy of the German *feldflasche* usually made of aluminum but also from Bakelite), bayonet frog and scabbard. For each squad one mess tin was carried in row. Later in the war it was replaced by individual boiler which was an exact copy of the German *kochgeschirr*. Total number of cartridges per person was 120; 90 cartridges at the ammunition pouches and 30 cartridges in the knapsack.

The standard infantry rifle was Mauser M 1903 (better known as small Mauser due to its 7.65x53 calibre) or it's a bit older versions (M 1890, M 1893) with the same calibre. Some infantry units were armed with old black-powder Mauser M 1887 (better known as big Mauser due to its 9.5x60 calibre). Although cavalry units were usually armed with either carbine version of Mauser M 1903 or M 1905, some still had old Mauser M 1877 or old re-chambered Winchester carbines. Due to lack of modern rifles combat service and combat service support units usually armed with assortment of old rifles such as Mauser M 1877, converted M 1874 Martini-Peabody, Winchester and Snider.

Art by Phillip Rutherford.

Officers

Essentially the officer's field service uniform was the same as the soldier's. However the quality of the clothing was better and instead of five Bakelite buttons it had six plain brass buttons at the front, two small buttons at the pockets and also two small buttons each at the shoulder boards. Professional officers usually preferred to wear tailored made uniforms whereas reserve officers mostly used issued ones. In 1909 the Ottoman army introduced simplified version of the German rank tabs for officers which was basically three different shoulder boards for company, field and general officers.

Officer's basic kit included; a soft woolen head gear (generally with a chin strap), two tunics, three pairs of pants, two pairs of fatigue shoes with leather leggings or boots, overcoat (with short collar), socks, shirts.

Officer's combat kit included; a leather belt (with a conventional single square frame and prong buckle, star and crescent with laurel wreath embossed brass plate buckle was introduced during 1916), leather shoulder straps for company grade officers, a leather map case (styled after German examples), a compass (usually Bezard) in leather pouch, binoculars (usually German Zeiss or Goerz) with leather case, brass whistle.

There was no standard pistol for officers at the beginning of the war. Officers used various different revolvers and semi-automatic pistols. According to regulation the pistol holster was placed at the left side but most officers preferred to carry it on the right side. With the 1909 regulation a short sword was introduced whereas old long sword became ceremonial weapon. However most officers preferred not to carry short swords and interestingly none was issued to reserve officers who were expected to carry bayonets with portepee just like German NCOs. Against the regulation it was common for the officers to carry carbine – especially captured British SMLE rifles.

Epilogue

General staff captain.
Art by Phillip Rutherford.

Infantry lieutenant colonel.
Art by Phillip Rutherford.

A NOTE ON TURKISH SOURCES

TURKISH ARCHIVES

The main repository of the Turkish military documents concerning the Gallipoli campaign is the Turkish General Staff Military History Directorate (ATASE) Archive which is in Ankara. The archive was established to preserve the wartime operational and intelligence documents of the Ottoman-Turkish Armed Forces. Thus ATASE holds only wartime documents and material directly related to the war effort. All war diaries, operational and intelligence documents and some of the captured enemy documents from the Gallipoli campaign are held on the inventory of the ATASE archive. While most of the documents have been catalogued and are available to researchers, the catalogue is relatively basic and its entries comprise short descriptions which are often difficult to decipher and may be misleading. While the archive is open to researchers, permission must be obtained to work there and the catalogues are only available on site.

Peacetime documents and most personnel, administrative and logistics documents are held at the Turkish Ministry of Defence (MSB) Archives in Lodumlu-Ankara. This archive holds important documents on the Gallipoli campaign including officers' personal files, unit registry log books, hospital records, prisoner-of-war documents, various logistic records, mobilisation records and those relating to the wartime economy. As a general rule, any file not deemed appropriate for the ATASE archive usually ends up at the MSB archive. Unfortunately the archive is closed to researchers and most of the documents have not been catalogued.

There are also other archives and libraries that hold documents relating to the Gallipoli campaign. The Prime Minister's Ottoman Archives (BOA) in İstanbul holds policy documents, diplomatic, financial and other papers relating to the general war effort. A selection of these documents was published in Turkish in two volumes in 2005. The Turkish General Staff College Library and the Military Museum Library (both in İstanbul) hold rare books, manuscripts, photo albums, maps and some private papers.

TURKISH *OFFICIAL MILITARY HISTORIES*

Military success against the Allied navies and armies prompted the members of Ottoman military circles to begin writing the official history of the Gallipoli campaign well before the Allied evacuation. Intellectual discussions within the military instigated in the aftermath of the Balkan Wars were instrumental in this decision. Enver Pasha assigned a small group of officers to write an official history and the group started work amid the heat of the campaign, finishing the draft volume on the naval phase in time for this work to be used internally in 1916. However the group was unable to produce subsequent volumes, possibly as a result of the deteriorating military situation.

A note on Turkish sources

In the difficult days following the Armistice, the Ottoman General Staff College (Erkân-ı Harbiye Mektebi) organised a series of lectures, inviting key staff officers of the Gallipoli campaign to present their experiences. These lectures were published for military use shortly after. The new Chief of the War History Commission, Major Süleymaniyeli Mehmed Emin, revived attempts to write the official military history of the Gallipoli campaign by publishing a preliminary introductory volume. Somewhat surprisingly, efforts to write a comprehensive official history continued in İstanbul during the heady days of the Turkish Independence War of 1919–22, although the final stages of the war put an abrupt end to this tenacious effort. Ottoman officers who did not actively take part in the Independence War were purged, including the members of the War History Commission.

The enduring popularity of discussions on the Balkan Wars by serving and retired officers saw interest in Gallipoli and other important campaigns of the First World War kept alive. The General Staff College occasionally published Gallipoli narratives for its own educational use, although these were not extended to a broad brush official history for public consumption. The newly founded Turkish General Staff War History Directorate capitalised on the growing enthusiasm for a Gallipoli history by asking selected veterans to write different parts of the official military history of the First World War. The purpose of these assignments was to blend personal war experiences with archival documents in similar fashion to the German '*die Slachten des Weltkrieges*' series. Şefik Aker, the famous commander of the *27th Infantry Regiment*, was given responsibility for writing an account of the initial Ottoman defence against the Anzac landing on 25 April 1915. He not only made use of his personal notes and archival documents, but also asked his former subordinates to contribute. Şefik's book resembles a memoir rather than an official history, unlike that of Ahmed Sedad (Doğruer) who wrote on the naval defence of the Straits and Bursalı Mehmed Nihad who covered the general land campaign. Both these veterans of the campaign preferred a more didactic style that included a number of personal anecdotes and experiences. Translating foreign works, particularly official histories, on Gallipoli also remained an important role of the History Directorate.

In the mid-1930s Kadri Perk, a young serving officer, was commissioned to write the first comprehensive official military history of Gallipoli. His selection was deliberate. While not a Gallipoli veteran, he was an ardent believer in the official Turkish historical and linguistic theses. The resultant book was completely different from previous official publications. He allocated one volume to cover the long military history of the straits and peninsula from prehistoric times to 1914 in order to illustrate both the 'long and uninterrupted Turkish presence' and the historical connections between ancient and current history. His second and third volumes constituted a concise and readable account of the campaign written in a popular style without the military operational descriptions that had characterised previous histories. However his approach and style did not suit the requirements of the professional military and his work was never treated seriously and lapsed into obscurity.

Fahri Belen was the real architect of the modern version of the official military history. As a junior staff officer he had a unique opportunity to witness developments as the campaign unfolded. At the end of the 1950s, several years after his retirement as a lieutenant general, he was tasked to write a concise official history of the war in five volumes. However Belen was reluctant to openly criticise his former colleagues and superiors. He also tried to distance himself from controversies such as the command void on 25 April, and the disastrous counter-attacks launched between 27 April and 19 May. Instead he focused on the tactical context and wrote his history using the description of a series of battles at the divisional and regimental level as his vehicle. Belen made use of previously published and unpublished official history books, memoirs, archival documents and Turkish translations of foreign official accounts. However his weakness was that he failed to use these sources in a comparative way and made no attempt to identify and seek answers to the problems, paradoxes, riddles and lack of information on various encounters and issues that have recurred throughout Turkish accounts of the campaign. Although largely forgotten, Belen's five volumes established a dominant narrative and style as the Turkish *Official Military History* of the First World War.

ATASE launched its major official military history of the First World War project during the second half of the 1960s. The project was divided into ten tomes which dealt with the various battlefronts and services with a large group of retired officers (most from the General Staff Branch) who could read the Ottoman script assigned as authors or researchers. Each tome was divided into several parts and given to small groups of authors. The Gallipoli campaign tome was divided chronologically into three parts: naval defence (June 1914–25 April 1915), defence against the landings (25 April–May 1915) and the final phase (June 1915–January 1916). The authors used previously published official histories, filling out the narrative using documents held by ATASE. The finished drafts were presented to committees which examined, evaluated and edited the work. In several cases the manuscripts were deemed unsatisfactory and found to contain errors of interpretation and the committees returned the drafts seeking major changes or assigned new authors to rewrite the works. The second volume of the Gallipoli campaign was the first to be published in 1978. The third volume followed a few years later in 1980, while the first volume's publication was delayed more than a decade until 1993.

The publication of the final volumes of the Turkish *Official History* of the First World War (better known as the 'White Series') was completed in 2002. The entire history consists of ten tomes in 18 volumes. The Gallipoli campaign is covered in the fifth tome across three volumes. The quality varies across the series, with some volumes better than others in their utilisation of sources, quality and flow of the narrative. The *Official Histories* follow the principles and style adopted by Fahri Belen — the narratives are generally uncritical, unreflective and non-academic. Their battlefield focus tends to be limited to a chronological day-to-day narrative of the combat actions below regimental level. Most often the operational context in which battles and encounters occurred remains largely unexplained and this lack of context remains a significant weakness, undermining the value of the history. In addition, the immensity of detail, the frequent jumps from divisions to companies and vice versa make the volumes difficult for the layperson to read. Against these criticisms these volumes remain the best and most complete historical narrative produced in the Turkish language on the Gallipoli campaign.

MEMOIRS AND DIARIES

One of the most established stereotypes of Ottoman officers and soldiers is their historical reputation as brave but illiterate fighters. According to this view, Ottoman military personnel simply did not have the tradition, culture and literary background to record their war experiences in narratives such as diaries, journals and letters. The illiteracy of a large percentage of the Ottoman peasant soldiers may seem to endorse the validity of this view, but makes no allowance for the officer and professional non-commissioned officer (NCO) corps. There has been little discussion of whether these men were sufficiently literate to keep diaries or write some sort of personal narrative.

In reality, the Ottoman officers and NCOs had a significant advantage over their Australian and British counterparts. Instead of forbidding or discouraging them, Ottoman military authorities encouraged their personnel to record their combat experiences. The new infantry manual of 1909 (*Piyade Talimnamesi,* 1325), the officers' handbook (*Zabitin Harb Çantası,* 1332) and the infantry soldier's handbook (*Piyade Neferi,* 1329) advised junior officers and NCOs to keep small journals (*muhtıra*) in their pockets and take notes on important events and orders. Most officers took this advice quite literally and diarised personal issues and feelings as an adjunct to recording events. In addition to keeping small journals, a percentage of officers (particularly generals and field grade officers) made copies of important orders, replies and messages. Some of them even retained personal copies of official war diaries.

The humiliating defeats suffered during the Balkan Wars prompted officers to openly discuss why they had failed and examine the apparent weaknesses of the army. New publications fostered further discussion and the production of even more publications. Thousands of officers and NCOs who had either been sacked or dismissed from the military for incompetence had strong motives for presenting their cases to the public. The so-called 'battle of the memoirs' continued uninterrupted and the First World War provided additional opportunities for disaffected former and current personnel to add their voice to the analysis of the conduct of Ottoman Army campaigns.

The Gallipoli campaign is well covered by such personal war narratives. A significant percentage of the Ottoman Army (17 of 40 numbered divisions) and its officers (slightly less than half the regular and reserve officers) served in the Gallipoli campaign. Furthermore, like so many troops from combatant armies who faced danger and hardship on a daily basis, their shared experiences in the trenches created a special brotherhood. Veterans of the Gallipoli campaign enjoyed a clear distinction and prestige. For these reasons many officers and NCOs took the trouble to record their experiences. Thus it is remarkable that as few as 32 of these personal war narratives were published in various book formats and serialised press articles. This small number is all the more surprising given the importance accorded to the campaign. Why more of these personal narratives were not published is an intriguing question.

The first reason for this lack of published war narratives is linked to the final collapse of the Ottoman Army. Most veteran divisions of the Gallipoli campaign eventually served either on the Palestine-Syria or Caucasus fronts where large numbers of officers and NCOs perished in a series of disastrous battles. Thousands were captured after the final rout and most of their personal papers were either destroyed or confiscated. British and Russian military authorities in particular destroyed almost all captured documents during or after the war. However it is still possible to find remnants of this body of material. Indeed some Ottoman military personnel rewrote their lost narratives, although most did not.

Second, several new political entities were born from the Ottoman Empire and the Turkish Independence War that followed soon after. Veterans of the First World War soon discovered that, in their home towns and villages, interest in their ordeal had waned. Ottoman Arab officers in particular found it best to remain silent on their war experiences so as to ease their transition in the new states of Syria, Iraq, Jordan and Lebanon under British and French mandates. These years saw the loss or destruction of hundreds of valuable personal narratives.

However, in the last few years the Turkish public has begun to show a renewed interest in the First World War. A number of small publishers rekindled public interest by quietly republishing long out-of-print memoirs. The initial response was promising and a subsequent spike in demand fuelled a search for more unpublished personal narratives. While scholars and enthusiasts delved through libraries, archives and antiquarian booksellers, families began to rediscover long-forgotten manuscripts written by their grandfathers. Every year more and more personal war narratives of the Gallipoli campaign are published in Turkey. The availability of better scholarship and editing has played an important role in the increased quality of the new publications. These recently published Ottoman personal war narratives may represent just the tip of the iceberg and there may be many narratives either in private collections or in archives and libraries waiting to be discovered or released for publication to an increasingly receptive readership.

SELECTED BIBLIOGRAPHY

ARCHIVAL DOCUMENTS

19th Division, Reports and Returns, March-May 1915, Turkish General Staff Military History Directorate (ATASE) Archive, Ankara

19th Division Personnel Registry Logbook, the Ministry of Defence (MSB) Archive Division, Lodumlu-Ankara

19th Division War Diary, ATASE Archive

27th Regiment War Diary, ATASE Archive

57th Regiment War Diary, ATASE Archive

77th Regiment War Diary, ATASE Archive

72nd Regiment After Action Report, ATASE Archive

OTHER UNPUBLISHED SOURCES

Deusche Offiziere in der Türkei, Reichsarchiv, 1940, ATASE Library.

Esad (Bülkat) Pasha, Çanakkale Hatıraları, 3 vols, Turkish General Staff College Library, İstanbul.

PUBLISHED SOURCES

Old Turkish (in Ottoman script)

Bursalı Mehmed Nihad, Büyük Harbde Çanakkale Seferi, Matbaa-i Askeri, İstanbul, 1337 [1921].

Celaleddin [Germiyanoğlu], Harbi Umumi'de Çanakkale Muharebâtı Berriyesi Kumkale Muharebatı, Erkân-ı Harbiye Mektebi Matbaası, İstanbul, 1336 [1920].

Dukakinzade Feridun, Büyük Harb Türk cepheleri, Çanakkale Cephesi, Section 2, Askeri Akademiler Komutanlığı Matbaası, Yıldız, 1927.

İzzeddin, 'Arıburnu Muharebesinden Edinilen Tecarib', Askeri Mecmua, no: 13, Nisan 1336 [April 1920].

İzzeddin [Çalışlar], Burhaneddin, Harbi Umumi›de Çanakkale Muharebâtı Berriyesi Arıburnu Şimal Grubu Harekâtı, Erkân-ı Harbiye Mektebi Matbaası, İstanbul, 1336 [1920].

Hafız Cemil et.al., Harbi Umumide Osmanlı Tarihi Harbi: Çanakkale Muharebatı (Müsvedde Halindedir), Dersaadet, Harbiye Nezareti, İstanbul, 1332.

Sedad, Boğazlar Meselesi ve Çanakkale Muharebeyi Bahriyesinde Türk Tarafı, Askeri Matbaa, İstanbul 1927.

Selahaddin Adil, Harbi Umumi'de Çanakkale Muharebâtı Bahriyesi, Erkân-ı Harbiye Mektebi Matbaası, İstanbul, 1336 [1920].

[Süleymaniyeli Mehmed Emin], Cihan Harbinde Osmanlı Harekâtı Tarihçesi: Cüz 1 Çanakkale Muharebatı, Matbaa-i Askeriye, Dersaadet, 1338 [1922].

Modern Turkish

Adil, Selahattin, Hayat Mücadeleleri, Zafer Matbaası, 1982.

Askeri Tarih Belgeleri Dergisi, year 38, no. 88, August 1989.

Ataksor, Halis, Çanakkale Raporu (ed), Serdar Ataksor, Timaş Yayınları, İstanbul, 2008.

[Atatürk], Mustafa Kemal, Arıburnu Muharebeleri Raporu, Genelkurmay Basımevi, Ankara, 2011.

Aker, Şefik, Çanakkale-Arıburnu Savaşları ve 27, Alay, Askeri Matbaa, İstanbul, 1935.

Belen, Fahri, Birinci Cihan Harbinde Türk Harbi, vol. 2, Genelkurmay Basımevi, Ankara, 1964.

[Belen], Fahri, Harb Akademisi 1934-1935 Tedrisatından Çanakkale Savaşından Alınan Dersler, Harp Akademisi Matbaası, İstanbul, 1934.

Bir Kahramanlık Abidesi 57nci Piyade Alayı Şahitler Alayı, Milli Savunma Bakanlığı, Ankara, 2003.

Çalışlar, İzzettin, On Yıllık Savaşın Günlüğü: Balkan, Birinci Dünya ve İstiklal Savaşları (ed), İsmet Görgülü, İzzeddin Çalışlar, Yapı Kredi Yayınları, İstanbul, 1997.

Mahmud Sabri, Seddülbahir Muharebesi ve 26. A. III. Tb. Harekâtı, Harp Akademisi Matbaası, Yıldız, 1933.

Perk, Kadri, Çanakkale Savaşları Tarihi, vol.1-3, Askeri Matbaa, İstanbul, 1939–1940.

Saral, Muhterem, Alpaslan Orhon, Şükrü Erkal, Birinci Dünya Harbinde Türk Harbi: Çanakkale Cephesi, vol. 5, section 1, Genelkurmay Basımevi, Ankara, 1993.

Tümerdem, İ. Hakkı, Osmanlı İmparatorluğu Devrinde Büyük Meydan Muharebeleri ve Çanakkale Deniz ve Kara Harbi, Çeltut Matbaası, İstanbul, 1941.

Yiğitgüden, Remzi, Muhterem Saral, Reşat Hallı, Birinci Dünya Harbinde Türk Harbi: Çanakkale Cephesi, vol. 5, section 2, Genelkurmay Basımevi, Ankara, 1978.

German

Feldmann, Otto von, 'Das Oberkommando der Meerengen in den Dardanellen 1914 bis 1918', Marine Rundschau, no. 7, July 1939.

Kannengiesser, Hans, Gallipoli: Bedeutung und Verlauf der Kämpfe 1915, Schlieffen-Verlag, 1927.

Mühlmann, Carl, Der Kampf um die Dardanellen 1915, Verlag von Gerhard Stalling, Oldenburg, 1927.

Prigge, Erich R., Der Kampf um die Dardanellen, Weimar, Verlag Güstav Kiepenheuer, 1916.

Ruge, Friedrich, 'Artillerie und Minen in den Dardanellen', Wissen und Wehr, no. 5, 1935.

Sanders, Otto Liman von, Fünf Jahre Türkei, Verlag von August Scherl, Berlin, 1920.

Wehrle, Heinrich, 'Aus meinem Türkischen Tagebuch', Die Schwere Artillerie, year 3, no. 3, June 1926.

English

Aspinall-Oglander, Cecil Faber, *Military Operations Gallipoli*, Vol. 1, William Heinemann, London, 1929.

Bean, Charles E. W., *Gallipoli Mission*, Australian War Memorial, Canberra, 1952.

——, *The Official History of Australia in the War of 1914–1918*, Vol. I, *The Story of Anzac*, Angus & Robertson, Sydney, 1921.

Broadbent, Harvey, *Gallipoli: The Fatal Shore*, Penguin Group, Melbourne, 2009.

Cameron, David W., *25 April 1915: The Day the Anzac Legend was Born*, Allen & Unwin, Sydney, 2007.

——, *Our Friend the Enemy: A Detailed Account of Anzac from both Sides of the Wire*, Big Sky Publishing, Sydney, 2014.

Chambers, Stephen, *Anzac Landing*, Pen & Sword, Barnsley, 2008.

Dolan, Hugh, *36 Days: The Untold Story Behind the Gallipoli Landings*, Pan Macmillan, Sydney, 2010.

Erickson, Edward J., Gallipoli: The Ottoman Campaign, Pen & Sword, Barnsley, 2010

Fewster, Kevin (ed), *Bean's Gallipoli: The Diaries of Australian's Official War Correspondent* (3rd edn), Allen & Unwin, Sydney, 2007.

Forrest, Michael, *The Defence of the Dardanelles: From Bombards to Battleships*, Pen & Sword, Barnsley, 2012.

James, Robert Rhodes, *Gallipoli*, Pimlico, London, 1999.

Prior, Robin, *Gallipoli: The End of the Myth*, Yale university Press, New York, 2010.

Pugsley, Chris, *Gallipoli: The New Zealand Story*, Spectre NZ, Auckland, 1990.

Roberts, Chris, *The Anzac Landing 1915*, Big Sky Publishing, Sydney, 2013.

Rudenno, Victor, *Gallipoli: Attack from the Sea*, University of New South Wales Press, Sydney, 2008.

Travers, Tim, *Gallipoli 1915*, Tempus Publishing, Stroud, UK, 2002.

Williams, Peter, *The Battle of Anzac Ridge*, Australian Military History Publications, Sydney, 2007.

Winter, Denis, *25 April 1915: The Inevitable Tragedy*, University of Queensland Press, St Lucia, 1994.

INDEX

A

Abdal Geçidi 123
Abdülhamid II 23, 25, 72, 75
Adana 14, 132, 134
Adrianople (Edirne) 10, 18, 34, 46–7, 72
Afyon (reserve divisions) 43
Ağıldere 66, 67, 70
Ahmed, Captain 147
Ahmet, Sergeant 101
alaylı (rankers) 15, 22
Albania 38, 63
Albayrak Sırtı (Pine Ridge) 107, 118, 131, 140, *142*, 154
Aleppo (Haleb) 14, 73, 137
Ali Remzi (Alçıtepe) *59*
Allied naval attacks 68, 78, 83–5, 114, 131, 157
  defence against 81–6
Anadolu Hamidiye Fort *46*
Anafarta 81, 120, 159
Anatolia 27, 34, 40, 73
Anderson Knoll (Kavak Tepe) 104, 107, 114, 129, 131, 132
Anzac 13, 14, 16, 56, 68, 70, 146
  1st Battalion 138
  2nd Battalion 131
  4th Battalion 147, *148*
  6th Battalion 140
  7th Battalion 107
  9th Battalion 103, 106, 107, 109, 131
  10th Battalion 103, 106, 107, 109
  11th Battalion 108, 131
  12th Battalion 102, 108, 131
  Auckland Battalion 131, 138
  evacuation 14, 153
Anzac Cove 103, 107, 120, 122, 123, 129, 146, 152
Anzac landing 72–3, 106–11, 120, 122, 127, *156*
  evaluation of Ottoman defence 150–7
  machine guns, Ottoman use of 96–8
  original Ottoman defence positions *95*
  Ottoman artillery units and positions 103–4, *105*
  Ottoman counter-attacks 124, *125*, 130–8, *130*, 138, 139, *142*, 143–5, 153–4, 156
  Ottoman observation of 99, 106–7, 110
  Ottoman reinforcements 112, *116*, 118, 128–9, 139
Arab soldiers 137, 170
Arabian Peninsula 26
archives 166
Arıburnu 63, 65, 66, 70, 112–13, 156
  Knoll 67, 96, 97, 100, *101*
Arif Fountain *92*

artillery units and positions 103–4
  loss of 109
Asım, 1st Lieutenant 102, 107, *151*
Asir 18
Ata (Erçkan), Captain Mehmed 123, 131, 143–4, *144*
Atatürk, Mustafa Kemal 7, 14, *40*, *47*, 48, 53, 69, 71–3, *74*, 94, 136, 137, 140, 145, *159*, 160
  background 71
  character 73, 79, 157
  defence against Anzac landing 104, 110, 114, 120–9, 131, 136–8, 143, 146–7, 149, 153–4
  military service 71–3
  19th Division 74–81
  political career 73
August offensives 14, 72
Austro-Hungarian Army 65, 81

B

Baby 700 (Kılıç Bayırı) 109, 117, 124, 131, 138, 154
Balıkçı Damları (Fisherman's Hut) 67, 96, 107, 131
Balkan Wars 10–11, 17, 18, 22, 23, 25, 27, 35, 38, 43–7, 53–4, 61, 63, 75, 96, 110, 133, 155, 156, 157, 169
  Composite Corps deployment *45*, 46–7
Battleship Hill (Düztepe) 109, 124, 125, 131
Bean, Charles 7, 96
Beersheba 73
Belen, Fahri 167–8
Belgium 33
Beşika 58, 88
Bigalı (Boghali) 81, *117*, *119*, 120
Bitlis 72
Bolayır (Bulair) 13, 48, 58, 59, 78, 116, 120, 128, 146, 150
  defensive line 46, 58, 110–11
Bolayır-Saros 58, 59, 88, 92, 110, 116, 128, 146, 150
Bolton Ridge (Keltepe) 106, 140
Bosphorus 18
Bouvet 85
Boyun Mevkii 99
Braund, Lieutenant Colonel G.F. 144
Breslau 62
Brighton Beach 112
British Army
  aerial bombing 94
  landing at Helles 129
  Royal Marines 84, *84*
  26th Indian Mountain Artillery Battery 133
British Expeditionary Force 14
British Naval Advisory Mission 81
British Royal Navy 146, 157
  naval attacks 68, 78, 83–5, 114, 131

175

Bulair (Bolayır) 13, 48, 58, 59, 78, 116, 120, 128, 146, 150
 defensive line 46, 58
Bulgaria 27, 34, 35, 43, 46, 81, 110
Büyükdere (Shrapnel Gully) 100, 102, 107
Büyükkemikli (Suvla Point) 66

C

casualties 103, *136*
 Anzac 100, 107–8, 133, 146
 Ottoman 48, 55, 84–5, 86, 94, 100–1, 102, *118*, *119*, 133, 135, 138, 143, 146–7, 154–7
Caucasus 34, 52, 55, 170, 170
Cemal Pasha 11, 34, 72, 75
Cemil, Major *152*
Cemil, Private Gelibolulu 99, 101
Cevad, Colonel Ahmed *151*
Cevad (Çobanlı) Pasha 56, *57*, 78, 83, 88
Cevdet, Lieutenant *152*
Chunuk Bair (Conkbayırı) 97, 101, 104, 109, 123–4, 136
Clarke, Lieutenant Colonel Lancelot F. 102
Committee of Union and Progress – CUP *see* İttihad *ve Terakki*
communications 88, 99, 107, 110, 126, 140, 153
Conkbayırı (Chunuk Bair) 97, 101, 104, 109, 123–4, 136
conscription 25–7, 55, 137, 143
Critchley-Salmonson, Captain A.C.B. 144
the Cup (Yeşiltarla) 70, 101, 103, 107, 109, 135
Çamburnu 104, 113
Çamtepe 70, 103
Çanakkale (Dardanelles) Provisional Army 38
Çatalca Fortified Zone 18
Çatalca line 10, 43, 46

D

Daisy Patch 118
Damascus 14, 18
Dardanelles Straits 8, 16, 18, 34, 37, 38, 43, 52, 55, 81, 167
 Allied naval attacks *see* Allied naval attacks
 Balkan Wars 43–7
 coastal defence concept 86–7, *90*
 Ottoman-Italian War 38–42, 43, 63, 72, 75, 86–7
 von Sanders' defence strategy 86–94, *89*, *91*, 110–11, 112, 157
de Robeck, Admiral John 85–6
Debre 63
deputy officers (*zabit vekili*) 31
dispatch riders *128*
'dugout' officers 27, 33
Düztepe (Battleship Hill) 109, 124, 125, 131

E

Ece Bay 66, 80–1
Edirne (Adrianople) 10, 18, 34, 46–7, 72
Edirne Sırtı (Mortar Ridge) 117, 138
education, military 18–22

Emin, Major Süleymaniyeli Mehmed 167
Enver Pasha 10–11, 14, 15, 25, 33–5, 36, 52, 72, 73, 75, 81, *82*, *160*, *161*, 162, 166
Erkân-ı Harbiye Mektebi (General Staff College) 19, *19*, 167
 Library 8, 166
 Military History Directorate (ATASE) Archive 8, 166, 168
Ertuğrul 42
Erzincan 18
Erzurum 18, 34
Esad (Bülkat) Pasha 48–53, *49*, *50*, 55–6, 80, *82*, 83, *83*, 86, 93, *117*, *121*, *127*, 146, *151*, 156–7, *158*, *159*, *160*
 ANZAC landing, defence against 110–11, 120, 126–9, 150
 background 51
 character 48, 53
 military service 51–2
Eskihisarlık 60

F

Fahreddin (Altay), Lieutenant Colonel 48, *49*, *117*, *158*, *159*, *160*
Fahri, Lieutenant *85*
Fahri Pasha, Çolak 43, 46
Faik, Captain 99, 101, 102, 106, 109, *152*
field maintenance 79
First World War 11, 73, 157, 168, 170
Fisherman's Hut (Balıkçı Damları) 67, 96, 107, 131
400 Plateau 67

G

Gaba Tepe (Kabatepe) 40, 58, 60, 62, 66–70, 78, 81, 92, 96, 97–8, 99, 101, 102, 103, 106, 107, 109, 113–14, 116, 120, 122, 129
Galacia-Poland 65
Galib Pasha *40*
Gallipoli Peninsula 38, 43, 52, 55, 61, 72, 73, 78, 92, 110
 artillery units and positions 103–4
 demographics 61–2
Gaza 73
gendarmerie *20*, 26–7, 35, *35*, 58, 62, 66, 69, 78, 81
General Staff College (*Erkân-ı Harbiye Mektebi*) 19, *19*, 167
 Library 8, 166
 Military History Directorate (ATASE) Archive 8, 166, 168
German Army
 General Staff 11, 33–4, 35, 73
 Ottoman commands, holding 16
German Military Advisory Mission 10–11, 15, 92
German mission command (*auftragstaktik*) 92–3, 120, 150
German Officer's Spur (Merkez Tepe) 16, 99, 101, 106, 116, 131
German Officer's Trench 16
German propaganda *86*
Göben 62

Greece 43, 51, 65
Gun Ridge *see* Third Ridge
H
Hacı Emin, Major Mehmed 140, 143, 145
Haig, Lieutenant James 106
Hain Tepe (Plugge's Plateau) 100, 101, 102, 107, 109
Hakkı (Tümerdem), Deputy Officer İsmail 106–7, 114, 131, 140, 143
Halil, Lieutenant 116
Halil Sami, Colonel 80, 110, 113, 120–2, 129, 150, 153
Halim Pasha, Grand Vizier Said 34
Halis (Ataksor), Captain Kör 117, 131, *133*, *152*, 154
Hamdi, Lieutenant *152*
Hamilton, General Ian 86, 157
Haydar (Alganer) *159*
Hayreddin (Ağıldere), Deputy Officer İbradalı İbrahim 107–9, *108*, 123
Hejaz 18, 34
Helles 13, 14, 16, 56, 77, 78, 84, 92, 98, 110–11, 120, 122, 129
    Seddülbahir 42, 58, 60–1, 84, *84*, 120
Hıfzı, 1st Lieutenant Hasan 103
Hill 180 117, 145
Hill 971 (Kocaçimen Tepe) 101, 104, 115–16, 122, 123
Hilmi, Lieutenant Mustafa 106, 117, 125
Hilmi (Sanlıtop), Captain Mehmed *85*
HMS *Ark Royal* 114
HMS *Bacchante* 103
HMS *Inflexible* 85
HMS *Irresistible* 85
HMS *Majestic* 147
HMS *Manica* 114
Hulusi (Conk), Major Mehmed 99, 113, *159*
Hüseyin Avni, Major 75, 122–4, *122*, 127, 131, 136, 138, 144, 146, 154
I
Imperial Engineering School (*Mühendishane-i Berri-i Hümayun*) 18
Imperial Military Academy (*Mekteb-i Fünun-u Harbiye-i Şahane*) 18–19, 27, 30, 51, 63, 71
Italy 38–42, 43, 63, 72, 75, 86–7
Izmir (Smyrna) 64
İrfan, Lieutenant Colonel 62
İbrahim, Major Malatyalı 118, 131, 143, 145
İdris, Bigalı 99
ihtiyat zabit namzeti (reserve officer candidates) 30–3, *31*, *32*
İhtiyat *Zabit Talimgâhı* (İstanbul Reserve Officer Training Corps) 29, *29*
İşkodra (Shkodër) 10
İsmet (İnönü) *160*
İsmet, Major Mehmed 99, 102, 109, *151*
İstanbul 11, 13, 14, 18, *21*, 22, 29, 34, 37, 43, 52, *54*, 63, 73, 81, *111*, 119, *160*, *161*, 166
İstanbul Reserve Officer Training Corps (İhtiyat *Zabit Talimgâhı*) 29, *29*
İttihad *ve Terakki* (Committee of Union and Progress – CUP) 11, 34, 75
İzzeddin (Çalışar), Major 75, *159*
İzzet Pasha, Ahmed 17
J
Jacobs, Captain Harold 138
Janina (Yanya) 10, 48, 51
Jerusalem 14
Johnston's Jolly (Kırmızı Sırt) 116, 118, 145, 146
K
Kabatepe (Gaba Tepe) 40, 58, 60, 62, 66–70, 78, 81, 92, 96, 97–8, 99, 101, 102, 103, 106, 107, 109, 113–14, 116, 120, 122, 129
Kadri, Lieutenant Colonel 120
Kaiser Wilhelm II 10–11, 13, *82*
Kanlısırt (Lone Pine) 106, 114, 116, 118, 126, 131, 132, 135, 140, 145, 146, 147, *152*, 153
Kannengiesser, Hans 13, *159*
Karayürek Deresi (Legge Valley) 106, 114, 117, 140, 145, 149
Kavak Deresi 114, 129, 145
Kavak Tepe (Anderson Knoll) 104, 107, 114, 129, 131, 132
Kazım (İnanç), Lieutenant Colonel *86*, 110, *117*, 151
Keltepe (Bolton Ridge) 106, 140
Kemal Pasha, Mustafa *see* Atatürk, Mustafa Kemal
Kemalyeri (Scrubby Knoll) 97, 104, 106, 114, 116, 135, 136, 147, *159*
Kesikdere (Mule Valley) 117
Kılıç Bayırı (Baby 700) 109, 117, 124, 131, 138, 154
Kırkkilise 43
Kırmızı Sırt (Johnston's Jolly) 116, 118, 145, 146
Kilitbahir Plateau 88, 127
Kirte (Krithia) 77, 129
Kocaçimen Bloc (Saribair Range) 66, 88
Kocaçimen Tepe (Hill 971) 101, 104, 115–16, 122, 123
Kocadere 69, 104, 106, 116, 123, 129
Koyun Limanı 70
Krithia (Kirte) 77, 129
Krupp artillery
    75mm L/14 M1904 70, *83*, *102*, 103, 109, 113, 136, 146
    75mm L/30 M1903 *25*, 69, 104, 126, *126*, 131
    87mm L/24 M1885 'Mantelli' guns 60, 76, 103, 105, *105*, 126, *147*
    150mm L/26 fortress howitzer 56
    150mm M1893 103
    150mm *schwere Feldhaubitze* M1902 70, 103, 105, *106*
    240mm L/35 fortress gun *56*, *85*
    355mm L/35 fortress gun *46*

Krupp field battery *23*, *25*
Kumkale 13, 16, 40, 58, 84, 92
   fort 42
Kumtepe 60, 80, 81, 98, 104, 127, 129

L

Lebanon 14, 34, 170
Legge Valley (Karayürek Deresi) 106, 114, 117, 140, 145, 149
Libya 38, 72, 75, 145
Limpus, Admiral 81
Lone Pine (Kanlısırt) 106, 114, 116, 118, 126, 131, 132, 135, 140, 145, 146, 147, *152*, *153*
Loutit, Lieutenant Noel M. 106, 114, 132
Lüleburgaz 43

M

Macedonia 43
machine guns 8, 9, 15, 17, 21, 46, 48, 60, 66, 76, 80, 88, 96–8, 103, 113, 114, 116–17, 123, 131–5, 138, 145, 146–7
   British Vickers *117*
   Hotchkiss M1900 97
   Maxim MG08 97
   Maxim MG09 21, *80*, *96*, 97–8
   Maxim MG99 *21*, 97
   Maxim-Nordenfelt 60, *61*, 98
   Nordenfelt guns 60, *61*, 97–8, 105
   Ottoman use of 96–8
Malta 14
Maltepe 81, 111, 114, 120, 126–7
Mantelli guns *see* Krupp artillery
Martini-Peabody rifles 22
Maydos 62, 63, 75–8, 81, *94*, 114
Mediterranean Expeditionary Force 86
Mekteb-i Fünun-u Harbiye-i Şahane (Imperial Military Academy) 18–19, 27, 30, 51, 63, 71
Merkez Fort *58–*, *110*
Merkez Tepe (German Officer's Spur) 16, 99, 101, 106, 116, 131
Mersintepe 120
Merten, Vice-Admiral Johannes 81, *82*
Military Museum Library 166
military service 25–7
Military Service Law 1914 25
mine belts 83, 85, 86
Ministry of Defence (MSB) Archive 8, 166
Ministry of War 15, 26, 27, 29, 53, 84
mission command (*auftragstaktik*) 92–3, 120, 150
mobilisation for war 25–33, 53–5
Monash Valley 138
Mortar Ridge (Edirne Sırtı) 117, 138
Mudros Armistice Agreement 65
Muharrem, Deputy Officer 100, 101, 107, 156

Muharrem, Sergeant Lapsekili 102
Mule Valley (Kesikdere) 117
Mustafa, Captain *152*
Muş 72
Mühendishane-i Berri-i Hümayun (Imperial Engineering School) 18
Mühlmann, 1st Lieutenant Carl 16
Münir, Major Mehmed 149
Münir, Refik *151*

N

Naci (Eldeniz), Major 30
Nazım, Mehmed *158*, *159*
Nazif, Major Manastırlı 104, 118
The Nek 138, 145
New Zealand Army *see* Anzac
Nicolai, Colonel Arthur 16
Nihad, Bursalı Mehmed 167
North Beach 112
Numan Pasha, Dr Süleyman *151*
Nuri, Deputy Officer 99
Nusayris 137

O

Oak Grove *see* Olive Grove
Ocean 85
Odessa 35, 37, 81
Ohrili Kemal *49*, *159*
Olive Grove (Palamutluk Sırtı) 70, 103, 105, 106, 127, 129
Orhaniye Fort *41*, *42*, *43*
Ottoman Army 10, *17*, *26*, *58*, *66*, *76*, *84*, *111*, *115*, *135*, *141*, *149*, *153*, *155*, 160
   First Army 13, 18, 52, 87
   Second Army 18, 72–3, 151
   Third Army 18, 37, 52, 55
   Fourth Army 18, 37, 73, 75
   Fifth Army 13, 16, 52, 87, *89*, 98, 110, 119, 120, 151
   Seventh Army 73
   I Corps 11, 55
   II Corps 38, 40, 51
   III Corps 16, 24, 38, 40, 48–60, *80*, 83, 103, 126, 151, 157, *159*
   VII Yemen Corps 18, 26, 55
   X Corps 37, 47
   XV Corps 16, 43, 65, 93, 159
   XVI Corps 72
   2nd Fortress Artillery Brigade 83
   3rd Division 16, 92
   3rd Fortress Artillery Regiment 83
   4th Fortress Artillery Regiment 83
   5th Division 16, 38, 43, 51, 83, 92
   5th Fortress Artillery Regiment 83, 85
   7th Division 58, 59, 83, 92
   8th Division 24, 53

8th Heavy Howitzer Regiment 83
9th Division 16, 38, 48, 55, 58, 60, 62, 69, 70, 80, 81, 85, 88, 92, 97, 99, 102, 110, 122, 127, 129, 161
9th Field Artillery Regiment 98, 103, 109, 113
11th Division 70, 92
14th Division 63
15th Division 76
16th Division 159
19th Division 16, 24, 48, 53, 63, 65, 69, 72, 74–81, 83, 92, 97, 110–11, 116, 119, 120, 122, 137, 146
21st Asir Division 18, 26
22nd Hejaz Division 18, 26
23rd Division 51
25th Regiment 70, 80, 81, 120
26th Regiment 53, 66, 78, 79, 81, 97, 120
27th Regiment 43, 48, 61–2, 63, 69, 70, 78, 81, 104, 109, 112–18, 120, 122, 124, 126, 129, *130*, 133, 138, 140, 143, 146, 149, *152*, *154*, 156, *160*, *161*, 167
39th Field Artillery Regiment 76, 104, 147
55th Regiment 53, 75
56th Regiment 53, 75, 81
57th Division 65
57th Regiment 72, 75, 76, 77, 80, 81, 104, 118, 119, 120, 122–5, 127, *130*, 133, 136, 138, 143, 145, 146, 149, 154, 156
72nd Regiment 53, 77, *94*, 126–7, 129, 136, 137, 138, 147, 149, 153–4
77th Regiment 53, 77, 79, 80, 97, 126–7, 129, 137, 138, 139–45, 146, 149, 153–4, 156
Bursa Division 38, 40
Composite Gallipoli Corps 38, 43, *44*, *45*, 46–8, 72
Çanakkale Division 38, 43
Dardanelles Fortified Zone Command (Çanakkale Müstahkem Mevki Kumandanlığı) 16, 38, 40–1, *40*, 43, 46, 47, 52, 55–6, *57*, 58, 60–2, 78, 81, 85, 86, 88, 98, 103
Eastern Army 43
Edremit Division 38, 43
Iraq Regional Command 37
İzmit Division 38
Janina Army Corps 51
Menderes Detachment 46, 62, 69
Ottoman Expeditionary Force 65
Southern (Helles) Group 16
Western Army 43
Yemen Expeditionary Force 63
Yıldırım Army Group (Heeres Gruppen Kommando F) 14, 73
Arab soldiers 137
cavalry *113*, 118, 122
conscription 25–7, 55, 137
depot regiments 24

deputy officers (*zabit vekili*) 31
discipline 149, 156
education and training 18–24, 30, *59*, *76*, *77*, *77*, *78*
field camp *68*
General Staff 15, 17, 18, 24, 25, 27, 33–4, 37, 38, 43, 46, 51, 53, 58, 72, 75, 81
German leadership 16
mobilisation for war 25–33, 53–5
NCOs 20–2, 31, 33, 55, 61, 133, 135, 138, 143, 145, 146, 155, 156, 169, 169–70
officer corps 20–2, 27–9, *28*, *29*, 133, 135, 155–6, *155*, 164
politics 15
post-Balkan War reforms 10–11, 15–22, 156, 157
reserve officers 29–33, *31*, *32*
strategy 33–5, 37
structure 15, 17–18, 53–4, 68, 70, 76–8, 87, 99, 100, 123
supplies 27, 54–5, 60, 66, 76, 80, 81, 83, *84*, 97, *129*, 133, *152*, 162, 164
triangular divisions 17, 18, 157
uniforms 162, 164
Ottoman-German agreement 11, 81
Ottoman-Greek War 1897 51
Ottoman-Italian War 1911–12 38–42, 43, 63, 72, 75, 86–7
deployment of Ottoman defence *39*
Owen's Gully 147

P
Palamutluk Sırtı (Olive Grove) 70, 103, 105, 106, 127, 129
Palestine 14, 34, 170
Pangaltı Barracks *20*, *35*
Perk, Kadri 167
Pine Ridge (Albayrak Sırtı) 107, 118, 131, 140, *142*, 154
Piyade Neferi, 1329 169
Piyade Talimnamesi, 1325 169
place names 6
Plan Number One 37
Plugge's Plateau (Hain Tepe) 100, 101, 102, 107, 109
Prigge, Captain Erich R. 16, 111, *151*
privates 162
Prussian Army 11, 13, 15

R
Rabe, Colonel Hans 30
Rafferty, Lieutenant Rupert A. 108
rankers (*alaylı*) 15, 22
Raşid, Deputy Officer Hasan 122
Rauf (Orbay), Lieutenant Commander *47*, *151*
Red Crescent Society 136, 150
reserve officer candidates (*ihtiyat zabit namzeti*) 30–3, *31*, *32*
Rhododendron Ridge (Şahin Sırtı) 109
Rıfat, Major 140, *143*, 149
Rıza (Sedes) Pasha, Ali 38, 40, 41, *158*, *160*

rifles 22, 162
    Martini-Peabody 22, 162
    Mauser 80, 162
    SMLE 164
    Snider 162
    Winchester 162
Rodosto (Tekirdağ) 51, 55
Romania 27, 34, 35, 37, 81
route marches 76
Russell's Top (Yüksek Sırt) 101, 102, 144, 154, 170
Russia 10, 11, 34, 37, 72, 81
Rüşdü (Sakarya) Pasha 40–1, *40*, *158*

S

Saadet, Deputy Officer 116, 134, 146
Sabri, Captain Hüseyin 106
Sadık, Captain 101, 103–4, 106, 109, 116
Saip, Major 127, 129, 137, 139–45
Salih, 2nd Lieutenant Mehmed 122
Salonika 51
Sancak Tepesi 104, 106
sanitation *24*
Saribair Range (Kocaçimen Bloc) 66, 88
Saros 92, *93*, 110–11, 116, 128, 146, 150
Sazli Beit (Sazlı Dere) 109
Scrubby Knoll (Kemalyeri) 97, 104, 106, 114, 116, 135, 136, 147, *159*
Second Ridge 115, 126, 138, 146
Sedad (Doğruer), Ahmed 167
Seddülbahir (Helles) 40, 42, 58, 60–1, *84*, 120
Serbia 37, 81
Shkodër *see* İşkodra
Shrapnel Gully (Büyükdere) 100, 102, 107
Sırça Tepe (Walker's Ridge) 96, 131
Smyrna (Izmir) 64
Sniper's Ridge 140
Sofia 72, 75
Sonderkommando Kaiserliche Marine Türkei 81
sources of information 7–9, 166–70
    archives 8, 166
    diaries 169–70
    memoirs 169–70
    military histories 166–8
strategy 33–5, 37
Strickland, Lieutenant Frederick P.D. 108
Suez Canal 37
supplies 27, 54–5, 60, 66, 76, 80, 81, 83, *84*, 97, *129*, 133, *152*, 162, 164
Suvla 14, 59, 62, 63, 80, 81
Suvla Point (Büyükkemikli) 66
Suyatağı Mevkii 104, 124
Süleyman, Sergeant Major Gelibolulu 102
Syria 14, 24, 34, 38, 53, 71, 73, 75, 137, 170

Şahin Sırtı (Rhododendron Ridge) 109
Şarköy 46, 48
Şefik (Aker), Major Mehmed 62–70, *64*, 78–9, 97, 104, 132, *152*, *160*
    Anzac landing, defence against 104, 107, 112–18, 120, 122, 124, 126, 131, 135, 136, 139, 143, 145, 146–8, 153–4
    background 63
    character 65
    military memoir 167
    military service 63, 65
Şevket Pasha, Mahmud 10, 40–1

T

Talat Bey 11, 34, 72, 75
Talbot-Smith, Lieutenant E.W. 103, 109
Tali, Dr İbrahim *151*
Taurus Mountains 14
Teke 60
Tekirdağ (Rodosto) 51, 55
Third Ridge (Topçular Sırtı) 69, *83*, 104, 109, 113–17, 123, 146, 149, 153
Thomas, Lieutenant G. 103, 109
Thrace 34, 37, 47, 81
Topçular Sırtı (Third Ridge) 69, *83*, 104, 109, 113–17, 123, 146, 149, 153
training, military 23–4, 30, *59*, *76*, 77, *77*, *78*
trenches 30, 41, 48, 60, 63, *66*, *67*, *115*, *135*, 146
Tulloch, Captain Eric W. 124, 125
Turkish archives 166
Turkish General Staff College Library 8, 166
Turkish General Staff College Military History Directorate (ATASE) Archive 8, 166, 168
Turkish Independence War 1919–22 73, 167, 170
Turkish Republic 73
Turşun 80, 120

U

Üçüncü Tepe 104

V

Vasıf, 1st Lieutenant 143
Vehbi, Mehmed 133
Vehib Pasha *151*
Viale, Vice Admiral Leone 41–2
Vittoio Emanuele 42
von der Goltz, Colmar 15, 20, 35, *36*
von Falkenhayn, Field Marshall Erich 14, 73
von Frese, Major 16
von Sanders, General Otto Liman 11, *12*, 35, 36, 58, 59, 72, 110–11, *117*, 126, 128, 150, *151*, 157, 160
    background 12
    character 14, 92–3
    Dardanelles defence 86–94, *89*, *91*, 110–11, 112, 120, 128, 146, 157

Ottoman Army, command of 13–15, 16, 52, 57, 73, 92–3
von Schellendorf, Colonel Friedrich Bronsart 33
von Sodenstern, Colonel Eduard 16
von Thauvenay, Lieutenant Colonel Perrinet 48
von Usedom, Admiral Guido 81, *82*, 83
von Wangenheim, Hans 11, 13

W

Walker's Ridge (Sırça Tepe) 96, 131
War History Commission 167
water supply *92*, *129*, *152*
Weber, Brigadier General Erich Paul 16, 93
Wehrle, Colonel Heinrich *57*
Western Front 37, 157
'White Series' 168
Willmer, Wilhelm *159*

Y

Yanya (Janina) 10, 48, 51
Yazidis 137
Yeldeğirmeni Plains 120
Yemen 18, 34, 63
Yeşiltarla (the Cup) 70, 101, 103, 107, 109, 135
Yüksek Sırt (Russell's Top) 101, 102, 144, 154, 170

Z

zabit vekili (deputy officers) 31
Zabitin Harb Çantası, 1332 169
Zeki (Soydemir), Captain Ahmed 124, *124*
Zığındere 60